IN SEARCH OF

THOMAS CHRISTOPHER

Thomas Christopher

LOST ROSES

SUMMIT BOOKS

NEW YORK · **LONDON** · **TORONTO** · **SYDNEY** · **TOKYO**

SUMMIT BOOKS
Simon & Schuster Building
Rockefeller Center
1230 Avenue of the Americas
New York, New York 10020

Copyright © 1989 by Thomas Christopher
All rights reserved
including the right of reproduction
in whole or in part in any form.
SUMMIT BOOKS *and colophon are trademarks*
of Simon & Schuster Inc.
Designed by Edith Fowler
Manufactured in the United States of America

10 9 8 7 6 5 4 3 2 1

Library of Congress Cataloging in Publication Data

Christopher, Thomas.
In search of lost roses / Thomas Christopher.
  p. cm.
 ISBN 0-671-66220-1
 1. Roses. I. Title.
SB411.C545   1989
635.9'33372—dc20
                                        89-11342
                                          CIP

Page 2: 'Géant des batailles' *rose* ("Giant of battles")

Title page and chapter illustrations courtesy of the Library of the New York Botanical Garden, Bronx, New York

To Suzanne,
beside whom all the queens,
countesses and *Kronprinzessin* pale

Contents

Introduction

IN MY GARDEN there are roses with wonderfully evocative names:* 'Queen Victoria,' "Giant of Battles," "Pearl of Gold,"

*Unfortunately, the nomenclature of roses is mired in controversy; a number of conflicting systems have evolved over the years, and it sometimes seems as if every botanist and nurseryman is intent upon developing his own unique variant. For the purposes of this book, I will identify rose species by their botanical names, Latin binomials, as listed in Cornell University's Hortus III. This handbook of plants in cultivation within the United States is not entirely free from error, but it is widely accepted as the standard within the American horticultural industry. With respect to common names of garden roses, that is, the names of cultivated varieties and hybrids, I will follow the rules laid down by the American Rose Society. If a cultivar has been duly registered with that body, the recognized name will be surrounded

"Rose of the King," 'Baroness Rothschild,' 'Marchioness of Lorne.' They read like a roll call of the ancien regime, and in fact these roses are a living link with the past. They are so-called old roses, the types beloved of our great-grandparents. Once the pride of gardeners from New York to San Francisco, they were for generations virtually unobtainable, lost entirely or preserved only in the gardens of a few antiquarians. Today, they are returning, once again filling gardens with their subtle, unfamiliar colors and perfumes. Behind their reappearance lies an extraordinary story, a tale of flowers that have persisted unchanged for centuries and of the unlikely band of experts who united to rescue them from extinction.

My own introduction to old-fashioned roses was accidental, but almost inevitable, since I discovered gardening through the pages of a two-thousand-year-old agricultural treatise. Classics were my first love, most particularly Latin literature and archaeology, but three years of chasing Caesar's ghost through the dusty stacks of the Brown University library left me ready for a change. In the fall of my junior year, I spent a semester in Rome. That city, where modern tenements and shops squat in the shells of ancient monuments, fascinated me. The obtrusion of a broken column or triumphal arch only accentuated the vitality of the streets, the colors, the noise, the smell of the foods and the bite of cold Frascati wine. One evening, a favorite professor and I climbed a hill on the outskirts to watch the sun set over the city. As I drank in the rich, hazy vistas of reds, grays and browns, he turned to me, smiled, and said, "What a pity we can't dig it all up."

---

by single quotes—thus, 'Marchioness of Lorne.' The use of double quotes indicates that the name is not officially recognized—the breeder may not have registered the cultivar, or the rose may have come to the present grower unidentified (this is often the case with old roses), and had a new name assigned to it provisionally. I've placed double quotes around several names in the first paragraph, "Giant of Battles," for instance, because I've taken the liberty of translating them from the original French.

A few days later in the library, I stumbled over a stray volume of Marcus Porcius Cato's De Agricultura—On Farming. Within a few pages, I knew I'd discovered my escape. Nicknamed "the Censor," Cato was the moral conscience of the second century B.C.; and in this book he urged his fellow Romans to abandon the baths and banquets and return to a simpler, rural way of life. "In his early manhood," the Censor contended, "the head of the household should be eager to plant his land." I found that I was, or at least I thought I was after reading Cato's advice on buying a farm and establishing vineyards, orchards and gardens. It was from farmers that the sturdiest men came, or so the old Roman led me to believe. Likewise, it was men engaged in this pursuit who were, according to the same authority, least given to thinking evil thoughts.

I didn't want to doubt the Censor. He was the man, I learned, who succeeded in banning all Greek philosophers and rhetoricians from the city of Rome, a coup that won my jealous admiration, since I was that semester waging a desperate battle with the devious complexities of their prose. Fired by Cato's vision of a return to the soil, I abandoned plans of an academic career and upon my return to Brown struck a deal with the dean for an early graduation so that I could enroll immediately in a horticultural training program at the New York Botanical Garden.

There the gardeners taught me never to call soil "dirt" (an unforgivable slight to that precious commodity), to swear in Sicilian and to work all day doubled over, because kneeling, even though it might ease my back, would decrease my productivity. They taught me, too—especially the older gardeners, Ralph, Dominic and Patsy—the dignity that comes from a life of collaboration with nature. In 1976, after a two-year apprenticeship, I graduated and had the good fortune to find immediately a job that called on all my skills, academic as well as horticultural. Columbia University commissioned me to restore an old estate it had been given, 126 acres of woods, lawns and gardens along the crest of the Hudson River Palisades.

The landscaping had been done in 1929; it was one of the few great gardens to emerge from the crash and subsequent depression, and it had been built in the grand style. Olmsted Brothers of Brookline, Massachusetts, the successors of Frederick Law Olmsted, the designer of Central Park, had drafted the plans. One hundred and eighty-seven sheets drawn in the most exquisite detail, the blueprints included the name and location of every tree, shrub or flower in the original gardens.

Though I recognized the species names, very few of the cultivars were familiar to me. Of the 27,500 bulbs planted in the fall of 1930, for example, I didn't know a single one. But that didn't surprise me. Fashions in flowers change as regularly as they do in clothes and cars, and nurserymen are quick to dispose of last-year's-model tulips or hyacinths. But roses were, and are, another matter. A bed of roses in full bloom, especially if it is a bit wild and overgrown, gratifies in me a repressed yearning for colorful, sensual disorder. Roses I had grown by the hundreds, and I prided myself on my ability to maintain them in an apparent state of romantic abandon while secretly cultivating them in perfect health. I thought I knew roses inside out, so I was piqued when I found one on the plans that I didn't recognize. What was this 'Île de France'?

I liked the name. It had an elegance that I missed in the 'Voodoos,' 'Razzle Dazzles,' and 'Just Joeys' I found in my contemporary catalogues. 'Tiffany'—now that was a modern rose. It sounded like something you would hear, followed by a slap and a wail, at the supermarket. 'Île de France' suggested other things: men in tuxedos and ladies in gowns, long summer evenings, champagne cocktails, and a party that never ended. That sounded like a rose I wanted, and, surely, it was the rose for this estate.

Besides, the idea of a classic rose suited my prejudices. Like most gardeners, I have an abiding mistrust of progress. Syn-

thetic fertilizers, turbo-charged tools and genetic engineering
may fill agriculturists and extension agents with visions of
utopia, but they are far less attractive to the practitioners of a
craft that has not changed in its essentials since Pliny the
Younger's slaves spelled out their master's name in boxwood
hedges. (Before leaving Brown, my horticultural education
had progressed as far as the end of the first century A.D., and
the letter in which this wealthy Roman man of letters described the landscaping of his Tuscan villa.) Unfortunately,
the nurserymen with whom I usually did business had never
heard of 'Île de France.' Nor had the librarian at the New
York Botanical Garden, but she was able to put me in touch
with someone who had, Lily Shohan.

Lily Shohan was Northeast Regional Coordinator for the
Heritage Roses Group, "a fellowship of those who care about
Old Roses." Lily was only too happy to answer my questions
about 'Île de France.' It was, she wrote me, a rambling rose
that had been introduced on the market in 1922. It hadn't made
much of an impression. Within eighteen years the name was
reassigned to another rose, and "as for Île de France, we can
but suspect it was thrown out—discarded as not being worth
the space it took up."* Lily sounded well worth meeting.

On a gray February day I arrived at her house in the Ta-
conic Mountains of upstate New York. Inside, there were
roses in bloom. Ranked in pots along a west-facing window
were four full-sized bushes, each one picked out with buds
and even a blossom or two despite the season. It was a saffron-
yellow blossom that caught my eye. Though large, it was a
simpler rose than the modern Hybrid Teas to which I was accustomed. I have since learned to call it "semi-double," mean-

---

* I have since learned that Lily was not entirely fair in her condemna-
tion of this rose. The reason that 'Île de France' disappeared so abruptly
from our catalogues was that American distributors renamed the rose
'Adoration,' presumably hoping that a more pronounceable name
would improve sales. It did not, and 'Adoration' gradually dropped
out of the nursery trade. 'Île de France' survives under the original
name in France.

ing that it has fewer petals than the typical florist's rose of today. One hundred and forty years ago, however, it held center stage in the shop windows. 'Safrano' was its name, Lily told me. It was "introduced" in 1839 (roses, like debutantes, do not appear unannounced: they must be formally presented to the public). The perfume was pleasantly odd—clean, fruity, almost acidic. It was supposed to recall the aroma of dried tea leaves, which was why this strain and its relatives were called "Tea roses."

Lily Shohan couldn't have presented a more striking contrast to the fragility of her flowers. She is the daughter of a dairy farmer, a sturdy countrywoman with a no-nonsense manner. Past middle age now, she still splits the firewood that heats her house and digs her own garden. An explorer by nature, she had recently returned from a tour of English gardens, and her conversation was filled with the discoveries and incidents of that trip. The novelties had impressed her most—the eucalyptus tree she had seen on the outskirts of London, a subtropical tree flourishing unprotected at the same latitude as Labrador.

Yet coupled with her enthusiasm for the new was an abiding appreciation of the way of life in which she was raised. I had interrupted her in a search through a pile of nursery catalogues; she wanted seed, she told me, of a particular dwarf basil to try in her garden. Dropping a catalogue back on the pile, she berated the nurserymen for advertising not what was proven and good, but merely what would sell. Her house may be new—she built it in 1976—but it's set on land she knows well, thirty acres she has kept from the farm her parents bought in 1933, land that fed and clothed her as she grew up. And she's surrounded the house with rosebushes even older than the farm.

She cannot recall just when she developed her enthusiasm for roses—she's grown them since childhood—but she remembers precisely the occasion of her conversion to the old-fashioned varieties. Her parents had said they wanted to grow

"roses like they have in the florist's window," so Lily bought
them a dozen Hybrid Teas. Then came the winter of '58-'59,
"a real heller," when temperatures dropped to thirty below.
Though she had spent her Thanksgiving burying the base of
each rosebush with a wheelbarrow-load of sandy soil, most
of them died. She was determined to replace the bushes, but
this time with something more persistent.

By reading through guides to rose growing, she learned that
roses needn't be ephemeral; that they have, in fact, been a
fixture of man's gardens since the days of the Pharaohs.
William Penn brought garden roses to America in 1699—but
according to Captain John Smith, the Quaker had been pre-
ceded by the Indians of the James River valley, who transplanted wild roses from wood and field to adorn their en-
campments. There are still roses the length of the Oregon
trail, brought there by Conestoga wagon.* Obviously, those
gardeners hadn't reordered from the nursery every spring. So
Lily turned her back on the roses of the modern hybridizers
and returned to the varieties country people had grown for
generations. They're tough, those old roses, and she likes that.

The roses Lily sought were not for sale then in any of the
mass-market nursery catalogues, but she found she was not

---

* The rose commonly planted by these pioneers was 'Harison's Yellow,' a vigorous shrub that makes a mound of foliage six feet high and
covers itself in June with deep-yellow, two-inch wheels of yellow
petals. This cultivar's popularity with westerners seems to have arisen
from its resilience. Bristling with needlelike thorns, 'Harison's Yellow'
could fend off the hungriest longhorn, and once well-rooted it is impervious to drought and cold. Best of all it spreads by suckers, providing a steady supply of rooted shoots that could be dug and packed in
a pot to ride in the back of a wagon. Often claimed as the "Yellow
Rose of Texas," it is, in point of fact, a New Yorker—it originated as
a chance seedling sometime before the year 1830 at the country home
of a Manhattan attorney named Richard Harison. Collectors who visit
the rose's birthplace, a stretch of Thirty-first Street between Eighth
and Ninth avenues, will find no memorial to the city's floral pioneer;
indeed, it is difficult today to imagine that landscape bearing a crop of
anything other than hand trucks and garment warehouses.

entirely alone in her interest. Lambertus Bobbink, a New Jersey nurseryman, had anticipated her by more than thirty years. His specialty was roses, and he had been intrigued by the antiques he had found in France. He'd amassed a collection of 3,000 plants which he shipped back to Rutherford; by 1932 he listed 200 types in his *Bobbink & Atkins* catalogue. In the booklet he distributed with these roses, Bobbink noted that conservative estimates placed the number of "Old Fashioned Roses" at a total of 6,500 distinct cultivars. Of these, he calculated, less than a tenth were still in existence.

The challenge implicit in this situation proved irresistible to Ethelyn Keays, a clubwoman from New York who summered in Maryland's tidewater country. Her affection for old roses sprang from the survivors she had discovered on the farm she and her husband bought in Calvert County. She began to supplement this collection with bushes recovered from neighboring plantations, and in 1935, she published a book, *Old Roses,* in which she described all her finds, together with brief histories and genealogies. This in turn sparked a minor renaissance, encouraging two or three other rose growers, most notably Will Tillotson of Watsonville, California, to advertise limited selections of antique varieties.

Since Bobbink & Atkins had gone out of business in 1957, Lily placed her order with Tillotson's. But that alone didn't satisfy her—she had taken to heart the "Challenge to Rose-Lovers" that was the preface to Mrs. Keays's book. It charged readers with the rediscovery, protection and preservation of antique roses, and sent them out into the field to rescue the survivors of old gardens, to make "a real American collection of old roses still alive."

The white rose that climbs the corner of Lily's house is evidence of her success as a rose collector. She found the creamy, fragrant blossom in the garden of a colonial-era farmhouse down the road. By checking the flowers against Mrs. Keays's descriptions and those of other rose handbooks, Lily eventually identified the bush as *Rosa alba* 'Maxima.' Once known as

the "Jacobite Rose," this blossom was the badge of supporters
of the Stuart kings after their exile in 1688.

Lily didn't bother to collect seed, since she knew that garden roses don't reproduce true to form from seed. Even seeds
taken from the same fruit (or "hip") rarely produce identical
plants; sow 100 seeds from a given bush and, if 100 percent
of them germinate, you will find yourself, almost certainly,
with 100 different bushes. Transplanting the entire bush was
not an option Lily considered very often, since that violates
one of the basic rules of old-rose collecting. Unless threatened
with destruction, the find must remain *in situ* and intact,
available to other collectors. Instead, the rose must be cloned.
That is, a piece of tissue is removed and induced to develop
into a new, but genetically identical, plant.

"Cloning" is a modern-sounding word, but in the case of
roses, the techniques involved date back, in a crude form, three
thousand years, and require no more sophisticated equipment
than a sharp knife. Chinese gardeners were the first to discover the principles of grafting and to use them to propagate
exceptional trees and shrubs. This is still the method of choice
for commercial growers: a bud is excised from the hybrid or
garden rose and inserted into a slit the grower has made in the
stem of the "rootstock," a rosebush of a type remarkable for its
hardy, vigorous roots. Once the new bud sends up a shoot, the
entire top of the rootstock bush is removed, forcing the roots
to feed only the new shoot. For the nurseryman, the advantage of "budding," as it is called, is that it lends itself to mass-
production. The procedure succeeds with almost every type of
rose, and it produces bushes of fairly uniform size and quality
in a predictable interval of time.

Amateur growers, however, generally prefer the simpler,
though less dependable, method of rooting a cutting, and that
is what Lily does. She's no expert, she's quick to point out;
she just does it. With a pair of pruning shears, she'll cut a
flowering shoot from a bush. She has found that the shoot has
reached just the right stage of maturity by the time that it

flowers: "Just as the bloom opens, or just as the petals fall, somewhere in there." A stem that's "blind" (without flower bud or blossom) she avoids, since "there's some indication that if you keep selecting blind wood, you're going to get a plant that doesn't bloom as much. At least that's the theory. If you keep selecting from a blind shoot, eventually you're going to get a blind bush."

Lily doesn't make the cut entirely clean either, preferring to take the cutting with a "heel," a sliver of the cane from which the shoot springs. Removing the flower, she cuts the shoot back to the "first true leaf"—a leaf that shows at least five leaflets. These cuts she then trims smooth with a razor blade, scraping the bark at the cutting's base, "wounding" it, to promote the formation of the callus that develops into roots. The only advantage that modern technology has given Lily over her Chinese predecessors is in the rooting hormone she uses, a synthetic duplicate of the chemical plants produce to initiate root formation. Dunking the cutting's base in this, she sticks it into a four-inch pot full of sterilized potting soil; though she uses a commercial blend of peat moss, vermiculite and perlite now, she thinks the soil she used to gather from her woods works better. It was in this homegrown "loom" that she rooted her Jacobite rose.

This process of cloning, a strange mixture of empirical plant lore, science, custom and superstition, makes Lily's roses, and those of other collectors, special. The rose Lily grew from that cutting is not a descendant of the rose Jacobites picked to wear in their buttonholes on the birthday of the Old Pretender (James III, the king who never reigned); it is a piece of the very same plant.

Lily's most important role in the revival of old roses, however, was not in collecting but in promotion. At rose shows and meetings of the American Rose Society, she met the handful of other rose growers who shared her interest in old roses, and she won a reputation as someone who not only knew her subject but also was generous with her time. This brought tangible rewards, as her collection swelled with gifts of unknown roses, "foundlings" sent to her for identification. In May of 1975, she collaborated with three other collectors, Carl Cato from Virginia, Miriam Wilkins from California, and Edith Schurr from the state of Washington, to found the Heritage Roses Group. She has been enrolling interested novices ever since.

One of my first questions to her was the definition of an "old" rose, and how it differs from a "new" rose. Lily couldn't give me any hard-and-fast rule, but then, neither could any other collector I've met since. The standard definition is that an old rose is any that appeared before the introduction of the first Hybrid Tea rose, 'La France,' in 1867. Previously, gardeners had grown roses of many different types or "classes." Besides Tea roses there were Portland roses, Bourbon roses, Damasks, Gallicas, Moss roses, Centifolias, Albas, Hybrid Perpetuals and a host of others. 'La France' and its offspring, the Hybrid Teas, eventually swept the others off the market, so their appearance is said to mark the end of the old roses.

Yet one of the roses that was blooming in Lily's house, a red blossom, was 'Monsieur Tillier.' This, too, is a Tea rose, for it shares 'Safrano's' bloodlines and surely deserves inclusion in the same category. But 'Monsieur Tillier' dates only to 1891. The best solution to this dilemma of definitions seems to be the one developed by New Zealander Trevor Griffiths. He prefaces his recent guide to old roses by noting the position of the purists, and then explaining his own rule of thumb. For the purpose of his book, an old rose is any that is not modern.*

* *The American Rose Society has dealt with this problem by creating a new term "old garden rose." Old garden roses include any rose whose class appeared before 1867; thus, 'Monsieur Tillier,' though arguably not an "old rose," does qualify as an old garden rose and may be displayed with his relatives at rose shows. Unfortunately, while the American Rose Society's innovation solves one problem, it creates another (at least in my opinion). There are private enthusiasts, even commercial hybridizers, who are breeding new roses of the old classes, new Teas, new Hybrid Perpetuals, etc. Should a reproduction of this sort be classed with a genuine antique such as 'Safrano'? I say no.*

Imprecise as this may be, it is only a reflection of the field. Old-rose collectors are connoisseurs, not academicians, amateurs in the best sense of the word. Their approach recalls that of Bernard Berenson, the pioneer of art history. When Berenson could not assign a painting to an artist he knew, he would create a hypothetical master, sometimes hypothesizing a school of students as well, to whom he attributed other paintings. This is a practice that outrages modern professors of art history. But so profound was Berenson's knowledge of the field, so accurate his intuition, that the scholars who followed in his wake have discovered previously unknown artists who proved to be Berenson's hypothetical masters. The collectors I have met may be unable to define an old rose except by negatives, but they know one when they see it.

That's not really such a feat. There is in the old roses a richness, a particular beauty that has been bred out of the modern rose. Rose production in the United States is dominated today by the judgment of the A.A.R.S.—"All America Rose Selections"—an organization founded by nurserymen in 1938 to impose uniformity on what was then a chaotic business. This body has worked with the American Rose Society to eliminate the willful renaming of roses that unscrupulous dealers practiced to pass off inferior stock as popular varieties. In addition, its annual selections of the best roses, the "All America Roses," have become the nurseryman's standard of reliability and favorites with the public. But they are all approved according to a single set of standards.

These new roses are admirable in many ways. They are everblooming; given adequate care, they bloom continuously from late spring until frost. That is something the hardy types of old roses, the ones that flourish throughout the United States, never achieved. The new roses offer a wider selection of colors, too. Sun yellows and oranges in particular are generally a product of modern times, since hardy roses of these hues descend, almost invariably, from a cross that the French nurseryman Pernet-Ducher made in 1900 between an old

Middle Eastern rose, 'Persian Yellow,' and a winter-proof Hybrid Perpetual. Finally, the best of the new roses are disease-resistant, less prone to the mildew and blackspot that are the plague of the rose grower. Unblemished, vivid and reliable—yet the new roses all look very much the same. They were all bred to the same set of criteria, to win the same prize, and as a result they lack character.

A hundred and fifty years ago, there were dozens, hundreds of nurserymen all working separately and toward different goals. Few understood the botanical basis of their breeding programs, and all guarded their methods with paranoid jealousy. The roses of each expressed a private vision of what a rose should be. One famous Frenchman, Monsieur Vibert, who had begun his career as an undergardener to the Empress Josephine, specialized in striped and spotted roses—"marbled roses" he called them—and his creations were famous throughout Europe in the first half of the nineteenth century. Three generations later, the Dicksons, Alexander senior and junior (the third and fourth in Ireland's leading dynasty of rose breeders), consistently won prizes at British rose shows. According to legend, the son achieved what has always been the rose hybridizer's unattainable dream: a blue rose.* His father, a stern old Ulsterman, when he learned of the accomplishment destroyed the entire stock. A blue rose, he said, would corrupt the public's taste.

As idiosyncratic as their creators, no two of the old roses are alike. Whereas modern roses almost invariably aim at the tight, high-centered blossom of the Hybrid Tea, the old roses may be flattened like architectural rosettes, or cupped, with the petals wrapped tightly round the center, or even as huge, fluffy and overblown as a crinoline petticoat. The colors are softer and subtler than those of their modern counterparts.

---

* Breeders have produced a number of bluish or lavender roses; but to date no true clear blue. The reason for this, it has recently been discovered, is that the genus Rosa lacks the genetic coding for delphinidin, the pigment that colors delphiniums and other flowers blue.

A cupped rose

A quartered rose

An imbricated or expanded rose

A globular rose

Delicate blends of pink, rose, lilac and mauve were what old-time nurserymen preferred, though they could, and did on occasion, also breed vivid scarlets and pure whites, even an occasional gold. Extraordinary roses were produced, blossoms whose hues are almost indescribable and certainly irreproducible.

Even the perfumes were stronger, richer and more varied. Besides the tea scent, there were roses that smelled of exotic spices, myrrh, cinnamon and cloves. Some were said to smell of apples, others of mangoes, oranges, pineapples and bananas. There are, to be sure, highly perfumed modern roses such as 'Chrysler Imperial' or 'Fragrant Cloud,' but too often the fragrance has been bred out in the pursuit of blue ribbons. In the heyday of the old roses, by contrast, it was said that a blindfolded expert could identify different varieties by fragrance alone.

The most obvious difference between the old and new roses, and one that bespeaks a basic difference in aesthetics, lies in their season of bloom. The old roses bore the bulk of their blossoms in a few weeks, with perhaps an occasional encore thereafter. Even the "Hybrid Perpetual" roses, latecomers among the old roses and a class that does continue to flower through the summer months and into the fall, yield 95 percent of their blossoms in June and July. Such a brief season does not reflect a poverty of bloom. Actually the average Hybrid Perpetual bears more flowers each year than the average modern Hybrid Tea, but the Hybrid Perpetual yields its blooms in a single exuberant burst, rather than doling them out, month by month.

Old roses, a collector once explained to me, are the most "people" flowers. People have loved them longest, and their history has always been the story of the people who grew them. Today, it is the story of the people who are rescuing them from extinction. To the extent that I have come to know the old roses, I have done so through the acquaintance of the collectors I've met through the Heritage Roses Group. I've toured their gardens, looked through their libraries, listened to their stories. I've accompanied them on collecting expeditions where their real work is done. In the cemeteries of backwoods Texas, in abandoned gardens in Vermont, and in the black neighborhoods of small Virginia towns, I've plunged my nose into perfumed blossoms, counted leaflets and pulled thorns from my fingers, as the collectors I was with looked for lost roses. Their quarry was blossoms of which perhaps they had only read or heard, but which nevertheless they were determined to find.

In my garden, among the queens, duchesses and other gentry are roses with incongruous titles: "Route 301," "The Hole Rose," "Petite Pink Scotch," and "Margaret Parton." These are gifts of collectors, roses they have rescued but never identified. So they named the bushes after the places or people from which the roses were obtained. These are the shrubs I guard most jealously. Who knows what rarities they may one day prove to be?

1

Of Musk Roses
and
Other Mysteries

Single musk rose

"It's very annoying, I find, after all these years for people not to put things right."

Graham Thomas, the Englishman who is generally conceded to be the world's foremost authority on old roses, spoke with measured severity. We were discussing the Musk rose. Exposing the impostor that masqueraded as this ancient flower was one of his most inspired bits of detective work. The day when he rediscovered the true Musk in 1963 was, he had told me twice, "certainly the most exciting" of a rose-collecting career that has lasted half a century. Naturally, he hadn't been pleased when I told him that America's leading old-rose nursery had yet to correct its catalogue.

A sitting room in Surrey and tales of an English rose hunt might seem a long way from home for an American gardener. But it would be impossible to write a story of these flowers without featuring Graham Thomas. Scholar, artist and dirt-under-the-fingernails gardener, he comes close to defining what an old-rose collector should be, and his pursuits of floral antiques, masterfully narrated in his own books, serve as manuals for American as well as British enthusiasts. Besides, his recollections could provide the final pieces for a story I'd been following through the American South for two years. Collectors there had escorted me backward, step by step, along the Musk rose's trail from the eve of the Civil War and North Carolina's Piedmont Plateau to Jamestown and the birth of the thirteen colonies. I had come to England seeking the thorny immigrant's roots and to speak with the man who set its revival in motion.

I was delighted but surprised when Graham Thomas readily agreed to meet with me. He's not only eminent, he's busy. Though he donated his personal collection of old roses to the National Trust in 1972 (I planned to visit them the next day, in their walled garden at Mottisfont Abbey), he continues to puzzle out the history of the rose. He has written three volumes about roses old and new that belong on any serious rosarian's bookshelf, and currently, at seventy-nine, he is corresponding with botanists in China, sorting out the confusion that surrounds some of that country's early cultivars.

Yet when he is described as a rose specialist, Graham Thomas betrays a trace of impatience. His interests are much broader than that—the quarter acre that surrounds his home, Briar Cottage, in Surrey is a horticultural jewel box. The carefully orchestrated borders of perennials and shrubs and the beds of alpines he showed me round are testimony to a lifetime of weighing and judging all sorts of garden plants. That was his occupation, of course, during his forty years as a nurseryman, during which he took plantsmanship to an extreme. Sunningdale, the nursery he managed for fifteen years, came to be known as "the most beautiful nursery in the country." A fellow nurseryman and admirer whom I asked about it thought perhaps Thomas's omnivorous appetite for beauty had been a liability for a businessman. Certainly it had run against the current of post–World War II horticulture, in which great collections were pared down to small lists of easily raised, easily marketed plants.

"Graham grew *everything*," the informant confided with a grin and a note of rueful admiration. He felt that Thomas had found his real calling in the National Trust, which he served as Gardens Adviser from 1955 until 1974 (he continues in retirement to serve as Gardens Consultant). In the beginning, he had the stewardship of just a handful of gardens, though these included several neglected masterpieces whose resuscitation required the greatest sensitivity. Plantings designed for the days of cheap labor had to be simplified to suit a postwar economy, and seasonal displays extended to keep the fee-paying visitors coming throughout the warm weather. Substantial changes were required, yet these had to be made in such a way as to fit the vision of the original creator.

Spare time and his three-week annual holiday sufficed to fulfill these tasks at first, but as death duties forced more and more stately homes into the National Trust's receivership, the job expanded to a nearly full-time position. Eventually the Trust became Britain's largest private landowner—today this charitable society manages 188 houses and castles, 533,000 acres of countryside and more than 100 gardens. It could be argued that Graham Thomas has had his hands on more of Britain's landscape than any gardener since Capability Brown began showing the gentry the "capabilities" of their properties in the mid-eighteenth century. But whereas Brown was a revolutionary, putting the axe to alleys of ancient trees and sweeping away parterres and terraces to make room for his essays in "naturalism," Thomas has been a restorer, an enlightened adaptor of the old to suit the constraints of a new day.

Thomas distilled his experiences in garden design and restoration into another book, *The Art of Planting*, which he published in 1984. His use of the word "art" in the title was significant. He came from an artistic family—his father had a deft hand with crayon, pen and pencil, and his mother a talent for watercolors, charcoal and chalk. And painting and drawing had been his field until age eight, when he was seduced by his first commissions as a garden designer (he built rockeries for his parents' friends, reinvesting the income in more plants for his own plot).

"I found gardening and playing about much easier and lacked the application for art," Thomas has explained in a biographical note accompanying one of his books. Actually, his training in horticulture was of the most rigorous, traditional kind. He apprenticed from age sixteen at the Cambridge University Botanic Garden, where he worked under the kind of master craftsman who no longer exists. There was a right way to do everything then, a way the elders had evolved through years of hard, unglamorous labor, and in routine operations every motion was prescribed. It was the *heel* of the boot you placed on the spade's shoulder when digging, so that you didn't break the instep; you learned to tell by the heft of a pot or the tone it made when it was struck whether the plant needed water; you never used your *thumbs* to firm the soil when potting plants. I remember Thomas Everett, an English horticulturist of the old school who presided over the New York Botanical Garden when I was a student even though he had retired a decade previously. If Tom Everett saw your thumbs in action when you were potting, he'd pick up your finished pots and smash them one by one against the potting shed wall, then tell you to do it all again, and this time to do it right.

Graham Thomas acquired the journeyman's technique without ever losing the artist's instinct. He has received the Victoria Medal of Honour, Britain's highest award for horticultural achievement, as well as an Order of the British Empire. Yet he seems much more interested in the yellow-and-blossomed honeysuckle that bears his name (*Lonicera pericly-menum* 'Graham Thomas'), which he found in a Warwickshire hedge, and the glorious yellow 'Graham Thomas' shrub rose that made its debut in 1983—"You'll see me at Mottisfont," he told me. "I'm blooming there." He listed for me a number of places where I should see him blooming, then remarked wryly that he doesn't perform very well in his own garden. Last year Thomas published a well-received collection of botanical drawings and paintings, and I noticed that his sitting room houses two pianos. When I asked why he chose gardening as his vocation, he replied simply, "A love of beauty."

It was a bad debt that introduced him to the Musk rose. In 1936, he explained, "Daisy Hill Nurseries in Northern Ireland owed our firm some money, and they were not in very good order." In fact, this firm which had made a business of supplying plants to the Anglo-Irish aristocracy, another vanishing breed, was bankrupt. Daisy Hill settled with Thomas's employer by sending over a large collection of old roses from Irish gardens. "Here was something utterly different from anything else in horticulture," Thomas recalls, "and they were worth looking after."

Perhaps so, but the war intervened, and the roses sat in a field full of couch grass and thistles until 1948, when Thomas had the leisure to begin sorting them out. He had stolen away from his war work to visit the odd garden where old roses were treasured—one gardener would pass him on to the next, for the horticultural world of England was still very much an upper-class club. A number of the estates Thomas visited on these expeditions later passed into his purview while he was working for the National Trust. During the first year of the war he had also acquired a second nursery collection, this one of species roses, plants collected from the wild. The bulk of England's old roses was coming to repose in Thomas's garden, and among them was a plant that purported to be *Rosa moschata*.

As I listened, I couldn't help reflecting on the circumstances under which I first encountered the Musk rose, long before I developed any interest in gardens. It was eighth-grade English class, and we were struggling through *A Midsummer Night's Dream*. Shakespeare's versifying held only limited interest for a fourteen-year-old boy, but a few of the passages stuck, as I suppose my teacher must have hoped. One was Oberon's lyrical speech in which he describes the bower of Titania, his fairy queen:

> *I know a bank where the wild thyme blows,*
> *Where oxlips and the nodding violet grows,*
> *Quite over-canopied with luscious woodbine,*
> *With sweet musk-roses, and with eglantine.*

I'm not sure whether it was the power of the language or the daydreams of summers in the country this verse stirred (though I recognized none of the flowers, only the mood), but I never forgot those lines. Much research has been expended on Shakespeare's flowers, and "Shakespeare gardens" are a common conceit, though there is no evidence that he ever lifted a spade. Shakespeare was, however, obviously fond of flowers, and he took a special interest in the Musk rose. In Act II, Scene 2, Titania, as she beds down in her bower, assigns to her attendant fairies the task of killing "cankers in the musk-rose buds."

That the poet considered this flower a fit ornament for royalty was not surprising, although it is in appearance a modest shrub. Its canes may climb to heights of ten to twelve feet, but the blossoms it bears in loose clusters are small and pale, bearing only five white petals apiece. But its perfume is remarkable; it mimics the secretions of the male musk deer, a costly but popular basis for perfumes since ancient times.

Finding its way about southern Europe with Arab invaders, the Musk rose travelled from there to England—according to one account, in the suite of a returning ambassador, Lord Cromwell, in 1513. Its fragrance guaranteed the rose an enthusiastic reception in Tudor England, where the scent of the rutting musk stag was the favorite deodorant of the court's unwashed dandies, and the perfume of choice for Elizabeth, the Virgin Queen. No doubt it was as a graceful bow to this royal patron that Shakespeare intended his reference to the Musk rose. There is only one problem, as I discovered when, armed with a new interest in roses, I returned to the play after twenty years. The Musk doesn't bloom at midsummer.

Graham Thomas was the one who pointed this out, in his book *Climbing Roses Old and New,* and he was sure of this because John Gerard had told him so. Gerard was a sixteenth-century barber and surgeon, and the author of *The Grete Herball.* In his day, medical men still compounded their own prescriptions, often from herbs they gathered themselves, and Gerard's knowledge of plants was so famous that it won him the superintendency of the gardens, in both town and country, of Queen Elizabeth's favorite minister, Lord Burghley. In his *Herball* (published in 1597, two years after the composition of *A Midsummer Night's Dream,* but in plenty of time for Shakespeare to have made the necessary revisions before the publication of the First Quarto in 1600), Gerard boasted of having grown more than one thousand different "herbes," including the "Muske Rose." He recommended the flower not as a garden ornament but as a purge, to be eaten as a salad dressed with oil, vinegar and pepper. This was a seasonal remedy only, since Gerard stated very definitely that "the Muske Rose floureth in Autumne, or the fall of the leafe."

Thomas learned of Gerard's observations through the program of reading he had begun. As he acquired old roses, he also acquired old-rose books. "I now have all the rose books, the worthwhile ones, that have ever been published," he told me, except for two pictorial works of the late eighteenth to early nineteenth century, which cost five to six thousand pounds when they come on the market, "and I haven't seen any advertised for donkey's years." I could well believe his claim when he took me into his study, where every wall was hidden behind serried ranks of bindings. For other materials,

Thomas commuted by train into London and the library of
the Royal Horticultural Society, a collection that has almost
never failed to supply the works he needed.

"I've stumped them twice, I think," he reflected. He knows
his way around the stacks so well that sometimes the librarians
will ask him where to find an errant volume.

In light of Gerard's information, Thomas believes that
Shakespeare's Musk was actually *Rosa arvensis,* a native English species. "Which I am adamant has a most delicious scent,
though certain people can't smell it. But that," Thomas continued firmly, "is because they haven't educated their noses."
Far more reprehensible than the poet's ignorance was the
carelessness of modern nurserymen. Thomas observed that all
the live roses he found under the label "Musk," even those at
Cambridge and Kew, bloomed in midsummer and not, as they
ought to, "at the fall of the leafe."

Additional trips to the booksellers and to the Royal Horticultural Society library revealed further discrepancies between
the Musk rose he knew and the original. John Parkinson,
Botanicum Regius Prismarius ("Royal Botanist Most Illus-
trious") to Charles I, had also described the Musk in his
Paradisi in Sole ("The Park-in-Sun"), a work published in
1629 and generally considered the first great English gardening encyclopedia. Parkinson stressed the height of the canes—
ten to twelve feet. Yet the Musk at Thomas's alma mater, the
University Botanic Garden at Cambridge, had heaved its
thick, thorny canes forty feet up a neighboring pine. Parkinson wrote of "small darke greene leaves," and Gerard of a
foliage "smooth & shining," but all the modern Musks flaunted
leaves long, drooping and grayish. An English nursery catalogue from 1843 recommended the Musk for "the autumnal
rose garden," and another from 1848 praised the "abundant
blooms, especially in autumn." The Musks Thomas knew had
all finished blooming by then.

Thomas spent the winter in 1962–3 stalking the Musk rose
through the literature. He checked herbalists against botanists,

and supplemented both with extracts from accounts of plant explorers. He watched the Musk rose drop from its place of honor in the garden—a character in a popular novel, *My Lady Ludlow* of 1859, observed that the old Musk rose was "dying out through the Kingdom now." He noted the appearance of a Himalayan relative, *R. brunonii,* in the popular gardening guides of the 1890s and watched as the rampant newcomer first joined the Musk in the catalogues and then gradually supplanted it. By 1914, it had become commonplace to confuse the two species—no doubt the confusion brought to the nursery business by World War I helped *R. brunonii* to assume the Musk roses's identity. However it had happened, Thomas became convinced that what was now selling as the Musk was actually the far eastern rose.

The search this discovery prompted and his rediscovery of the true Musk Graham Thomas has related in his book *Climbing Roses Old and New.* Thomas drew on his wide acquaintance with the horticultural establishment to locate the Musk rose. He found it at the home of the late E. A. Bowles, a gentleman gardener who had satisfied his taste for oddities with the "lunatic asylum" he kept for eccentric plants. The exact circumstances surrounding this discovery the reader will find in Mr. Thomas's book; I don't intend to enter into a competition with him. Instead, I will return to the United States, the hunt Graham Thomas inspired there, and a Musk rose as rich in history as any in Britain.

Thomas had a reader in Lynchburg, Virginia, named Carl Cato. Carl claims (not too seriously) descent from my mentor, the Censor, and like the noble Roman, Carl is a practical man, an engineer by profession and a farmer by upbringing. One of the founders of the Heritage Roses Group, Carl believes sincerely in the fellowship that organization espouses. He's a skilled propagator and has helped to return a number of roses to the nursery trade, but when I met him he was very definite about the fact that he had never *sold* a rose; he had given them all away. (The last time I spoke to Carl he confessed that he had at last gone into business: he had rooted and sold ten cuttings of his 'Spanish Beauty' to raise funds for a medical research institute.)

Carl could hardly fail to take an interest in heritage in Lynchburg. The traditions of the Old South are strong there—most agreeably in Carl's courtly manners, his soft-spoken civility. Strictly speaking, the foothills of the Blue Ridge do not lie in the land of cotton, but I did spy a fluffy white boll on the Catos' sideboard, a reminder of the snowy beauty of the fields in bloom. And old times are not forgotten: the Shenandoah Valley was the scene of some of the Civil War's hardest-fought campaigns, and battlefields, monuments and graveyards dignify every corner. Carl knows the significance of every one. All in all, it is an environment in which old roses seem perfectly at home.

There is the rose Carl found at Appomattox Courthouse, for example. By the door to that shrine stands a venerable rosebush whose pink blossoms Carl had little trouble identifying as those of 'Old Blush.' A stubbornly tenacious shrub, 'Old Blush' is the most common rose in the dooryards of Southern cabins and shotgun shacks. 'Old Blush' Carl knew to be an antebellum variety which came to Virginia with the tobacco planters. On a hunch, he scrutinized the Matthew Brady photograph of Lee's surrender, and found the same shrub growing in the same spot by the doorway. As a Southerner, Carl takes great pride in having located the last surviving witness to that fateful event.

Unlike Graham Thomas, Carl Cato didn't come upon old roses as a part of a general horticultural exploration. Of course, he'd raised vegetables as a child on the family farm in South Carolina, but he never paid much attention to roses until he moved to his present home in a Lynchburg subdivision. At each corner of the house he found a rosebush. "In spite of receiving no care," he recalls, "they insisted on producing some extremely beautiful bloom every summer."

Carl was impressed and he went down to the garden center

to add to his collection. The process of selection was simple: he ordered "a white 'un, red 'un and a yaller 'un," he explained, deliberately dropping into a deep back-country drawl.

After a few years and many more purchases, he began to feel what he describes as a "surfeiture."

"The modern rose grower is entranced with the magnificent beauty of the Hybrid Tea, especially the exhibition type. That's what he strives for, and although there are many colors and many modifications of form, he admires only one kind of beauty," Carl says. "We," he adds, meaning the old-rose growers, "have many, many kinds of beauty to admire, to study and to treasure."

Carl discovered the old roses in 1970 at the prompting of a New Jersey rose fancier who challenged him to read a catalogue from Tillotson's (the nursery that supplied Lily Shohan's first old roses) *without* becoming addicted. Soon thereafter, he was.

From reading catalogues, he went on to an in-depth study and, inevitably, Graham Thomas's books. Carl was intrigued by the author's account of Musk-rose hunting. He began to drive up and down the streets of Lynchburg and surrounding towns, finding "that roses have a magnetic attraction to the eye."

He found especially good hunting in the older black neighborhoods. Around the weather-beaten frame houses and sagging verandas he'd find glorious blossoms—later, with catalogues and handbooks he'd identify these as roses of the most distinguished European descent. Few of the owners he interviewed knew what they had, though many had a lively appreciation of the flowers. It is Carl's belief that the roses found their way into those neighborhoods generations ago as cuttings that black gardeners took in their white employers' gardens. It is testimony to the black gardeners' taste that they kept the roses long after their employers succumbed to the itch for novelty.

Though an outgoing man, Carl is not the type to buttonhole

a stranger in the street. But rose hunting, he says, has given him "a lot of brass." If he spots a rose that interests him, he feels no hesitation about stopping the car and crossing over into a yard to inspect it—almost invariably, the householders seem to enjoy his interest. Maybe it is the sincerity of his manner, but Carl can remember only two rebuffs. Once the lady of the house was willing to share a cutting, but the husband intervened. Greed was his motive, Carl told me with disgust, for the man showed no interest in the bush until Carl told him how old and rare it was. Then the man wanted to know the rose's value, and abruptly countermanded his wife's offer. His memory of the second rebuff still causes Carl to laugh. Seeing a rose he admired, he called over a backyard fence to an elderly man who sat smoking on the porch. Pointing at the flower, Carl asked if the man knew its name. Taking the pipe from his lips, the old man observed mildly that it was called a rose, and went back to his meditations.

As soon as he read the descriptions Graham Thomas had culled from Parkinson and Gerard, Carl realized that he had already discovered not one but two specimens of Musk rose. What was more, he had done it by smell alone.

Carl had a unique advantage over other Musk-rose hunters in that respect, and it derived from his South Carolina childhood. South Carolina was also the birthplace of a once-popular class of old roses called "Noisettes." These roses take their name from a French nurseryman, Philippe Noisette, who was their commercial promoter, but they began as the hobby of a Charleston rice planter named John Champneys. Champneys, the first American to breed a rose of lasting fame, produced the founder of the line, 'Champneys' Pink Cluster,' about 1811. He accomplished this, according to modern rosarians, by crossing a Musk with a China rose (R. chinensis).

Reconstructions of such crosses are difficult, both because the hybridizers rarely kept records and often did not understand the genetic basis for what they were doing, and because of their suspicion. Not realizing that a given cross was a fluke, one of thousands of possible offspring of two parents, hybridizers regularly concealed or misrepresented the blood-lines of their roses. Otherwise, they feared, rivals might duplicate their work and steal their roses. That the Musk played some part in producing the Noisettes, however, is obvious in these flowers' musky perfumes. The Noisettes still persist in the older gardens of the South, especially, of course, in South Carolina, so long before Carl Cato ever encountered the Musk rose, he was familiar with its fragrance.

In 1975, this knowledge stood him in good stead. Like most old-rose collectors, Carl had become an habitué of old cemeteries. These are one of the great repositories of old roses, for whereas each generation is apt to relandscape the garden, few of us would root up the rose that was planted by grandmother's grave. So on a business trip through North Carolina, Carl stopped to prospect in the Elmwood Cemetery of Charlotte. Strolling through the rows of crypts and headstones, he smelled a perfume he recognized at once, the familiar odor of musk. Thoroughly intrigued, he traced the fragrance to its source, twenty-five feet away. There he found what appeared to be two bushes, one with single white flowers, the other with double blossoms.

From Peter Lewis, a past president of the American Rose Society and his mentor in the art of rose identification, Carl learned the habit of studying each new or unfamiliar rose until he had recorded a complete picture of it in his mind's eye. A decade later, I watched him perform this operation on a Rambler in a Lynchburg cemetery. Methodically, he checked the thorns, since the shape of these, hooked or straight, and their relative abundance, varies with the class of rose. Then he scrutinized the stipules, the leaflike appendages that flank the leaf-stem, since these also differ from rose to rose. The shape and color of the leaf itself, he explained to me, and whether it is silky or smooth, are also characteristic, as is the shape of the blossom.

Picking a flower, he turned it over to examine the sepals,

the five leaflike structures that shield the flower's base, since
the sepals' configuration is another clue to a rose's identity.
With his penknife, he split the flower to check its sexual
parts, the stipules, pistil and ovary, their configuration and
arrangement within the floral tube. Finally, leaning over the
bush for a last, comprehensive look, he suddenly plunged his
nose into the heart of a blossom, snuffing deeply and with
obvious satisfaction to absorb and file away in his memory that
particular perfume. Having completed all these steps, Carl
told me, he could be sure of knowing any rose when he encountered it again.

In the case of the Elmwood rose, this mnemonic routine paid
off handsomely, for three years later, when he read Graham
Thomas's description of the Musk, Carl was sure he had
found a match. One detail in particular raised Carl's hopes:
Thomas repeated an observation of Parkinson's that sometimes
the Musk bears single (five-petalled) and double (multi-
petalled) blossoms on the same bush. Carl hurried back to
Elmwood Cemetery and checked the base of the twin white
roses. They were connected; what Carl had thought were two
bushes was actually one. He had found an American specimen
of Parkinson's Musk.

Even in the midst of his excitement, Carl's well-trained
memory recalled two more sightings, one in Lynchburg and
another in the garden of "a lovely lady," Helen Watkins of
Hillsborough, North Carolina. Upon returning home, he
found the Lynchburg rose had died. His call to Hillsborough
was even more deflating. Mrs. Watkins told him that of course
she had the "old Double Musk"; she'd found it in 1971 when
as chairman of the Hillsborough Historical Society Horticulture Committee she had directed an inventory of every old
garden in town. She was sure she had told Carl about it.

Carl can take pleasure in the fact that it was cuttings from
his rose that restored the true Musk to American nurseries—
those that have recognized their former error. So the Musk

rose that wreaths a column in my garden at Lamont is a clone of the Elmwood rose. Carl also takes pleasure in another, less tangible dividend of his discovery, the new light it sheds on the Musk rose's history.

When Carl told Helen Watkins of his discovery, the mere fact of the Elmwood rose's identity didn't impress her, but its location did. The ground on which the bush happened to be growing was the burial plot of a family named Burwell; Helen's Musk rose had a Burwell pedigree, too. Her bush had come from the grounds of the Burwell School, a women's academy founded by a Presbyterian minister, Robert Burwell, in 1837. Convinced that the connection could not be coincidental, the rose hunters turned to genealogical records. Eventually they located a surviving member of the Burwell clan, an elderly lady who furnished them with records reaching all the way back to the arrival of one John Burwell in Jamestown in 1607.

It was the minister and educator, Robert Burwell, who furnished the link between the three separate specimens of the Musk rose in Hillsborough, Charlotte and Lynchburg. Before moving to Hillsborough, he had resided for a time in Lynchburg; Carl has found a record of his ordination there. The Burwell plot in Elmwood Cemetery was his, too, for Robert moved his family to that town in 1850. Obviously, it was this footloose minister who was the evangelist of the Musk. He must have brought slips with him whenever he moved, planting them wherever he settled.

Why Robert Burwell so loved this rose will never be known. Perhaps it was a family heirloom, a memento that the minister's ancestors brought with them from England. If so, it was one of the first garden roses to come to the colonies. Whatever its significance to Robert Burwell, however, it seems to have been a favorite not just of his but of the whole family. John and Marie Butler of Chesterfield, Virginia, subsequently found another specimen in the Hollywood Cemetery at Richmond. This bush was not growing on a Burwell grave, but Helen

Watkins wonders if the rose had been introduced to the area by Mrs. Burwell's Aunt Bett, who kept a large garden in nearby Petersburg.

The Musk rose is not nearly so common in England. Graham Thomas found it only once more, in a garden in the Lake District of Cumbria. His is the most luxurious specimen I have seen. It climbs to the top of a south-facing wall in Mottisfont's brick-enclosed garden. When I visited in mid July, the bush showed hardly a promise of bloom. Its cozy location against the sun-warmed bricks had teased open only a single cluster of the long, pointed buds.

The head gardener, David Stone, very generously clipped the stem and handed me the sprig so that I might examine the flowers more closely. They were single, I noticed, the five white petals folded back at the tips to give the blossoms a slightly dog-eared look. Not showy, but the fragrance was remarkable: warmly spicy, a touch of clove and something else, indefinable but unforgettable.

If I wanted to see the Musk rose at its peak, Stone told me, I'd have to return in late August or September. Graham Thomas, he added, would be keeping a particularly vigilant watch over the rose this year. Last year, someone had yet again displayed R. brunonii as the Musk rose at a Royal Horticultural Society exhibit. This year, Graham Thomas was going to bring a vase full of sprays cut from the real article to the Late-Summer Flower Show. Twenty-five years after rediscovering the true Musk, he is still putting things right.

2

"An Awful Yet Pleasing Treat"

'Maréchal Niel'

I'VE NEVER BEEN to the Elmwood Cemetery to view Robert Burwell's rose, but I've been through every burial ground in Lynchburg with Carl Cato, and dozens more from Vermont to Texas. The municipal cemetery has become a regular stop whenever I visit a new city or town, and when I pass an old church, I usually turn in for a tour of the churchyard. I like sampling the regional differences, as distinct in their way as the flavors of the indigenous cuisine. Because the water table runs so close to the surface around New Orleans, the people of that city have traditionally buried their dead in marble vaults above the ground; they shrank from drowning them or polluting the groundwater, already notoriously unhealthy in that home of yellow fever. There may be trees, shrubs and flowers of all descriptions in a real Southern graveyard, but no grass; the bereaved gather on Decoration Day every May to hoe it out, a custom they seem to have inherited from snake-fearing Africans. In my own Hudson highlands, the cemetery is almost always set high on the side or at the peak of a hill, to secure the best panorama of the wide, misty river. Whether it was the meditative quality of the view the founders sought or the reminder of another river, the one they believed we all must one day cross, I don't know. But I don't go there looking for redemption, I go in search of old roses.

An older graveyard, one where the groundsmen are not overly conscientious and where the foreman is too conservative to trust in herbicides, is a bonanza for the old-rose fancier. Generally, such a find remains a jealously guarded secret. Certainly, the Heritage Roses Group outraged a collector of my acquaintance when it published an account of her favorite cemetery in a recent edition of the society's magazine, *The Rose Letter*. This preserve, whose name my friend had revealed to me only under the strictest promises of secrecy, had provided her and her close friends with a steady supply of choice cuttings for eighteen years. She said she worried about inexperienced and greedy collectors overtaxing the shrubbery. And indeed, the article did describe an expedition during which the author took a whole ice chest full of cuttings, of which she succeeded in rooting not a single one. My pique arose from a less altruistic motive: It annoyed me to have my new secret garden opened to the public.

Curiously, though, the publicity didn't disturb the discoverer of the cemetery, Douglas Seidel. A Baptist minister in the nearby town of Macungie, Pennsylvania, he reports that many roses have disappeared, but he blames this on the hard winters of the late '70s. Though he wonders how the cemetery's superintendent will react to an invasion of clipper-wielding collectors, Douglas feels that their attention has been a blessing—the cuttings already taken, the ones that did root, are in many cases the only survivors of unique roses. "Things that we found there were *priceless,* incredibly beautiful. . . . With a lot of things, we almost felt, and you have to forgive me for bringing my profession into this," he says with only a trace of a smile, "we almost felt like there was divine guidance bringing us to some of these things to rescue them in time, before they disappeared."

Whatever role a higher power may have played in preserving these graveyard roses, it was youthful restlessness that instigated Douglas's first visit to the cemetery in the spring of 1968. He was eighteen at the time and, according to his own recollection, a moody boy. His main recreation was long and solitary rambles through the countryside around his home at the edge of Easton, Pennsylvania; otherwise, his only enthusiasms seemed to be ancient Greek literature and his garden.

At age twelve, Douglas had gone with his father to visit The Cloisters, New York City's museum of medieval art. The boy was intrigued by an herb garden he found in one of the museum's courtyards. The history behind the plants, the things people had done with them, fascinated him, and he returned home determined to recreate the planting in his own backyard. This proved to be more than a childish whim. When he found no American source for some of the plants he needed, he got a permit from the Department of Agriculture to import live plants from abroad. Among the specimens he ordered to plant around the family's tract house were several roses, varieties like the "Apothecary Rose," *Rosa gallica officinalis,* whose petals medieval pharmacists had used to scent their salves and lotions (this flower was said to possess the unique virtue of actually increasing in fragrance as it dried—a modern authority I consulted disagrees with that claim but agrees that this rose keeps its fragrance longer than most).

Something about these primitive roses tugged at Douglas's memory; he recalled having seen similar bushes when he had ventured past the borders of his development and off into the Pennsylvania Dutch farmlands. It wasn't until the spring of his freshman year in high school, however, that he borrowed his brother's bicycle, and pedalled out to an area of abandoned estates. Down an overgrown road, he found a row of roses struggling up through a field of wheat, the pale pink blossoms cupped like anemones. Later he discovered that these were bushes of 'Shailer's Provence,' a China rose from around 1790, but at the moment he knew only that he wanted one. He talked his father into driving him back under cover of darkness, and that night, at age fourteen, Douglas pried a rooted stem from the soil to collect an old rose for the first time.

That was the beginning. Their religious beliefs had isolated his Pennsylvania Dutch neighbors from the mainstream of American life and all its changes; old roses were one more aspect of the old ways to which they clung. When they learned of Douglas's interest, they shared their roses with him. The cleaning lady brought him a piece of her Moss rose, a strange white flower whose buds were encrusted with a mosslike growth of resinous glands. This proved to be 'Quatre Saisons Blanc Mousseaux' ("Four Seasons White Moss"), a French novelty of 1835. The receptionist at the dentist's office brought him a start of 'Tuscany,' a rose notable for both its pedigree, which has been traced back (fairly certainly) to 1596, and the rich maroon of its petals, which long ago earned it the common name of "Old Velvet Rose." And all the time, Douglas was supplementing these donations with his own finds.

Because he rarely succeeded in his attempts to root cuttings (a skill he admits he still hasn't mastered completely), he collected "suckers," the rooted shoots that emerge from the base of old rosebushes. This is not a technique that would succeed with most modern, commercially produced rosebushes, since they are almost invariably propagated by budding; any suckers that emerge from their roots are offshoots of the rootstock, not the hybrid above-ground growth.* Luckily for Douglas, he

* *This, incidentally, is the explanation of the many stories I have heard from disgruntled gardeners of the miraculous "reversion" of their garden roses to wild species. In every case I have found that a*

could depend on the thrifty habits of the Pennsylvania Dutch, who, rather than purchasing roses from nurseries, had grown their own from cuttings. Such "own-root" roses are hybrids down to the tips of their root-hairs, and so are their suckers.

Douglas's greatest discovery came at the end of his senior year of high school. After finishing his final exams, Douglas rewarded himself with one of his long jaunts. He set out to investigate a spot that he had long suspected might harbor roses, the heights that rise up abruptly at the confluence of a fast-running creek and the Delaware River to force a wedge through the center of an old red-brick town. As he rode round the foot of one hill, he found the entrance to a tunnel. Scenting adventure, he walked in and emerged onto a scene whose memory still quickens his voice twenty years later, a place where it "seemed time had stood still." It was a cemetery, an old and wonderful one full of roses. The very first rose he came to, "a huge, very double pink," he says, "was like nothing I'd ever seen with *my* eyes before—I'd only seen pictures of things like that. And then, every other grave seemed to have a rose on it." There was also a sizable crew of caretakers in view, so Douglas hurriedly pried up a couple of suckers and left. Later, he decided he would need help in sorting out the cemetery's roses, so he wrote to a friend, an experienced rose grower and authority on rose identification.

When they returned together to the cemetery the next June, this time driving, they saw, through the main entrance, a scene from a Victorian sketchbook. A triple gothic arch of stone framed the gap in the tall black iron fence. Within was a descending hillside shaded by giant oaks and maples, and ornamented with an endless variety of marble vaults, columns, obelisks, urns, and classically draped maidens in poses of de-

---

hard winter or clumsy pruning killed all growth above the point of budding. When new growth sprang up from the roots, it wasn't the 'Tropicana' or the 'Peace' rose the gardener was expecting, but shoots of some rootstock, a primitive interloper whose coarse, rampant shoots bear only negligible flowers.

spair. Most exciting from the two sleuths' point of view, however, was a detail no ordinary visitor would have noticed. There
were no bald spots around the monuments, no rings of brown
grass. That meant the groundsmen trimmed and edged the
turf by hand, without the help of "Kilzall," "Kleen-up,"
"Perma-Trim," or other chemical vegetation killers or "growth
inhibitors." Such sprays may streamline the job of mowing,
but unless handled with extreme care, they are the death of
graveside roses.

Wandering amid the graves, the pair had to keep calling
their attention back to the roses, for they found the arcane
symbolism of the monuments irresistible. The oldest stone, an
obelisk sporting a top hat, led them to believe that the cemetery had been founded by Masons. Other monuments were
elaborately carved like tree trunks, indicating, they supposed,
that the deceased had been cut down in the prime of life. For
wives, there were smaller stumps.*

For little girls, there were lambs. Often, a family plot would
include a row of stones for children who had died in infancy:
an upright stone with name and date, the next one flat with

---

* Later I learned the true meaning of these monuments: they mark
the resting places of the Woodmen of the World, members of a fra-
ternal order that guaranteed to erect a monument over any Woodman
who lay a full year in an unmarked grave. The lodge would send
$100.00 together with appropriate designs to a local stonecutter, and
then dispatch lodge brothers to install the stone. In the Woodmen of
the World Magazine of June, 1978, a Mr. Clee Woods recalled wit-
nessing an installation as a boy at Lick Creek, West Virginia in 1904.
"I was filled with wonder and admiration," he wrote, "as the Woodmen, all resplendent in gray uniforms, stood by the grave and performed the solemn burial rites. Most vividly I remember how they
popped their hands on their arms repeatedly in an amazingly disci-
plined unison." Forty thousand of the Woodmen's monuments were
erected from the day in 1890 when "Sovereign" Root founded the
order until the 1920s, when cemetery associations put a stop to the
practice because the groundsmen complained that it complicated mowing. Today the Woodmen, still 950,000 strong and headquartered in
Omaha, Nebraska, continue to mark the graves of brothers, but the
current model is a modest bronze plaque set flush with the ground so
that groundsmen can ride right over it with their tractors.

just a name and after that a string of smaller stones, flat and without any mark. Among these somber memorials, the sleuths found roses, so many roses that they could not collect them all at once. So they resolved to concentrate on the pinks. The red-blossomed bushes were just too numerous. Douglas, as was his custom, dug for a piece of root, while his companion took cuttings, no more than two from each bush.

Rather unexpectedly, most of the neglected roses were in flourishing condition. Many leaves had been reduced to a tissue of holes by hungry caterpillars and beetles, but the growth was compact and vigorous, remarkably free of disease. This, they learned later, was the result of the cemetery superintendent's unconventional maintenance program. His crew hadn't the time to prune the roses properly, so every third year he cut all the bushes back to the ground and burned the clippings. This inadvertently exterminated parasitic bacteria or fungi before they could reach epidemic proportions and forced from the shrubs a flush of healthy new growth.

It also provided the first clue to the roses' identities. Old roses fall into two general categories: remontant or non-remontant. Non-remontant roses are like the old-fashioned Ramblers that climbed our grandparents' fences—they yield only one crop of blossoms each year, blooming for a period of just a few weeks, generally in the late spring. This habit is a function of their physiology; only the "old wood," canes that matured the previous year, are capable of bearing flowers. Remontant roses like the so-called Hybrid Perpetuals, another class that persisted well into this century, bloom more or less repeatedly through the growing season since they can bear flowers on new wood, the current season's growth, as well as the old. So when the two collectors found blossoms or buds on the new shoots springing from the base of a decapitated shrub, they knew they had found a remontant rose.

When they arrived back at Douglas's house, his mother was making dinner, but they cleared the kitchen table to sort out their finds. Five pairs of cuttings had come from remontant pinks, and two of these they recognized as the Hybrid Perpetuals, 'La Reine' (the Queen) and 'Baronne Prévost.' Not ancient by rose standards, both varieties date back only to 1842, but they nevertheless marked a milestone. Among the first of their class, they caused a great stir when they first appeared on the market. Henry Curtis's albums of lithographs, *Beauties of the Rose,* began to appear eight years later in 1850; beside his portrait of 'La Reine' he noted that "a greater sensation had rarely been excited amongst florists than was caused by the announcement of the Floral Queen, to which title its style of beauty lays no mean claim." But this rose and 'Baronne Prévost' offered an even more potent attraction to rose fanciers of that era: a new season of bloom in the rose gardens of northern Europe.

Previously, if a Scot or a German or a Dane wanted blossoms after midsummer, he was confined to the greenhouse, because the only roses to bloom reliably through summer and fall were exotic species or hybrids from the Middle East or Asia, and these would not tolerate northern winters without protection from the cold. By intermarrying them with hardier native stock, European nurserymen sought to produce what they called "perpetuals," shrubs with both longevity and repeating blooms. One Jules Laffay of Bellevue, France, was the most successful at creating perpetuals, and 'La Reine' was his masterpiece. It did not bloom all the time—through the heat of the summer it produced only leaves and shoots—but come fall and cooler weather it rose again, *"remontant,"* like Lazarus, to yield a smaller but significant flush of lilac-washed and crimson-touched blossoms, each tightly cupped like the bowl of a wine glass.

'La Reine' was not the only rose of this type. Laffay's countryman Romain Desprez, an amateur, produced 'Baronne Prévost' through similar crosses, and Laffay himself bred several lesser examples, including 'Princess Hélène' (1837), 'Madame Laffay' (1839), and 'Duchess of Sutherland' (1839). Other nurserymen followed suit to introduce some 3,000 more

Hybrid Perpetuals over the next fifty years. Their success anticipated to a degree the tyranny of the Hybrid Tea rose; an authority of the time, Shirley Hibberd, complained in his *Amateur's Rose Book* (1864) that "This class is like Moses' serpent, it swallows up all the rest." To it, Douglas and his partner eventually discovered, all of their five remontant pinks belonged.

Return visits to the cemetery yielded other old roses of various colors and strains, twenty-eight in all, though many were never identified. Methodically, the collectors moved from one area to another, taking photographs and drawing detailed maps. At least one of the roses they recovered has found its way back onto the market. A compact, lightly fragrant white rose they found in the Pennsylvania cemetery matched the descriptions of 'White Pet,' a rose of 1879 bred by Peter Henderson, a Scottish florist who had settled in New Jersey to grow roses for the New York City trade. It fit the original descriptions far better than the specimens of 'White Pet' offered by old-rose nurseries, and it has since replaced the impostor. Other varieties circulated only informally, as Douglas and his friend established specimens in their own gardens and passed along cuttings from their stock. As the originals in the cemetery disappeared, Douglas came to feel that the preservation of these roses was a sacred trust. When he moved to Macungie, he moved his collection with him, and they grow outside his house still. He and his friend never took more than two pieces from a single specimen, and they shared the location of the cemetery only with those few collectors whose judgment and discretion they trusted absolutely. For eighteen years the spot remained a place of pilgrimage to the inner circle and an important, if obscure, source of stock for the old-rose revival.

The cemeteries of the last century have been such a haven for old roses not only because they have provided a peaceful, stable environment in the midst of America's changing landscape, but also because they have played a special role in the history of this nation's horticulture. Until well into the Vic-

torian era cemeteries were often the only green spaces open to
city-dwellers. Reverence for the dead is a far more primal sentiment than the philanthropic impulse to provide for the recreation of the poor, and the landscaping of cemeteries anticipated by a generation the appearance of the first urban parks.
It was in cemeteries that America's first landscape architects
learned their craft, and it was cemeteries that provided the
model for such parks as Central Park in New York and Golden
Gate Park in San Francisco. Lavishly planted with ornamental
trees, shrubs and flowers, these "rural" cemeteries were the nation's first public gardens. Indeed, the prototype, Mount Auburn Cemetery in Boston, actually began as the joint effort of
a visionary named Jacob Bigelow and the Massachusetts Horticultural Society.

Bigelow was a man of impressive, though oddly assorted,
talents, a near genius whose accomplishments veered from the
eccentric to the truly grand. For forty years (1815–1855) he
was a professor of medicine and botany at Harvard, justly proud
of his medical writings, notably the essay on "self-limited diseases" that did much to discredit bloodletting as a therapeutic
measure. Other titles strike a less impressive note, though I'd
like to believe that "On Coffee and Tea, and Their Medicinal
Effects," and "On the Poisonous Effects of the Partridge, or
Ruffed Grouse" included information important to past generations of hunting and shooting country squires. But I find it
hard to credit the report he submitted in August of 1817 to
the New England Linnaean Society concerning the sighting
of a sea serpent off Cape Ann, and the discovery of its supposed young.*

His contemporaries took Bigelow very seriously. His lectures on the application of science to the "useful arts" drew
packed audiences, from not only the university community

---

* I was familiar with one of Bigelow's works long before I developed
an interest in cemeteries. That was a translation into classical Latin
and Greek of Mother Goose, a volume that had a secure place in the
Classics Department library at Brown.

but the general public as well, and when the Harvard regents resisted incorporating applied sciences in their curriculum, Bigelow helped to found the Massachusetts Institute of Technology. "Technology" itself is a term his biographers have credited Bigelow with coining. In fact he did not, since the Oxford English Dictionary cites a use as early as 1615, but he could be said to have redefined the word in his own person. As a boy, he confessed in his autobiography, he took "delight in the construction of miniature sawmills, [and] machinery for entrapping rats and squirrels." As an adult, he haunted the workshops of Boston, mastering the rudiments of every craft from blacksmithing to glassblowing. When he published his *American Medical Botany,* a landmark guide to medical plants, in the years 1817–1820, he decided to illustrate the work with the first color-printed plates ever produced on this side of the Atlantic. Since no printer in Boston knew how to produce them, Bigelow invented a color-printing process himself.

The plight of American cemeteries caught Bigelow's attention in the 1820s through his study of infectious diseases. At that time, the nation's burial grounds remained much as they had been in the days when the settlers used to camouflage them to hide the ill health and weakness of their communities from the Indians. The haphazard collection of churchyards and family lots continued to serve the needs of country folk more or less adequately, but it could not cope with the exploding population of the cities and towns. By the opening decades of the nineteenth century, space was at such a premium in urban cemeteries that churches regularly removed the elder dead from vaults and yards to make room for new corpses. A few benefited from this seller's market; by dumping a three-foot layer of earth over its graveyard, the Methodist church in Lancaster, Pennsylvania, managed to sell its lots a second time. Hunting for an odd corner into which to shoehorn the loved one, however, can only have increased the sufferings of the bereaved.

It was the disregard for sanitation that appalled Dr. Bigelow. Warehousing the dead in crowded urban neighborhoods seemed to him a positive invitation to epidemics. Moreover, as an apostle of progress, he found intolerable this slapdash treatment of the dear departed. When the city of Boston ignored his calls for reform in 1825, Bigelow summoned eight friends to a meeting at his home. How he happened to select these particular men he never made clear, but the roster included both a Lowell and a Nathan Hale, names to conjure with in nineteenth-century Boston, and one imagines that they were all individuals of a progressive frame of mind. In any event, they were receptive to the project Bigelow suggested, the establishment of "a suburban cemetery in which the beauties of nature should, as far as possible, relieve from their repulsiveness the tenements of the deceased." After formal ratification of this proposal, a committee of two was appointed to locate a suitable tract of land.

This task proved more difficult than anticipated, for the searchers found themselves frustrated by both the high prices of the real estate and a popular abhorrence of their goal. The bereaved resisted the removal of their loved ones' remains to an inconvenient distance, and no one wanted a cemetery in their backyard. After a series of aborted deals, the search returned to its originator, Bigelow, who alone had kept his enthusiasm. In 1829, he paved the way for success by a particularly shrewd move. He adopted as his partner a civil engineer named Henry A. S. Dearborn, a man who also happened to be the founding president of the Massachusetts Horticultural Society.

The establishment of this society had been a project particularly dear to fashionable Boston, and by borrowing its prestige Bigelow at last made headway. He and Dearborn settled on a parcel on the outskirts of Cambridge, seventy-two acres of hilly woodland, pasture and swamp known to Harvard undergraduates of that period as "Sweet Auburn." The owner, foreseeing the city's growth, had bought the land some years before to hold in trust for some worthy project. When Bigelow

explained his goal, and added that he intended to give thirty-
two acres to the Horticultural Society for use as an experimental garden, the owner agreed to sell at cost. Turning to the
Horticultural Society, Bigelow and Dearborn persuaded that
institution to raise the necessary funds by selling lots to 100
subscribers at sixty dollars apiece.

Having taken title to the property, Bigelow and Dearborn
decided to draft plans for the Brahmin Valhalla themselves.
As an engineer, Dearborn's qualifications were obvious, and he
could be trusted to do the grading, drainage and roadways. Bigelow, who had just finished revising his *Florula Bostoniensis,*
the first systematic study of New England's flora, felt qualified
by his knowledge of plants and a certain facility at sketching
to turn his hand to landscape design. The plan they developed
looked nothing like any existing graveyard. Yet unlike many
of Bigelow's other projects, it was not at all revolutionary.
What they had designed, in essence, was an English ducal
park, with carriage roads winding around artificial lakes and
through manicured woods and broad meadows.

The marriage between cemetery (rechristened with the more
imposing title *Mount* Auburn) and Horticultural Society began promisingly. Bigelow ringed the grounds with a palisade
fence (to be replaced with wrought iron as soon as finances
permitted) to forestall raids by "resurrectionists," those grisly
individuals who supplied cadavers to the laboratories of medical schools (including, presumably, his own). The Horticultural Society meanwhile collected 450 varieties of seeds and
scionwood (material for grafting) from as far afield as Turkey
and the botanical garden in Naples. When Supreme Court
Justice Joseph Story delivered the opening address on September 24, 1831, he promised that on this site would grow an
outdoor school of history and philosophy which would "preach
lessons to which none may refuse to listen, and which all that
live must hear."

The high-water mark of this unlikely partnership between
reformer and society came in June of 1833 with a produce

show that featured such homely products as peas, lettuce and strawberries. None was fertilized with graveyard mold, however, since the projected garden had never gotten off the ground. When the Horticultural Society, which for legal purposes had been given title to all the land, tried to use income from the sale of lots to pay its own operating expenses, Bigelow and the other cemetery trustees demanded a divorce. In 1835, they and the Society's officers worked out a settlement by which the Society relinquished its claim to the land in return for a handsome share of any surplus income. Even though the association had proved only temporary, it was to have important consequences for both the Horticultural Society and the cemetery. The continuing income would enable the Society to grow into the most dynamic body of its kind in the United States, and the influence of the horticulturists still persists at Mount Auburn. By the date of the Horticultural Society's withdrawal, 1,300 ornamental and fruit trees had already been planted, together with uncounted masses of flowering shrubs. This program of planting was one that Bigelow and the cemetery's board continued and expanded.

Mount Auburn proved an enormous popular success, not only with those seeking a last resting place but also with those simply in search of recreation. Regular visits to the graveyard were an old custom in Massachusetts—the Puritan fathers had encouraged them in the belief that such melancholy spectacles served as a useful reminder of life's fleeting nature. Indeed, Samuel Sewell, an early diarist, recorded that he celebrated Christmas Day of 1696 with such a visit (more traditional festivities then being prohibited by law). To view the graves of his parents-in-law, cousin Quincey and his six children, Sewell wrote, "Twas an awful yet pleasing Treat."

When combined with an opportunity for fresh air and bucolic scenes, this melancholy pleasure proved irresistible. As the editor of the *Atlantic Monthly* observed, "Bostonians generally seem to have two notions of hospitality—dinner with people you never saw before nor ever wish to see again, and a drive in Mt. Auburn Cemetery." Others were less critical. As Andrew Jackson Downing, America's first great authority on landscape architecture, testified in 1849, "Travellers made pilgrimages to the Athens of New England, solely to see the realization of their long-cherished dream of a resting place for the dead, at once sacred from profanation, dear to the memory, and captivating to the imagination." Mount Auburn had spawned a wave of copies, so that by the time of his writing, Downing noted with approval, there was "scarcely a city of note in the whole country that has not its rural cemetery."

Attendance records suggest the impact these new landscapes had on the life of the average townsman. Laurel Hill on the outskirts of Philadelphia entertained 30,000 visitors in 1848, Greenwood in Brooklyn twice that number. In 1855, to accommodate the traffic to its Hollywood Cemetery (already planted, perhaps with Burwell Musk roses), the city of Richmond, Virginia, ran an omnibus line to this "future Mekha [sic] of the Old Dominion." And all this was accomplished without cost to the taxpayer, since the sale of lots provided a continuous source of income. Nor were the sums involved inconsiderable—Downing noted that $1.5 million had been expended on cemeteries in Philadelphia alone.

No private individual could compete with the scope and variety of planting in these public gardens. In the spring of 1858, for example, Hollywood planted 700 trees, including hollies, weeping willows, maples, cedars, poplars, cypresses, and oaks. Trees, especially exotic species such as the Cedar of Lebanon or novelties like the Colorado Blue Spruce, received the most notice from visitors and absorbed the largest part of the landscaping budgets, but flowering shrubs were not neglected. Mount Auburn ordered 500 flowering shrubs from an English nursery in 1859, and along with "Camellia," "Kalmia" and "Andromeda" paths, it boasted an "Eglantine," named in honor of another of Shakespeare's fancies, the Sweet Brier rose (*Rosa rubiginosa*), which came to Massachusetts with the Puritans. J. W. Russell, the superintendent at Mount Auburn, became something of an authority on roses. Articles with his by-line ("On the Repotting and Management of Chinese Roses"; "Some Remarks respecting the treatment of the Yellow Noisette Rose") appeared regularly in *The American Gardener's Magazine and Register*. Laurel Hill, Philadelphia's showplace, in July was, according to Downing, "a wilderness of roses."

"Wilderness" may seem a strange word to describe a plantation of anything so formal and artificial as garden roses, but certainly not to anyone who has cultivated old roses. Modern roses are the ultimate remontants, bearing the largest, most perfect blooms on the new growth of the current season. Accordingly, it is accepted practice to prune them back to stumps each spring, leaving just three or four canes, a foot tall or less, so that the bush is forced to renew itself annually. Such drastic measures eliminate all bloom from the non-remontant old roses, however, and even the remontant types respond better, I have found, to a gentler, more sophisticated treatment.

Actually, my treatment for roses derives from the more general pruning program I was drilled in at the Botanical Garden by a tyrannical old Irishwoman, Bridey McSweeney, whose hands might shake but whose tongue was still sharper than any rose's thorn. The three D's are what Bridey told me to look for in springtime, just as the buds begin to swell. *D*ead wood, canes killed by winter's frost and cold, dry winds, you remove first, then *d*amaged and *d*iseased ones. At this point her mnemonics broke down, but Bridey was no less certain of how to continue. Weak shoots, spindly canes that show no promise of future performance, are cut back all the way to the ground (I delay this part of the program until after bloom, since to remove old wood in the spring, at least in the case of non-remontant roses, is to remove also summer's flowers). After that, she would thin the bush, snipping away twigs and whole canes here and there to give the shrub an open, spreading structure. Let in the air and light, Bridey maintained, and

you'll have a healthy shrub, with a greater resistance to pests
and diseases.

Far more difficult than the simple lopping performed on
Hybrid Teas, Bridey's style of pruning is also far more painful,
since it involves creeping into the heart of each thorny shrub.
I've never questioned it, though. Timed as it is to the natural
calendar, and taught to me in a Celtic brogue, this ritual has
the uncanny wisdom of a Druidic mystery, a blood sacrifice I
must make to the spirit of spring. Practicing it without fail for
thirteen years now, I've always been granted a good crop of
roses; the only innovation I've introduced is to shorten straggling canes to keep paths free and to prevent bigger bushes
from smothering smaller neighbors. As much as possible,
though, I prefer to let my roses wander.

And wander they do, often building a flowering mound six
feet tall and as many feet across. My 'American Pillar' roses,
climbers of a 1902 vintage that were planted decades ago as
replacements for 'Île de France' (the Rambler Lily Shohan so
disparaged), bury a nine-foot trellis in rude, thick canes and
lustrous foliage; in June, the flowers, bright pink rounds
with a white eye, hang in swags to the ground. Every year the
spectacle draws admirers armed with cameras, but I know that
it is modest by comparison with the gigantic size old roses may
reach if left undisturbed. In Tombstone, Arizona, I've heard
there is a 'Lady Banks Rose' that puts all the competition to
shame.

'Lady Banks Rose' is an evergreen rose of Chinese origin
that found its way west in 1807 with an East India Company
tea merchant. This importer assured his find a warm reception, at least in horticultural circles, by naming it for the wife
of Sir Joseph, the Royal Botanic Garden's superintendent.
Like many Chinese roses, the 'Lady Banks' had difficulty cop-
ing with the cold, damp British climate, but when planted
against a south-facing wall, it would survive to bear a foam of
small violet-scented white blossoms every spring. Arizona's

dry heat proved much more congenial to its rather delicate
constitution—ironically, it was brought there as a souvenir of
Scotland.

Mary Gee was a new bride in 1884 when her husband
Henry moved from Scotland to Tombstone to supervise his
company's mining interests. The young woman followed, but
she missed the cool, lush greenery of home. So she wrote to her
parents for cuttings of the old white rose that grew in their
garden. When the bits of rooted cane arrived in 1885, Mary
planted one behind "Cochise House," the adobe boarding-
house where she and her husband had first stayed when they
came to Tombstone. There, the formerly delicate 'Lady Banks'
began to behave in a very unaristocratic manner. It soon smothered the woodshed against which it had been planted, climbing
so fast that the owners had to build a special trellis to which
they added prop after prop. By 1968, 'Lady Banks' had begun
to make headlines. The *American Rose Annual* reported that
this rose's trunk had reached a girth of ninety-five inches, and
in a photo it dwarfs the stout figure of its current owner. *Rip-
ley's Believe It or Not,* and *The Guinness Book of World
Records* also took note of this floral monster, which has now
spread its branches over eight thousand square feet to bear
"millions" of blossoms annually. I've never been to Tombstone, but should I decide to go, I'll time my visit for the peak
of bloom, mid-April, and I'll make my way to the corner of
Fourth and Toughnut Streets to the old adobe, now a museum,
where the diorama of Wyatt Earp's shoot-out at the OK Corral
takes second billing to a 'Lady Banks Rose.'

Institutions such as Laurel Hill may have planted roses
wholesale, but judging by their proximity to headstones, most
of the cemetery roses I have found were planted not by grounds
crews but by individual lot holders. Bigelow recommended this
in 1860, in a history of Mount Auburn Cemetery he published
that year. A living memorial was a beautiful gesture, he acknowledged, but the trees that the lot holders insisted on planting were turning his meticulously planned park into a wilder-

ness. Roses, he pleaded, were a far more suitable tribute. Little urging was necessary to ensure the popularity of this shrub. For just as there was a rivalry among neighbors to erect the most imposing monuments on their lots, so there was a rivalry for the showiest floral display, and nothing could compete with roses in this respect.

Not just any rose would do, though, as witnessed by one gardening guide from the turn of the century, *Everblooming Roses* by Georgia Torrey Drennan* which devoted a whole chapter to a discussion of the best roses for this purpose. 'Souvenir d'un Ami' (Remembrance of a Friend), a large fragrant salmon-colored Tea rose, the author judged particularly suitable because of its name. 'Marie Pavié' and 'Clotilde Soupert,' two pale pinks of modest stature (the shrubs stand at two to four feet), were ideal for children's graves, though the 'Marie Paviés' in my backyard memorialize nothing more than an empty spot along a sunny walk. 'Maréchal Niel,' a bold yellow climber of 1864, was one of the very few really good old garden roses of this color, and consequently famous in its time; it had been named for a hero of the Crimean War, so Drennan judged it appropriate for the grave of a soldier. 'Cornelia Cook,' a white Tea of exceptional purity and waxy camellia-like blossoms, had been the rose tossed at the feet of Jenny Lind, the "Swedish Nightingale," during her American concert tour in 1850. The glamour that reflected on the rose was attested, the author noted, by the many graves of that era that still sported a venerable specimen of 'Cornelia Cook.'

Different varieties moved in and out of vogue, but the rose remained the flower of choice for mourners, as it had been, in fact, since prehistoric times. One doubts that even Bigelow with his classical education was aware of the antiquity of this gesture; such an apostle of enlightenment could not have approved of the shrub's original role, which was to furnish offerings to the earth goddess. But the trail of evidence is easy

* *New York: Duffield & Company, 1912.*

enough to follow. In his excavations of medieval crypts, the French architectural historian Viollet-le-Duc found the skeletons resting on litters of herbs and flowers, the flowers' spiny stems identifying them as roses, a flower then sacred to the Virgin Mary. Saint Jerome, the translator of the Vulgate Bible, wrote in the fourth century of widowers scattering roses over the tombs of their wives; he admitted that this was a custom Christians had adopted from the pagan Greeks and Romans, though Jerome insisted that to those heathens the rose was an emblem of grief, while to Christians it was the joyous symbol of the second life.

Actually, the use of the rose at funerals was as much a celebration of rebirth for pagans as for Christians. Among the early peoples of the Mediterranean world, this flower was a necessary prop in their worship of the Mother Goddess, a deity known by a variety of names, according to the country. She was Cybele in Anatolia, Cotytto in Thrace, Corinth and Sicily; she was Demeter throughout most of Greece, Isis in Egypt and Magna Mater, the Great Mother, in Rome. Everywhere she showed a predilection for roses: Demeter and Isis were commonly depicted riding a rose-wheeled cart, and the Corybantes, the eunuch priests of the Magna Mater, wore rose garlands during their processions through Rome. According to myth, it was a rose that lured Demeter's daughter Persephone into the grasp of Hades, the god of the underworld. As the flower of funerals and rebirth, the rose was a most appropriate bait for Hades' trap, since it was Persephone's kidnapping that plunged the world into winter, and it was her release that prompted the return of spring.

Surely this explains the rose's incongruous connection with death, since the Mother Goddess as the goddess of the earth governed not only fertility but the afterlife. Only through reunion with her, through burial, could man achieve immortality. So it was with rose-scented oil that Aphrodite anointed the dead hero Hector in Homer's *Iliad*, to preserve his body from corruption. And it was with roses that the mortals of

Greece and Rome wove wreaths for their dead. To ensure a supply of blossoms, they planted beds of roses in *necropoli,* their cities of the dead. Even in the days of the Caesars, this was already an ancient practice, as the English archaeologist Flinders Petrie proved in 1888. A man who would never have styled himself an old-rose collector, Petrie nonetheless recovered the very oldest specimen of a garden rose, a blossom 2,000 years old.

Unprincipled collectors may be a threat to the cemeteries of eastern Pennsylvania, but my friend should take comfort in the fact that her rivals don't dig with dynamite. This was Petrie's pet grievance. By nature a most careful, methodical man, he favored a camel-hair brush as his tool for excavation, and he deplored the ruthless tactics employed by those who, he charged, dug "simply for the sake of plunder," individuals like Auguste Édouard Marriette, Egypt's Director of Excavations who had used explosives in his ransacking of ancient temples. Mariette found the treasure he sought, but in the process, he destroyed the archaeological record. Petrie, through his greater patience, recovered not only treasure but also a host of fragile, insignificant-seeming artifacts, objects without the glitter of gold that, placed in context, revealed a wealth of information about bygone societies. Such a find was the ancient funeral wreath he unearthed during his excavation of the Egyption necropolis of Hawara in 1888.

In the dry desert air, the wreath's petals had shrivelled, but they still kept their color, and when placed in warm water, the blossoms seemed to come back to life. Buds swelled, and the pink petals spread, unfolding to reveal the knot of golden threads at the center just as they must have on the morning of the funeral. A botanist at Cambridge had little trouble in identifying Petrie's flowers as roses, specimens of *Rosa richardii,* a species already known as "the Holy Rose of Abyssinia" because at that time it was still a fixture of Coptic Christian churchyards in that country.

Grave robbers aren't the worst threat to cemetery roses, nor

are irresponsible collectors, as I learned in Central Texas. I'd
gone there in pursuit not of roses, but of a woman, a scientist
who had, perversely I thought, chosen a landlocked university
on the prairie at which to study the geology of the ocean floor.
On the recommendation of Lily Shohan, I looked up Miss
Pamela Puryear while I was there. The editor of *The Old
Texas Rose,* the quarterly publication of the "South Central
Texas Old Garden Rose Enthusiasts," Pam is a polymath with
a sharpshooting wit and the born truant's readiness to set out
on a cross-country ramble at a moment's notice. She can talk
with humorous erudition on topics ranging from Victorian
couture to the steamboats that used to ply the Brazos River
(she's written books on both those topics); she also proved to
be the most dedicated student of cemeteries I have ever encountered. She took me in hand—her weakness for strays has
made her the sole visible support for sixteen cats—and escorted
me to Central Texas's choicest burial grounds. There she introduced me to all her favorite roses. All, that is, that still survive. The roses lived under a constant threat of extinction,
Pam told me, the enemy was "perpetual care."

Perpetual care is yet another chapter in the history of the
groundsmen's campaign to shape cemeteries to their convenience, since it makes all landscaping the monopoly of the
institution's own staff. First instituted at the Oakwood Cemetery of Albany, New York, in 1873, it has since spread
throughout much of the country. It guarantees neatness, of
course, and by simplifying grounds maintenance cuts costs,
which has made it popular with boards of trustees and municipal councils; but it also bars the bereaved from planting anything on a grave themselves. When an existing cemetery converts to this plan, usually the existing graveside plantings are
not disturbed but gradually eliminated through intentional neglect and natural attrition. It is a rule that might have been
aimed directly at rose collectors, Pam complains, and it flies in
the face of Texas tradition.

There, in years gone by, the custom was to plant Mother's

favorite flower by her grave. More often than not, that was a
rose, in many cases an exotic variety of great antiquity. Central Texas was settled largely by Germans, Poles and Czechs,
brought from the old country by entrepreneurs like the German Prince Carl zu Solms Braunfels, who in 1845 imported a
whole town's-worth of inhabitants for his community of New
Braunfels. Naturally conservative, this transplanted peasantry
found itself further isolated by the enormous distances of its
new home. The result has been a remarkable persistence of
the old ways. Until this generation, New Braunfels's newspaper was published in German, while the town of Snook,
110 miles to the northeast, is known throughout the surrounding area not only for the rodeo it hosts every summer but also
for its *kolaches,* poppy seed or fruit-filled pastries whose recipe
the pioneers brought with them from Czechoslovakia. Along
with language and cuisine, the residents also preserved and
propagated the roses their grandparents and great-grandparents
brought with them from the old country, making their cemeteries a particularly fruitful hunting ground for collectors.

Pam knows every one of these old graveyards in Grimes,
Washington and Brazos counties. An eighth-generation Texan,
she takes a keen interest in the doings of her ancestors and
other pioneers of the region. Carrying an old saber to dispatch
either brush or snakes, as the occasion demanded, Pam came
to the cemeteries originally to collect genealogical information.
In the process, she fell in love with the roses. As we drove the
back roads in the fall of 1985, she would interrupt her instruction in local customs and usages (raise just the forefinger from
the wheel to wave as you pass a native; over there's the spot
where great-uncle James died in a duel he fought to protect
the honor of his horse) to stop and check on the status of her
finds.

We paused in William Penn, a town settled by an errant
company of Pennsylvanians, now entirely vanished. Only the
graveyard remains and this, despite its name, is a pure vestige
of the Old South: huge gnarled live oaks dripping Spanish

moss, wrought-iron railings surrounding plots of staggering, drunken tombstones. No roses there, so on we went to Shelby, another Anglo cemetery. Though less picturesque, Shelby's cemetery kept closer to tradition—there was no grass, the neighbors still come to hoe it out, and there were roses. 'Cramoisi Supérieur' was one Pam pointed out to me, a low-growing, wiry-stemmed bush with globular blossoms of brilliant crimson. Though the descendant of a Chinese species (*Rosa chinensis*), this particular cultivar is the work of a French breeder who introduced it in 1832.

Nearby was another, even more Gallic rose, a variety of *Rosa gallica* in fact, and so a close relative of Douglas Seidel's "Apothecary Rose." The leaves, leathery and furrowed as a farmer's neck, and the still straight shoots, sparsely armed with a stubble of straight, sharp prickles, were unmistakable badges. They marked the Texan bush as a member of that ancient race of European garden roses, roses that were already old when medieval monks planted them in cloisters. The color of the Shelby roses, a cerise that fades to a slate purple among the older blossoms, reminded Pam of 'Empress Josephine,' a rose of mid-nineteenth-century vintage, but she admitted that an exact identification was beyond her. Gallica roses are a difficult group to sort out, since all the nurseries of the world offer only a handful of Gallica roses today, and the collector cannot easily check his guesses against other specimens. The situation was far different in 1848, when William Paul, the leading English rose breeder of the time, set out to distill his experience into a single volume, *The Rose Garden*. "The French or Garden Roses [Gallicas] as they are so often termed," Paul asserted, "form the most extensive group belonging to the Genus Rosa." In proof of this statement, he appended a *select* list of some 523 varieties. He continued: "All hues are here, and the flowers are remarkable for their brilliancy, fullness, perfect outline and the regularity in disposition of the petals." A description that should set any gardener to ransacking old cemeteries.

How could some Texan mother, I wondered, develop such a taste for these exotic flowers that her family would plant them on her grave? I'd imagined those women as more accustomed to rifles than roses. Pam's answer completely changed my vision of pioneer life. Even while Comanches raided these parts, Pam assured me, French roses, the latest Teas and Hybrid Chinas, arrived within a couple of years of their first appearance on the international market. Nurserymen in New Orleans purchased direct from Europe or from New York, then shipped the shrubs across the Gulf and up the Brazos River in the steamboats that came to fetch Texan cotton.

The next stop was La Grange, which, despite its name, was pure German. It was near there I met the old gentleman who informed me that German had been the only language at his public school until the First World War, and Pam, while interviewing another senior resident, had heard her refer to the neighbors down the road as "those Americans." In La Grange's cemetery we found, predictably, precision and neatness, baroque monuments of great elaboration but little grace in ordered rows. The roses, however, revealed another, more sympathetic side of La Grange's burghers.

'Cécile Brünner' was one we found here, a compact shrub of 1881 named for the daughter of a family of Swiss nurserymen. I had heard it called the "Sweetheart Rose," and looking at the blossoms, I understood the reason: tight little buds of shell-pink, they were as innocently sentimental as an old valentine. All around we found scarlet sprays of 'Skyrocket.' This is a rose that claims a distant descent from the Musk rose but shares more of the habits of another parent, *Rosa multiflora,* a tough, sprawling east Asian species whose thorny thickets have been planted along parkway shoulders up north to serve as a self-perpetuating car-proof barrier. 'Skyrocket' bears semi-double blossoms, flowers of twenty-four to thirty petals, that I found cheerful but unimpressive. Nor could these bushes claim antiquity, since the variety was introduced only in 1934. Still, they did testify to the enduring ethnicity of the town, since 'Skyrocket' is a German rose, the creation of Wilhelm Kordes' Söhne of Sparrieshoop, Holstein. Apparently, as recently as a generation ago, the people of La Grange still looked to the fatherland for flowers.

In Anderson, we stopped at the Odd Fellows Cemetery, a patch of grass half-overgrown with Red Cedars and Crepe Myrtle on a rise outside of town. There Pam introduced me to a four-foot bush of 'Old Blush,' another Chinese rose that is, despite its delicate appearance, one of Texas's most durable pioneers. When exactly it entered the state no one knows. Undoubtedly though, this occurred while the lands between the Rio Grande and Red rivers were still a province of Mexico.

An old rose even by that time, 'Old Blush' had bloomed in Chinese gardens for a century at least before 1752, when the physician of a Swedish ship brought a specimen back to his friend in Upsala, the botanist Carolus Linnaeus. As one of the very first remontant roses to reach Europe, 'Old Blush' was admired as a novelty by gardeners in England, but like the 'Lady Banks Rose,' its susceptibility to cold limited its success there. Once again, the rose really came into its own only when it reached the Southern states of America, where the regularity of its bloom won it names like "Common Monthly" (because it flowered on a monthly basis through the growing season) and "Old Pink Daily." This habit more than compensated for the small and unspectacular quality of this "Daisy Rose's" blossoms. As rough-and-ready as the frontiersmen themselves, 'Old Blush' also proved indifferent as to soil and impervious to drought, at least once a bush had had a couple of years to spread its roots.

Another custom of the old Southwest frontier was for a bride to take a few roots or slips of flowers with her when she joined her husband. As these grew, they would keep fresh in her mind the sights and smells of the family "homeplace" and might be her only luxuries for many years as she helped her husband carve a plantation from the wilderness—in those days, Pam confided with a grin, Texas "was heaven for men and dogs, but hell for women and oxen." So it was that 'Old Blush' had come to Texas in the trousseaux of young women. Generations later the rose's fluttering petals, palest pink at the center and blushing darker toward the edges, continue to bear witness to frontier brides' irrepressible femininity.

Three more roses we found in Anderson's cemetery, sad gray flowers that had bloomed continuously for more than a century. These were only effigies, rosebushes carved onto the limestone monuments of the Thompson family plot. Mother Rosa O., "a loving wife and patient mother," had died first, on July 9, 1878, aged "29 Years, 11 Mos and 28 Days," as her headstone noted with pitiless accuracy; on her stone Pam pointed to a relief of a rosebush, in full bloom but lacking the bud second from the top. This had snapped off and was falling, tumbling to the ground, just as Mother had. Thirteen years later, on September 2, son Dion followed at age nineteen; on his monument the rosebush lacked a lower bud as well. One wonders who were the other children who stripped the bush; they aren't buried here, but on the last stone, Father's, only the topmost bud remains. Its stem snapped on April 1 of 1896. In the stone's inscription lies one more hint of his loneliness: "His many virtues" may well have "formed the noblest monument to his memory," but this stone was erected by his lodge brothers at the Woodmen of the World, for Father Thompson was all alone.

Every rose collector I have known has taken many, if not the majority, of their finds from cemeteries. Most, like Douglas Seidel, show their respect for both the roses and the deceased by taking care not to injure the shrubs. Yet of all the collectors in this country, only Carl Cato, to my knowledge, is making any effort to repay his debt. In the municipal cemetery of Lynchburg, Virginia, there's a section dedicated to Civil War casualties. Not all the deceased died a hero's death on the battlefield, as I discovered when I began reading inscriptions. Smallpox had felled more soldiers than shot and shell, though of the two, I'm sure a bullet provided the quicker, less painful end. Carl intends to honor all casualties, regardless. He's working now with the local garden club to collect specimens of every old rose he has located in Lynchburg. These they will plant along the cemetery's perimeter in a perfumed hedge of antiques, as an enticement to modern-day strollers and a graceful bow to tradition.

3

Rose
Rustling

Bourbon rose

PAM AND I had been riding the La Bahia Trail all morning,
scouting for the upcoming rustle. Bumping along the rutted,
red-dirt track, we passed ranch after ranch stocked with sleek
horses and humpbacked Brahman cattle. Pam spared them
hardly a glance. When the rustlers assembled from all over
Texas in two weeks, it wouldn't be livestock they'd be after.
They'd be looking for roses, the roses of Texas's past.

That past had seemed close at hand all morning. I doubted
that the trail had changed much since conquistadores drove it
in from the coast four centuries ago, following Coronado into
this remote province of New Spain. Along the ridges the road
wound, then dipped down to wet our tires in a ford and

dragged us back up through dusty tangles of yaupon holly and post oak. Every few miles we emerged briefly onto black- top as we passed through some little town, but these were hardly more than ruins, lines of empty storefronts, customers and money sucked from them by bigger highways and distant malls. A half-mile of surfaced road, maybe, a church, a bar- becue and a convenience store, and we'd reenter the lonely but comfortable vistas of low grassy hills and threadbare woods.

Nor had the inhabitants changed, at least in one respect, as I'd learned a few days before: their conviction that lost trea- sures lie hidden in backwoods Texas, waiting for a person with the right kind of wit or luck. It was this same conviction that lured Coronado into this territory; the Indians who greeted him at the Rio Grande with cries of *"tejas"* (friendly) had promised him cities of gold beyond the prairies to the north. The middle-aged woman I'd sat next to on the People Express flight from Newark to Houston had stirred my inter- est with her high cheekbones and dusky skin. But when she tried to start a conversation, I buried my nose in a notebook. Flying People Express was like riding the subway to Texas— the vista of shopping bags and tired faces was just the same— and I knew better than to talk to strangers on the subway. My neighbor had persisted, though, informing me that she was one-quarter Indian and telling me stories of her grandfather, the last full-blooded member of the family.

Grandfather used to find signs carved into aged hollies when he was squirrel hunting, and these had eventually led him to an enormous altar rock outside the town of Crockett. He'd contracted with a local well-digger to drill through the rock to the treasure hidden below, when an ancient curse killed both grandfather and his son. All of this was fact; I'd find it recorded in a book her uncle had deposited in the Crockett school library before his death. Then, seizing my pen, she drew a map in my notebook. She marked the center with an X and told me that was the spot where I'd find the lost treasure of the Aztecs.

I had no intention of haring off to Crockett, but Pam and I were nonetheless infected with Texan treasure-fever. For us, the lure was not bullion but an opportunity to reach backward. We wanted to look at the same colors and smell the same perfumes as the long-dead uncles, aunts, cousins, friends, neighbors and rivals of whom she spoke with such familiarity. I knew, though, that in this preoccupation we would be in a minority among the Texas old-rose rustlers. Texans are proud of their special heritage and customs. "Native Texan," proclaim the bumper stickers on their cars, and the D.R.T. (Daughters of the Republic of Texas) is a far more active society there than the D.A.R. Yet the group Pam would be hosting, The Texas Old Rose Symposium, was looking forward, not backward. They were laying the foundation for the future gardens of the Sunbelt.

Texans, I had learned in the course of repeated visits to my geologist, are still very close to the experience of the frontier, and they have the pioneer's confidence that any challenge can be overcome, given enough energy, imagination and perseverance. Texan gardeners have kept, as well, the frontiersman's attitude toward natural resources. Resources, they believe, were put on this earth to exploit. Old roses are most definitely a resource, one that is begging for exploitation in the battle against the Texan climate.

My W.P.A. guidebook describes the Texan climate as "remarkable for its salubrity," but this leads me to conclude that the writer never met a Texan. Quiz a Texan on this subject and he, or she, will reply with perverse pride that in fact their state has no climate, only weather. Six months are dry and the other six without rain, residents of West Texas claim. Even in the eastern half of the state, where the average precipitation may average forty-five inches per year, the water comes in bursts, as the weather veers from drought to desperate storms, "gully washers" that may dump eight inches of rain in a single day. "Blue northers," the frigid winds that blow in from the north, figure in countless tales of birds freezing in mid-flight and cattle in mid-step, and when a norther does hit, you can feel the wind strike the house all of a sudden like a slap. Yet winter is not the worst season for the garden. That comes in midsummer, at least in Central Texas, when the temperatures break 100°F most afternoons, and a stifling humidity combines with monthlong stretches of rainless weather. "In Central Texas," as Pam remarked, "God is sparing with his watering can."

In such conditions, the average Hybrid Tea rose lasts no more than a season or two. If diseases—blackspot and mildews—don't strip the bush of its foliage, and the thrips and mites don't devour it, the return of the rains in October will almost certainly tempt the bush to bloom itself to death. It isn't the expense of replacing these shrubs that frustrates Texan gardeners (no one could accuse them of stinginess), it is that the sickly bushes never yield a really satisfying, flashy "Texas-style" display. As a result, many Texan rose growers are abandoning the mail-order nurseries and returning to the country-side to search for survivors. In the old cemeteries, of course, and round the weathered cabins of little towns, on the home-places tucked away on back roads, the gardeners look for old rosebushes, plants that came in with the pioneers to outlast generations of Texan weather. If these roses will bloom in conditions of complete neglect, Texan gardeners reason, what won't they do in the garden?

Pam asked herself this question back in 1969, when she found a huge specimen of 'Old Blush,' the first old rose she had ever seen, in front of an abandoned log cabin in rural Grimes County. She had gone there to photograph the building, which she could date by its architectural detail to the 1820s. She stayed to admire the rose. "It was August," she recalls. "It had not rained in five weeks." Yet the rose was "blooming its head off; you couldn't put your fingers between the blooms." Newspapers Pam found inside the cabin fixed the farm's abandonment to the 1940s, so obviously this rose-bush had received no care for more than a generation. Rue-

fully, Pam thought of 'Sterling Silver,' her pampered Hybrid
Tea, back home. Despite all her cosseting, it had degenerated,
she says, into "three brown sticks."

Admittedly, the old rose could not compete in grandiosity
of display with a modern rosebush. The flowers were smaller
and simpler, the colors paler. But the rose did exhibit the
virtue Texans admire most: it obviously loved Texas. Pam
stepped over to a nearby cotton mill, where she borrowed a
grub-hoe and the assistance of two men. They returned with
her to the cabin, dug the bush free from the soil and loaded
it into the trunk of her car. Pam transplanted it to a sunny
spot in her yard and the rose, completely indifferent to the
change of scene, never ceased blooming.

A half-hour's drive to the north of Pam's home in Navasota
lies Texas A & M University, the state's leader not only in
football but also in agricultural research. In the university's
library, Pam unearthed old gardening books that helped her
identify her find. As a historian, Pam found the rose's ties to
Texas's history intriguing; as a gardener, she found its rugged
vitality irresistible. She began bringing home other, similar
survivors, and as stories of her unconventional roses spread,
other gardeners joined her search. Meeting at Pam's house,
the searchers would set off together on a rural tour, stopping
wherever they saw a rose. If the bush proved to be of a type
they hadn't previously encountered, the gardeners would help
themselves to cuttings. It was their exuberance in doing so that
led a visitor from Missouri to dub the proceedings a "rustle."

In my previous experience, rose collecting had always been
a rather staid activity, pleasant and peaceful, definitely not a
pursuit to set the heart pounding. Pam had shaken me, however, when she warned me to wear snake-proof boots, and she
had described the Texan expeditions as a horticultural version
of Sherman's march to the sea. "We drive out in our cars and
just ravage the countryside," she explained. "Last year we
made it all the way to the Gulf." Though she had tried to prepare me for the event, still I was amazed at the string of cars,

trucks and RV's (recreational vehicles) that began to pull up in front of her house that fine November morning of my first rose rustle.

The yellow rose of Texas proved to be these collectors' totem, and in the crowd that assembled on Pam's porch, I spotted yellow-rose tee shirts, yellow-rose caps, even a yellow-rose bolo tie. Each collector had brought a bucket of cut roses from his or her garden to show off, and a plastic pail of cuttings to swap. On many of the buds there was still dew; the rustlers had cut them long before dawn, for some had driven almost two hundred miles from Dallas to be in Navasota by ten o'clock. Along with the samples of their roses, all had brought stories, tall tales of Texan rose collecting.

"I almost rustled your property, Pam, the first time I came through Navasota," a young man from Houston boasted. Horses, a middle-aged woman confided, are better transportation for rustling than a car. Easier to hide, a horse is also more difficult to trace. Another woman complained of a faint-hearted husband. If only he would cooperate, he could be so useful as the driver of her getaway car. Her neighbor, a respectable dowager, recalled the time she joined forces with a stranger to rustle a rosebush from a vacant lot. Only upon leaving did she discover that her impromptu assistant was actually the landowner.

Early November, Pam told me, was the customary date for rose rustles because it helped the Texans avoid non-remontant roses. Some representatives of the ancient spring-blooming European strains, the Gallicas, Albas and Centifolias, will survive in Texas—the 'Cramoisi Superieur' in Shelby's cemetery is an example—but since they do not rebloom in the fall, the Texans disdain them as ungenerous "Yankee roses." Far more desirable in their eyes are the old Tea and China roses, bushes that may not be proof against northern winters but that bloom whenever the weather grants moderate temperatures and sufficient moisture. In Texas, the Teas and Chinas bloom not only in spring and fall but into early winter as well. Actually, it is proverbial among Texan gardeners that the very finest roses are cut at Christmastime.

When I asked the young Houstonian about his collecting technique, he assured me that the days of grub-hoe collecting were over; the rustlers never took a whole bush anymore unless it was abandoned and threatened with destruction. Like the other collectors of my acquaintance, the rustlers take cuttings, but they treat these in a manner that was entirely new to me. Eschewing commercial products, they won't use off-the-shelf rooting hormone. Instead they stand their cuttings for twenty-four hours in "willow-water," a potion they make by chopping willow twigs into a bucket of water and leaving them to soak overnight. The rustlers themselves, the young man hastened to add, didn't invent this brew. It was developed by Dr. Makoto Kawase of the Ohio Agricultural Research and Development Center. Willow cuttings are notoriously easy to root; stick a willow shoot into moist soil, and soon you'll have a tree. The reason for this, according to the doctor's research, is that the willow twigs contain a root-promoting substance called rhizocaline. Water saturated with this natural product, the Texas rustlers maintain, is far more effective than commercially available products, and they use willow-water exclusively.

Pulling on the bill of his "gimme cap," the young man took me over to the tailgate of his pickup to show me the apparatus he had developed for hit-and-run rose propagation. From a stack he grabbed a three-inch plastic pot and plunged it into an adjacent barrel to fill it with a compost of screened peat and sand. Then he leaned over and selected a likely-looking cutting from the bunch soaking in a bucket of murky willow-water. Next he stripped all but the terminal leaf from the pencil-sized length of rose cane and stuck its base one and a half inches deep into the pot of rooting medium. With a watering can he sprinkled the pot and sealed it, cutting and all, into a plastic bag before setting it down next to a row of its fellows. Upon his return home, he told me, he would plunge the pots into a shallow cold frame on the north side of the house; two or three weeks later the cuttings would be rooted.

The time came to mount up. Pam tied a yellow ribbon to the radio antenna of our car, and we pulled out, followed by a motorcade similarly marked. The town of Bryan would be the scene of our collecting today, and the first stop was to be Miz Shirlireed Walker's house for sand cakes and cider. You can't miss it, I was told; there'll be a Lone Star flag flying over the front door. On the way, Pam lamented the absence of Bill Welch.

Though she'd been rustling roses, alone and with friends, since the 1960s, Pam dates the birth of the Texas Old Rose Symposium from the day in 1981 when she met Dr. William Welch. Bill told me later that he hadn't been entirely unprepared for Pam's visit. Mutual friends had told him of the rustles because they knew that as the director of the horticultural extension service at Texas A. & M., Bill shared Pam's interest in garden flowers suited to Texas. In fact, when not consulting with nurserymen or lecturing to garden clubs, Bill devotes most of his working hours to research on that very subject. Besides the trials he has made of exotic plants, Bill has taken an active role in promoting the native flora to nurserymen, persuading them to include select varieties of yaupon, purple sage and other Texan shrubs in their sales yards. Old roses, though not exactly native, certainly are naturalized Texans, and Bill found them promising. With material collected on Pam's rustles he hoped to introduce a new class of low-maintenance flowering shrubs for local landscapers and park systems.

Calling on his acquaintance with gardeners all over the state, Bill had helped Pam enroll a host of new collectors who'd scoured the country from Navasota to North Zulch. He had also interested a local nurseryman, Mike Shoup, in the rustlers' discoveries. Mike had given their cuttings a home and used them as stock for a new nursery business that he christened The Antique Rose Emporium. In two short years, Mike had assembled a collection of 400 different rose cultivars, and he calculated he'd sell 100,000 rosebushes that year. Many he'd sell locally, but he had issued a mail-order catalogue as well, for he'd set his sights beyond the borders of Texas. The rustlers' roses, he believed, would prove the ideal flowering shrubs for all the Southern states.

After our courtesy call on Miz Shirlireed, it was on to Mrs. Seaman's property to admire her specimens of primitive Hybrid Teas, in particular a scarlet-red 'Étoile de Hollande.' Dating only from 1919, it lacked the antiquity of the other roses I had been seeing in Texas, but it obviously shared their affinity for a Southern climate and soil. Only a generation or two removed from its Tea rose ancestors, this Hybrid Tea retained a durability since bred out of the class. 'La France,' a lush silver-pink introduced in 1867 as the very first Hybrid Tea, also grows well throughout Texas, as does 'Radiance,' an enormous pink blossom dating from 1908. The rustlers' stock of the latter derives from a bush they found not far from Pam's house in Navasota. It had been planted, the owner related, by his grandmother in the first year it appeared on the market.

Nearby, two rustlers faced off over a handsome deep-pink blossom. A lady who sported a pair of red-handled pruning shears in a leather holster identified it as 'American Beauty,' the famous Hybrid Perpetual florist's rose. This assertion was emphatically denied by the gentleman in the yellow-rose bolo tie. Before the dispute could be resolved, it was on to the next stop, the home of an elderly Polish lady with a choice selection of Tea roses.

I'd grown accustomed to disputes over rose names, but I was to learn that the problem of identification was particularly troublesome in Texas, since the collectors there have found few experts to whom they can turn for help. Graham Stuart Thomas's books, for example, offer little information of relevance to Texas. The reason for this is, once again, the Texan climate. The roses that flourish there belong, of necessity, to heat-, drought- and sun-loving classes. They don't perform well in the British Isles, and if they've received any attention at all from English experts, the result has usually been no more than a curt dismissal. With no one to guide them, the rose rustlers have had to fall back on their own resources in naming their finds. The solution they have arrived at demonstrates the special blend of pragmatism and flamboyance that I was coming to think of as peculiarly Texan.

To each of the roses the rustlers find they give a "study name," a sobriquet they distinguish by surrounding it with double quotes (the mark of a cultivar's official name is, of course, a brace of *single* quotes). Generally, the study name recalls some circumstance of the rose's discovery: the place, the time, maybe the name of the bush's owner or discoverer. In theory, this study name is temporary and will give way to the true name if and when the rustlers discover it. The blush-white rose they'd found in a Navasota yard, its blossoms flat and quartered, their faces powdered pink, the rustlers called "Miss Mary Minor" in honor of its owner, an elderly black lady. Years later, someone recognized it as 'Souvenir de la Malmaison,' a Bourbon rose from 1843 that the French hybridizer had named in honor of the garden of Napoleon's empress, and that is the name under which this variety now sells in the Antique Rose Emporium catalogue. Often, though, the study name proves so much more apt to a Texan garden that it lives on side by side with the official title. 'Marie van Houtte,' a Tea rose of 1871, pale yellow at the center, the petals stained lilac, will always remain the "Hole Rose" to the Texan collectors who found it lurking in a roadside hollow.

I liked to leaf through the lists of Texan rose names in the Antique Rose Emporium catalogue, and every time a rustler mentioned a new one, I had to know the provenance. "Petite Pink Scotch," "November Surprise," "Navasota Noisette," "Baptist Manse," "Jessie Mae," "Highway 290 Pink Buttons," "Pam's Pink"; all by themselves these names furnished a complete history of old roses in Texas. My favorite was the "Burglar Rose" that Tommy Adams, Mike Shoup's foreman, had contributed to the Antique Rose Emporium's catalogue. A red-flowered climber, this had covered a fence around the chicken yard at Tommy's old family homeplace across the border in Louisiana. When a thief tried to force his way into the house one night, Tommy's father chased him out at gunpoint. The fleet-footed criminal would have escaped had he not run into the fence and the rose's thorny embrace. "Daddy come up on him," Tommy recalled for my benefit; "he pulled a knife on Daddy. Daddy knocked him on the head with the revolver and knocked him out cold. So it became the Burglar Rose."

I'd thought of this method of naming as typically Texan, but in looking through guides to old roses later I learned it was as much a survival as any of the rosebushes we were seeing on the rustle. Unknowingly, the Texans had fallen into the same habits as the nineteenth-century Frenchmen who had bred most of the old roses found in Central Texas. When, armed with a French/English dictionary and a file of old gardening journals, I began to investigate the roses' "true" names, I found that they were just as much a record of the flowers' past as the Texan study names, and often no more authentic.

The French nurserymen had looked upon their roses more as children than as products, and they had self-consciously resisted standardization in the matter of nomenclature. Indeed, the man who seems to have been the first to make a living from rose hybridizing, Monsieur J. P. Vibert of Chenevieres-sur-Marne, put it this way in his catalogue of 1830: "It is the privilege of beautiful roses to have many names." In his opinion, a noble rose was like a nobleman; the more important he was, the more titles he should bear. Some of the roses Vibert grew had ten names, every one as good as another. One particularly fine rose, a blossom he advertised that year as "Rouge Formidable" (Bold Red), came eventually to have fourteen. Who was to say which of these was the right one?

Many of the pet names Vibert and his colleagues gave to their roses were, like "Pam's Pink," a proud announcement of ownership, while others were, like "Jessie Mae," gestures of friendship. 'Souvenir de la Malmaison' wasn't the only old rose to bear that title; there were many "souvenirs" in the catalogues, and these are often the only mementoes of people who were very important to the development of the flower. There are several "Viberts," for example. There's 'Blanc de Vibert," a white Portland rose from 1847, 'Georges Vibert,' a purplish Gallica the breeder named for his brother in 1853, and 'Souvenir de Pierre Vibert,' a memorial to a dead son that was introduced in 1867. The most successful of these "Vibert" roses was 'Aimée Vibert,' a Noisette rose Monsieur Vibert named for his daughter in 1828. She must have been a most beautiful child; the rose, like all of its kin, bears small loose flowers but in bunches, large trusses, which in the case of 'Aimée Vibert' were a pure and virginal white. Vibert wrote about the rose to a British nurseryman, promising him that "the English when they see it will go down on their knees." Other nurserymen who adopted the flower called it "Nivea" (Snow Rose) and "Bouquet de la Mariée" (Bride's Bouquet).*

Vibert was also the man who introduced a very famous old Moss rose, 'Chapeau de Napoléon' (Napoleon's Hat) in 1826.

---

* *An interesting sidelight on this matter of naming roses for loved ones appeared in the May 1836 issue of* The Gardener's Magazine. *Among the "Gardening Notices" supplied by an English nurseryman, Thomas Rivers, upon his return from a tour of France was the following reflection: "A custom in France among rose-growers gives rise to many (to us) very uninteresting names. An amateur who raises roses from seed is regularly besieged by his lady friends to name one after them. He therefore keeps a book in which applications are duly registered, and this is only deviated from under very peculiar circumstances; hence we have Madame Desprez, Madame Hardy, &c. I often think that some of the fair applicants have not been in high favor when I find very bad roses honored with their names, which are soon confined to oblivion. On the contrary, if you find a cultivator names one after his wife, it is generally a very fine flower, as is the case with those above mentioned. I think this is generally a very safe criterion for judging the goodness of the flower, merely by the name; for if the unfortunate grower has a termagant wife, I am quite sure (from the active part French women take in business) that she would not allow her name to be attached to a bad rose; and, if an affectionate partner, his feelings will prompt him to honor her name with a fine flower."*

The pretext for that name was the shape of the blossom's calyx, the cup of green sepals that encloses the bud and later the flower's base. In 'Chapeau de Napoléon,' this structure spreads into three wings like a cocked hat. The name reveals something of the breeder as well as the rose, and it is this I value most, since it was almost the only insight I have been able to gain into that man's experience. Secondary sources connected him to the circle of rose growers who worked for the empress Josephine on her estate, Malmaison, but in Vibert's writings I found no reference to those days, no acknowledgment of a debt. The Moss rose, however, bears witness that Vibert's brush with greatness remained on his mind long after Waterloo.

Nurserymen, their friends, families and employers are not the only people memorialized in rose names. Miss Mary Minor is dead now and might be forgotten outside Navasota were it not for the rose the rustlers named after her, but that is a fate she shares with others once far more renowned. Maréchal Niel, for whom the yellow rose Georgia Drennan recommended for a soldier's grave was named, owes the considerable reputation he maintains in Texas to his rose's prominent place in the Antique Rose Emporium catalogue. Nurserymen gave names of this sort to their flowers because they hoped the person's fame might serve as a sort of endorsement; now it is the flower that rescues the personage from obscurity.

Sometimes, of course, the reverse has also held true. In 1900 the German National Rose Society sponsored a competition to select the rose that would bear the name of the recently deceased chancellor, Prince Otto von Bismarck. The winner has vanished without a trace, while Bismarck's fame has, of course, survived. The contest's runner-up, a white Hybrid Perpetual, continues to enjoy great esteem, but only among a select group of connoisseurs. This rose was named 'Frau Karl Druschki' in honor of the wife of the Rose Society's president. Nurserymen in other lands complained that the unmelodious title kept the rose from the sales it deserved. When a wave of anti-German sentiment struck Britain and the United States in 1914, gardeners in those countries rechristened the rose, respectively, "Snow Queen" and "White American Beauty," but after the armistice, the rose returned to its proper name. A gesture with the forefinger and a "look at that" is the way this nearly perfect white is usually identified for me during visits to old-rose collections, and even among collectors, 'Frau Karl' hasn't achieved the popularity its quality deserves.*

"Navasota Noisette," "Caldwell Yellow Tea" and "Giddings' Pink Cluster"—the rustlers' names furnish an atlas of forgotten small-town Texas. I was learning a new geography in the company of these collectors, learning that Navasota lies in Central Texas even though it is in the eastern third of the state. Other rustlers were equally sensitive about the boundaries of their regions: West Texas, Gulf Coast, the Big Thicket, Cross Timbers, Piney Woods and East Texas, not to be confused, of course, with Deep East Texas. Rose names were the signposts to this unfamiliar map, as they would be to the map I would subsequently draw of nineteenth-century Europe.

From the old gardening journals I learned that a particularly fine new cultivar might be a source of considerable income to a nurseryman; but more, it was also a source of intense local pride. 'Gloire de Dijon,' an exceptionally handsome yellow Tea rose, *was* the glory of Dijon. A pink cabbage rose that appeared in the Netherlands sometime around the year 1800 bore only small blossoms (one and one-half inches across), but because it rebloomed intermittently through the fall, it aroused intense interest among the gardeners of the day. It survives as 'Petite de Hollande' (Holland Dwarf). 'Belle Vichysoise' (Beauty of Vichy), and 'Belle Poitevine' (Beauty

---

* When relating this story to a garden club on Long Island, I was brought up short by a voice from the back of the room. "It's not ugly," I was informed in a tone of withering Germanic scorn, "if you pronounce it right." The lady applied her more educated tongue to the name, and it did sound quite distinguished.

of Poitou) both enjoyed the support of their provinces, while the city of Lyon was especially well represented in rose names, boasting, among others, 'Étoile de Lyon' and 'Gloire Lyon-naise.' Rose production was a big business in that region;* Lyon's climate was temperate and sunny, and its industrialization was an additional asset. In that age of coal, the factories filled the air with sulphur, a natural fungicide that helped guard rosebushes against blackspot.

Synthesis of a sort between Texan and European traditions was achieved at the next stop on the rustle, as we inspected the Polish lady's Tea roses. With the crowd of collectors milling about the yard, Pam had climbed the steps to knock on the front door. It opened a crack, enough to let a suspicious eye peer out. Pam introduced herself and explained our visit, not once but twice, the first time in a normal speaking voice, the second in a shout more suited to the old lady's hearing. "Don't you want to come out and say hello to everybody?" Pam asked. A firm no and a slam of the door was all the answer she got. Then a collector whom I will not name noticed the yellow rose climbing a porch post and came over furtively to introduce me. I was finally to meet the famed 'Maréchal Niel.' Only, by changing the accent, softening the syllables and drawing them out, my rustler friend transformed the old field marshal of Napoleon III's army to Marshal Kneel, Texas lawman.

Speaking softly, she told me the reason for her secrecy. Marshal Kneel's a common rose in Texas, throughout the whole of the South, but the cultivar that was originally praised for its exceptional vigor has been infected with virus and now performs poorly. This I knew to be a common problem among older roses, because of the way they are cloned. Any viral or bacterial disease present in the parent is almost sure to be

---

* So expert were the nurserymen of Lyon that they considered their region the rose capital and Paris the provincial backwater—and rightly so. 'Maréchal Niel' is one of their creations, and so is 'Cécile Brünner,' the "Sweetheart Rose" and 'La France,' the first Hybrid Tea.

passed along to the offspring through the cutting or grafted bud. If a conscientious nurseryman becomes aware of the infection, he or she will discard the stock. A nurseryman in a hurry may miss the symptoms, and an unscrupulous one may choose to look the other way. Once passed off to the unsuspecting customer, the infected rose may serve as parent to more cuttings or grafts, and an epidemic is born. Yet somehow, this particular Marshal Kneel looked remarkably fit; could it be an early, uninfected specimen that had survived unnoticed in this remote spot?

She'd like to share her discovery with the other collectors, my would-be accomplice continued, but there wouldn't be enough cuttings to go around. Now the other rustlers were watching her; but who would notice a Yankee? So if I would kind of wander over r-e-e-al slow. . . . In my best imitation of a mosey, I did as I was bid.

It was the sighting of a 'Duchesse de Brabant' that put an end to the day's organized activities. Following the rush to the yard of an abandoned house, I found a sturdy shrub covered with cupped salmon-pink Tea roses. This, Pam informed me, was the rose that Teddy Roosevelt (another New Yorker who succumbed to the lure of the West) favored above all others as a boutonnière. Then a shout from across the street announced the discovery of "Maggie," a China-Bourbon cross that bears rose-pink blossoms of extraordinary fragrance. With this, all semblance of order vanished. The fistfuls of cuttings contributed by the rose's startled but smiling owner seemed only to whet the rustlers' appetites. Climbing into their cars, they separated, each one going his or her own way in search of undiscovered treasure.

Graduating from onlooker to participant, I rustled my first rose that afternoon, an antique Hybrid Tea with graceful, long-stemmed blossoms of vivid pink. With proverbial Southern gallantry, my hosts insisted on giving this flower the study name "Suzanne" in honor of my fiancée, who had accompanied me on this expedition. Tired at last, having scoured every cemetery, churchyard and alley in the town of Bryan, we re-assembled at Pam's house for an evening of cucumber sand-wiches and reminiscences of former rustles. I listened and tried to put my observations into perspective.

Pam's house led me to think again about Texas's past. An imposing frame building with a columned portico, the house was testimony to the energy of her great-grandfather Jesse, a Welsh immigrant who'd built his home from a pattern he'd found in *Scientific American*. Much of the furniture was Jesse's work, too, unpretentious in design but elegantly simple and solid, fashioned from walnut and curly pine that the Welshman milled himself. In the attic, Pam told me, there were twenty-two trunks of family clothes, a collection that began with a wedding in 1804. I'd seen samples of these, faded parasols and frock coats, and I had thirty dollars from the box of Confederate currency Pam found there. The bouquets of floral antiques she and I had cut that morning were in perfect harmony with this setting—it was I who seemed like an anach-ronism. I kept thinking of a story Pam had told me of the roses' introduction into Texas.

Washington-on-the-Brazos was the town from which Pam's people had come, and it was there in 1836 that fifty-one dele-gates had signed the Texas Declaration of Independence, the document that announced the Texans' determination to sepa-rate from Mexico. One of the most ardent supporters of this step, Lorenzo de Zavala, was also a fervent Mexican patriot. Zavala had begun his revolutionary career fighting for Mex-ico's freedom when the nation was still a colony of Spain. He was in Madrid, representing the interests of his home state, Yucatan, in the Spanish *Cortes*, when Mexico won its freedom in 1821. He had promptly resigned to return to Mexico and serve in various senior capacities in his nation's government. He had been serving as ambassador to the French court in 1834 when his president, Santa Ana, overthrew Mexico's re-publican constitution. Resigning his post once again, Zavala made his way back to Mexico's northernmost province, Texas, to throw in his lot with the new republic being formed there. This intransigent idealist resigned repeatedly from his post in the Texan government, but to little effect since each time his superiors ignored the gesture and sent him back to work. No doubt they'd recognized the impractical streak in his character the moment he entered Texas, for with him the ex-ambassador had brought a highly unusual baggage—a collection of the finest French roses.

Lorenzo's granddaughter, Adina de Zavala, wrote an article for the society page of the *San Antonio Express* in 1934, on the occasion of Texas's upcoming centennial, in which she described her grandparents' garden. "In Grandmother's Old Garden," she titled the piece, "Where the Rose Reigned as Queen." Although she dwelt on the rich variety of her grandmother's garden—the magnolias with their white flowers, the crepe myrtles, the violets, the pansies, the Johnny-Jump-Ups, and the sweet-scented herbs—one flower held center stage. "Though grandmother loved all flowers and plants, her favorite was the rose."

Adina remembered her grandmother speaking of "the beautiful gardens of France, which she much admired when she was at the Court of St. Cloud, as the wife of an ambassador plenipotentiary." The granddaughter had seen the relics of those days, the old roses Lorenzo had brought from France, "the crimson Gloire des Rosomanes, the Louis Philippe, the rosy flesh-colored Madame Bosanquet, and perhaps others." Adina de Zavala urged her readers to prepare for the centennial celebration by planting roses, "so that every vacant spot shall produce a rose plant. Visitors must needs exclaim then," she concluded, "over the quantity and beauty of our roses, and name us—the State of Roses—the Lone Star State."

This was a rousing, flag-waving endorsement, but despite the nostalgia, it was not a call for old roses. Adina knew the old family home was gone, and with it the original French bushes. Yet the rustlers could have told her that was not the end of the story. They would have reminded her of an anec-

dote buried near the bottom of one of her columns of print:
"I remember a Negro cabin that was still in existence, occupied by 'Old Uncle Early,' an ex-slave, one of those who had
refused to leave grandmother. His house was fairly covered
with different-colored climbing roses." No doubt Uncle Early
had acquired his rosebushes by the least expensive means, taking cuttings from his mistress's plants; he and his fellows were
the ones who preserved such historic roses for the present
generation.

Bill Welch finally came to Pam's house that night; he
brought dessert. I already knew his verdict on the rustlers'
finds, though. "The roses of Texas," I'd read in one of his
articles, "are like the early pioneers—hardy, dependable, and
usually beautiful." When a bearded and smiling Mike Shoup
showed me round his nursery the next morning and the
100,000 bushes that represented a year's crop, he likened the
roses to Texas itself. "It's still a young state," he said, "settled
originally by outlaws, and they're a tougher breed. We've got
a gene pool that's a little different."

But it was Pam who put it best. Guiding me through the
nursery yard, she stopped by a climbing Tea rose of 1851
vintage, 'Sombreuil.' I recognized it, for it grows in my northern garden, though the Texan giant put my struggling specimen to shame. Handing me a flawless cream-and-pink-tinted
blossom the size and shape of a large saucer, Pam smiled. "You
have never lived," she drawled, "until you've seen 'Sombreuil'
in the South." A fitting epitaph for a Texas rose rustler.

4

'Gloire de Dijon'

Heirloom
Roses

TEXANS, SKILLED as they may be in identifying roses, are completely unable to distinguish between different breeds of Northerners. They lump us all together under the single epithet "Yankee." They even call me a Yankee, and as a New Yorker I know that is an honor I don't deserve. Though I grew up within commuting distance of Manhattan, I've got grandparents who hail from New Hampshire. I've been aware since infancy that "Yankee" is a term that properly applies to only a very select group.

Just who qualifies is, of course, subject to some debate even among New Englanders. My wife, who was raised in the Berkshire hills of western Massachusetts, in her heart does not believe that my relatives from Connecticut truly belong, and when my grandmother complains of the southerners who throw their weight around in Exeter, she is referring to week-ending Bostonians. Then too, there are "swamp Yankees," those unfortunate individuals who may fulfill the residency requirement but whose low morals and trashy standards bar them forever from full membership. By any criterion, though, Caroline Ferriday is a Yankee among Yankees, even though she has chosen to live in Connecticut, in the quiet village of Bethlehem. She is also an extraordinary gardener.

Caroline's house is set back from the road within an easy walk of the town green; tall, square and white, the house stands as a remembrance of another age. The circular drive swings around the front in the broad sweep required by a horse-drawn carriage, while the building's wooden cornices, pediments and dentils bespeak both a classical taste and the seemly thrift of Dr. Bellamy, the minister who built the house in 1754. The pastor aimed at substance, obviously, but he wouldn't have contemplated building in stone. White pine and oak can, after all, be milled to look almost like stone, and good timber was abundant and cheap in Colonial New England. The choice wasn't stingy; it was, as my grandfather would say, careful.

To this tradition of prudence, Caroline Ferriday has added a seasoning of elegance. When she greeted me, she wore a tweed skirt and wool blazer that were beautifully cut and tailored but not new. That would have been ostentatious. The dim stillness indoors smelled of polish; the rooms I could see were furnished with handsome antiques. Caroline told me they were old family property. The price of antiques today: "Unbelievable. . . . I think that's because they've run short. There isn't anything anymore to collect." Except old roses. They are priced to a Yankee's satisfaction, handsome enough to suit Miss Ferriday's cultivated taste and, as she points out, more appropriate to her garden than modern ones.

Caroline and her parents came to Bethlehem in 1913. Previously they had lived in New York, though she added that some of her family "are Connecticut; the Howlands are Connecticut." The reason for the move?

"Well, I was really responsible. I was a very nervous child, and the family doctor at Southampton, where we always spent the summer, told my parents that I must be taken away from the sea air. We settled in this part of the country because we had relatives in Litchfield—the Winkles, whom you've perhaps heard about if you know Litchfield at all. Well, they are an old, old family."

Bethlehem was a remote place, the roads so bad in some seasons as to be impassable. Now, of course, it has joined the Boston/Washington metroplex. But, Miss Ferriday remarked with satisfaction, "this town has done a very good job, I think, of remaining, as far as looks go, about the same."

The house the Ferridays bought, the one in which Caroline still lives, needed a complete refurbishing inside and out, and Caroline's mother was kept very busy that first year. So when a maid announced that the men were coming to lay out the garden, Mrs. Ferriday was caught unprepared. She must have been a woman of poise and decision, however. With paper and pencil she simply traced the pattern from the parlor carpet and gave this to the workmen to use as their plan. The arabesque of beds they cut into the terrace behind the house did remind me of an oriental rug, only the flowers here were real, the colors brilliantly alive.

Though its design is strictly symmetrical, the garden is set six feet off the axis of the house. A large maple tree that blocked the central view was the reason for this. When a friend who helped with the landscaping recommended cutting the tree down, Mrs. Ferriday adamantly refused. "My mother went on at a great rate," Caroline recalled, "about how no one was going to touch the trees that the Lord had put there—I don't think he had, but never mind—and so it was not exactly centered. . . . The curious thing about the maple down be-

low is that it came down of itself two years later. So we had
our vista without working for it."

If the outlines of the landscape reflect Mrs. Ferriday's con-
victions, the planting is purely Caroline's. Her mother let her
do what she wanted with it, and she responded by combining
perennial flowers and shrubs in the style that Gertrude Jekyll
was making fashionable in England. And like the town of
Bethlehem, the garden has done a good job of remaining the
same ever since.

My conversation with Caroline Ferriday kept yielding
scenes of the past, just glimpses but extraordinarily vivid ones.
She comes from a family of horticultural importance, as I
learned when I made the mistake of praising a gracefully cas-
cading evergreen I could see through the parlor window.
"That's a fine specimen of a 'Sargent's Weeping Hemlock,' I
said, more than a little smug at my identification of this classic
tree (which was introduced at Boston's Arnold Arboretum
and which I had always assumed to be named for the institution's founding director, Charles Sprague Sargent). "Sargent's?
There's nothing *Sargent* about the tree," she told me crisply.
It had been discovered by the husband of her favorite great-
aunt. "Uncle Joe Howland, he found that in his neighbor-
hood. He went to some friend"—Henry Winthrop Sargent,
the arboretum director's brother—"who was in *business*"—so
much for science—"and told him about it." Being a businessman, the friend of course took unfair advantage, distributing
the tree without a word of credit to its real discoverer. "So it
has the friend's name, but we have the history of it."

Caroline offered a unique perspective on the subject of rose
collecting; I had never met anyone before who acquired roses
through inheritance. The pair of 'Katharina Zeimets' at the
foot of the garden, two-foot shrubs liberally sprinkled with
white blossoms, had been her mother's—an old rose now, this
cultivar had been on the market only twelve years when Mrs.
Ferriday began the garden. Classed as a Polyantha rose,

'Katharina Zeimet' is a shrub with a truly cosmopolitan background.

Though the evidence is far from complete, the class of Polyantha roses seems to trace back to a bush that the Scottish plant collector Robert Fortune sent back from Japan in 1865. Fortune, who had already won fame as a horticultural collector in China (see chap. 6, pp. 144–52), went to Japan on a shopping expedition; American warships had opened the Mikado's empire to Westerners for the first time in two hundred years, and a prominent English nursery firm, Standish and Noble of Bagshot, hired Fortune to see what their Japanese colleagues had been growing. Among the plants that caught Fortune's eye was a low-growing variety of *R. multiflora,* a species that he had known in China in its natural form as an expansive Rambler. The dwarf bore bunches of small, pink flowers in early summer, and it was tough—the block of plants that Fortune purchased survived a deck passage to England of several months. Upon their arrival, one of these plants was passed along, as a courtesy, to the mayor of Lyon for distribution through that rose-breeding center. The new rose does not seem to have impressed the Lyonnais—perhaps they could not believe that any important roses could come from *that* side of the Channel—and though the mayor installed the present in a local park, it was ignored and eventually dug up and discarded.

But one nurseryman with more vision than the rest, Jean Sisley, saved Fortune's Japanese dwarf and transplanted it to his field, where it produced many interesting seedlings. In 1875, a friend of Sisley's, J. B. Guillot, introduced a cluster-flowered dwarf hybrid, 'Pâquerette,' that seems to have derived from Sisley's seedlings; contemporary records do not indicate what Guillot used for breeding stock, but at least one specialist in the history of roses, Roy E. Shepherd,* has suggested that the two men might easily have traded bushes back and

* Roy E. Shepherd, History of the Rose. *New York: Macmillan, 1954, pp. 202–21.*

forth. What is certain is that 'Pâquerette's' panicles of bloom resemble those of the Japanese import. Somewhere along the line, Guillot's rose had picked up a repeat-blooming habit, probably from a cross with R. *chinensis,* but what contemporary growers found most exciting about 'Pâquerette' was the bush's size. At a time when rosebushes commonly sprawled seven or eight feet, a two-foot hybrid was quite a novelty.

A French horticulturist dubbed the new cultivar a Polyantha rose, rather optimistically setting it apart as the founder of a new class. Actually, French and English nurserymen were rather slow to capitalize on Guillot's introduction. Only a handful of dwarves were produced until Peter Lambert of Trier, Germany, took an interest in the class around the end of the century. He introduced a number of Polyanthas—'Katharina Zeimet' was one of the earliest (1901) and the best, and it was timely. The appearance of a new breed of gardener, the commuter, brought with it a trend toward smaller gardens (the Ferriday establishment, though opulent by my standards, was modest by those of the pre-income-tax era). These compact landscapes created a need for more compact plantings.*

Miss Ferriday had equipped me with a map before sending me out into the garden, and with this I was able to identify many other antiques. In beds neatly outlined with clipped boxwood, roses competed with spikes of blue delphiniums and bouquets of pink and white phlox. I found 'William Lobb,' a Moss rose of 1855 whose sticky green fur that covered the buds (actually a thick growth of resin-producing glands) did look like moss. This rose, despite its name, is French in origin,

---

* For insights into the adjustments this shrinkage involved, I turned to a popular book of 1911: The Garden of a Commuter's Wife (New York, The Macmillan Company). Despite the promising title, this anonymous diary of life in the suburbs concentrated chiefly on the difficulties of finding faithful, obedient servants (gardeners were a special problem, apparently) and lampoons of wealthier neighbors. Interspersed with the venom, the author included breathless passages about the planting of her "Garden of Dreams"; her husband, a landscape architect, did most of the digging and, understandably, kept beseeching her to scale down her plans.

as is 'Louise Odier,' a bright pink, perfumed specimen of a
Bourbon rose that I spotted nearby. I found 'Tuscany,' too, one
of the oldest cultivars of the French rose, R. *gallica*, a species
that has flourished in France since it was known as Gaul.
'Tuscany' seems to have been grown by John Gerard, the herb-
alist and observer of the Musk rose, since he included the
"Old Velvet Rose," one of 'Tuscany's' aliases, in his *Catalogus*,
the list of his plants that he published in 1596. Miss Ferriday,
I noticed, grew not only 'Tuscany' but also its offspring,
'Superb Tuscany,' whose flowers have the same soft luxuriance
and maroon-crimson color as the parent, but more petals, as
well as larger blossoms and foliage.

In my rambles down Miss Ferriday's gravelled paths, I de-
tected a definite prejudice in favor of the French. Later I
learned that she kept an apartment in Paris for many years
and employed as her companion a woman whose language
was as charmingly Gallic as the roses. Francophilia aside, it
would be impossible to assemble a collection of old roses without giving pride of place to the flowers of France. One of
the very few points on which old-rose collectors agree is that
the French nurserymen were the premier rose breeders of the
nineteenth century—perhaps of all time.

The leadership of the French was due to the encouragement of another great lady: Napoleon's consort, the Empress
Josephine. That Creole from Martinique could not have been
more different from my hostess; certainly no Yankee could
approve of such an extravagant character. Yet the two women
shared an enthusiasm for roses. Indeed, they even grew some
of the same types. To both, I believe, the roses served as a kind
of spiritual refuge. To Miss Ferriday the roses are remem-
brances, and planting them is her way of rescuing a gracious
past from oblivion. Josephine's need for roses was much more
immediate. For her, they were an escape from the fatiguing
routine of her husband's court.

Rose was, quite literally, Josephine de Beauharnais's middle
name; she had been born Marie-Joseph-Rose Tascher de la

Pagerie. Friends and family called her Rose until she was married to Napoleon in 1796 after a passionate affair. In 1798 she bought a country house nine miles west of Paris, an old but modest chateau inauspiciously named Malmaison (evil house). Napoleon had opposed the purchase, on the ground that the price was too high, but she borrowed the down payment and closed the deal while he was away on his expedition to Egypt. He paid the balance of 300,000 francs upon his return, comforting himself with the thought that he could operate the property profitably as a stud farm.

Josephine had other plans, and she got her way. She spent millions on the redecoration of the house, and many millions more on the improvement of the grounds. "I wish Malmaison soon to offer a model of good cultivation," she wrote, "and to become a source of riches for the rest of France. It is with this in mind that I am having a very large quantity of trees and shrubs from southern countries and South America cultivated. I want each *département* within ten years to possess a collection of rare plants that have originated from my nurseries."

One lady-in-waiting, Madame de Rémusat, described Josephine in her memoirs as a skillful, effective liar and belittled the empress's contribution to the work of the garden. After describing the planting of a cypress at Malmaison, Rémusat noted that "Mme Bonaparte . . . threw a few handfuls of dirt on the roots of the tree, so that she might say that she had planted it with her own hands."

Naturally, Josephine's position prevented her from getting down on her knees in the mud, but other observers confirmed her very active interest in the extension and care of her plant collections. Another book of memoirs, ostensibly the work of Josephine's *femme de chambre* Mademoiselle d'Avrillion,* testified that the empress's "taste for botany was no caprice, but the basis of study, and serious study at that. She soon knew the names of all the plants, the family they were classified as

* *Actually, it was the work of a contemporary historian, Charles Maxime de Villemarest.*

belonging to by naturalists, their origins and properties. She took great pleasure in visiting her greenhouses; her little walks always led in that direction." A lady-in-waiting, Georgette Crest, recalled Josephine's devotion to her plants in even stronger, though less admiring terms:

> When the weather was fine, the greenhouses were in-spected; the same walk was taken every day. On the way to that spot, the same subjects were talked over. The con-versation generally turned on botany, upon Her Majesty's taste for that *interesting* science, her wonderful memory, which enabled her to name every plant—in short, the same phrases were generally repeated over and over again, and at the same time, circumstances well calculated to render the promenades exceedingly tedious and fatiguing. I no sooner stepped on to that delightful walk, which I had so admired when I first saw it, than I was seized with an im-moderate fit of yawning.

As Napoleon became increasingly absorbed in affairs im-perial and extramarital, Josephine withdrew for longer periods to her country home. It is significant that 1804, the year in which he (formerly First Consul) was crowned emperor of the French, was also the year in which she conceived her most ambitious horticultural project. She decided to assemble in her garden a sample of every living rose. As empress, however, she also had advantages no ordinary collector could match. An indulgent husband put all the resources of his empire at her disposal. His conquest of Egypt netted not only the Rosetta stone but also rare specimens for the Malmaison gardens, and the emperor instructed the captains of his privateers to search every ship they captured for exotic seeds and plants.

Even more important were the contributions of Napoleon's arch-enemies, the British. Though they detested Napoleon's politics, this nation of gardeners could not but admire his wife's horticultural enthusiasm. Britain's strategy called for a strict naval blockade of France and her allies, yet the Ad-miralty ruled that Josephine's plants, if intercepted, should be forwarded at once, and the Prince Regent issued special passports to British nurserymen and gardeners so that they could work at Malmaison. Josephine, in turn, ignored her husband's strictures against trade with the British. She ordered many of her roses from English nurseries, principally Lee & Kennedy of Hammersmith, where she spent £2,600 in 1803 alone.

The sexuality of plants was poorly understood as yet, but an English horticulturist, Andrew Knight, had by trial and error developed crude but effective techniques of hybridization. He had applied these with some success to fruit trees, currants and spinach; the French gardeners presently turned them to the breeding of new roses. The 197 different roses Josephine finally succeeded in collecting is a modest number today, but it was unique at the time. It was also a genetic gold mine: from Middle Eastern roses the breeders could introduce new and luminous colors (yellow in particular), and by crossing Chinese roses with native European species, they could create roses of an entirely new type, roses that combined the Europeans' hardiness with the oriental roses' generosity of bloom. No one seems to have grasped the possibilities of the situation all at once, but experiments were set afoot in the nursery yard that could only tend that way.

Admittedly, the Frenchmen's methods were haphazard. André DuPont, a nurseryman who was part of Josephine's circle, had learned the technique of pollinating flowers by hand, apparently from Dutch florists, but most of his colleagues relied on honey bees; the nurserymen would plant different species or cultivars in close propinquity and hope that the insects would transfer pollen from one to another.

The blossoms that resulted proved as revolutionary in their impact as any of Napoleon's reforms. Previously, roses had occupied a secondary position in the garden. They were widely cultivated for their perfume and supposed medicinal properties, but they did not enjoy the prestige of the so-called florist flowers, tulips, hyacinths, pinks and primroses. The new roses from France changed that, bringing the genus to the pinnacle of popularity, especially in Britain. When Napoleon's empire collapsed and the allies closed in on Paris, the British officers issued orders that Malmaison was not to be molested—one wonders if the motive was purely chivalry, or if the conquerors hoped to secure the empress's roses as spoils.

As it turned out, one of her disciples, Jean-Paul Vibert, forestalled the invaders. His mentor, Monsieur Descemet, another of Josephine's protégés, had bred 10,000 seedlings from the new roses. During the confusion of the French retreat, Vibert decided this stock was in danger and evacuated it to his own establishment; this provided the basis for some 600 hybrids of marketable quality. Vibert sold his roses at what were then remarkable prices, often to his erstwhile enemies, the British. For where Napoleon's armies had failed, the roses of Josephine's heirs, Vibert and the other French nurserymen, succeeded, taking England by storm. The leading English nurseryman of the period, Thomas Rivers, wrote with an envy that bordered on despair of the English lord who purchased 1,000 French rosebushes in a single order, even though they cost him a guinea apiece.

Rivers disparaged the lack of system in the French nursery industry. In his report to *The Gardener's Magazine* of 1836, he wrote:

> Nothing can be more insignificant, both as to size and stock, than the commercial rose-growers near Paris; they seldom exceed one acre, and more frequently contain but half that quantity of ground; in which standard roses of all heights, and dwarfs of all sorts, are grown in the same rows; presenting, to a stranger, an inextricable mass of confusion. It would be difficult to execute an order for a general good collection from any one of these nurseries; but they are so numerous, that twenty may be visited, for twenty sorts of roses, with but little difficulty.

While admitting the skill of the French growers and recommending several of their techniques to his readers, Rivers treated them personally with disdain. Of the rose beds of Monsieur Hardy he wrote:

> Some most superb varieties were among them; but M. Hardy is rather chary of his roses, and does not like them to be distributed hastily, patronising the old-fashioned idea of possessing what his neighbor have not. It is amusing to find very prevalent here the little jealousies and envyings that at one time were so common among our florists. If a rose that has been raised from seed by M. Hardy is praised in the presence of another celebrated amateur near Paris, it is always responded to with "Bah!" and a shrug of contempt. Reverse this, by praising the amateur's rose to another, and you will find the same effect produced. It is therefore most prudent, if you wish to remain in the sunshine of favor, to limit all your admiration to the roses present, forgetting that there are any other roses or rose amateurs in the world.

Nothwithstanding Rivers's sneers, history has been on the Frenchmen's side. I've read about Rivers's 'George IV,' a Hybrid China rose that was the Englishman's pride, but I've never seen it. 'Madame Hardy,' the cool, pallid damask with a green pip at the center that was the Frenchman's tribute to his wife, I have admired in fine growth in many California yards, and together with a number of much better qualified authorities, I would rate this as the most exquisite white rose of all time.*

America followed Britain in the enthusiasm for French roses, though the revolution took longer to penetrate to what

---

* *The French nurserymen's success irritated their English rivals, but it was part of a larger economic pattern. France lacked the necessary coal and iron ore to compete with Britain industrially, and was forced to fall back on its artisans to balance payments. Luxury goods such as cosmetics, jewelry and fashionable women's wear remained the mainstay of the French export trade through the nineteenth century; British mechanization couldn't compete with French chic in those areas. Silk was France's largest single export—it is no accident that Lyon, the rose capital, was also the center of silk production. Both industries emphasized handwork and the craftsman's instinct.*

was then a horticultural hinterland. French roses are not especially well represented in Bernard M'Mahon's *American Gardener's Calendar* of 1806. M'Mahon was an Irish nurseryman who had settled in Philadelphia, and his book is important as the first comprehensive gardening guide adapted to North American conditions. Among the eighty-three kinds of roses included in the catalogue of plants appended to the book is a "Lisbon Rose," a "Dwarf Austrian," a "Pennsylvania" and a "Hudson Bay Rose," but the only roses with French names are ancient types such as the "Common Province Rose," a rose that had been established in the Provence region of southern France since the Middle Ages.

The change in roses becomes apparent a couple of decades later in the catalogues of America's oldest commercial nursery, Prince's Linnaean Botanic Garden of Flushing, New York. This firm had operated since 1737, supplying grape vines and fruit trees to settlers and native American plants to European customers. The third proprietor, William Prince, Jr., interested himself in roses, and by 1822 he and his son William Robert listed 170 kinds in their catalogue and offered to provide customers a list of 200 further types upon request. All of Prince's names were English, but many read like translations: "Charming Beauty," "Triumphant Bizarre" and "Spineless Virgin" have a pronounced Gallic flavor. George Washington had been among Prince's customers, and at prices of as much as two dollars a plant, his roses were for the wealthy.

Prince's chief rival was another Philadelphian, the Scottish-born nurseryman Robert Buist. Roses were his specialty, too—he published the first American guide to rose growing, *The Rose Manual,* in 1844 (William Robert Prince replied with *Prince's Manual of Roses* in 1846). Buist returned to Great Britain and the Continent every year or two, visiting rose breeders and acquiring the latest introductions for his customers in the United States. He bought 'Madame Hardy' from Monsieur Hardy himself in 1832, the year of the rose's introduction, and in 1839, he bought 'Aimée Vibert' from the proud father.* Buist proudly labelled Philadelphia *"a very hotbed of roses"* in an era when every gardener knew at first hand what a hotbed was;† but he freely admitted that the French were "the leading spirits in everything connected with the rose."

Another rival set up shop in Prince's own backyard, in Flushing, in 1838. This was Samuel Parsons, a nineteen-year-old nurseryman who dared compete with the Princes in the Long Island rose trade. Parsons made *his* European tour in 1845 to "form contacts with earnest rose lovers abroad," and published *his* rose guide, *Parsons On the Rose,* in 1847. (One wonders that the gardening public didn't tire of making trips to the bookstore in those years, but all three books sold well, each running to several editions; Parsons's book saw twenty-four printings, the last in 1923.) Parsons praised from first-hand experience "the force of Hardy, the industry of Vibert, and the charming manners of Laffay," but it was Thomas Rivers with whom he formed the closest friendship. Still, his judgment came down on the side of the Continental nurserymen. "The French are constantly searching for improvements in horticultural science and practice," he wrote, "with an enthusiasm rarely found in the more cold Englishman whose skill seems to consist less in the creation of new varieties, than in growing perfectly those already known."

Without a doubt, however, the most eloquent testimony to Josephine's influence is to be had from a simple comparison

---

* *"Whilst discoursing upon roses,"* Buist wrote in The Rose Manual *of his visit to Vibert, "he directed my attention with great enthusiasm to this plant, and said,* 'Celle ci est si belle, que je lui ai donné le nom de ma fille chérie—Aimée Vibert.' *This enthusiasm can be easily understood by those who, like myself, have been so fortunate as to see the two 'Áimée Viberts'—the rose and the young girl—both in their full bloom, and both as lovely as their sweet name."*

† *A hundred years ago a hotbed was more than a cliché, it was the glass-covered pit in which gardeners grew their winter greens and started flower seedlings in the spring. The heat came from a layer of fresh, fermenting manure that the grower buried at the pit's bottom. Both quotes are drawn from Earl Coleman's reprint of the original edition of* The Rose Manual (*New York: Earl M. Coleman, 1978*).

of numbers—the number of garden roses that existed before her planting of Malmaison, and the numbers available in the years afterward. The *Histoire Naturelle de la Rose,* which J. L. M. Guillemeau published in 1800, lists 100 species, varieties and cultivars. William Robert Prince advertised 1,600 in 1846 (the American probably maintained the world's greatest collection), while by 1900 the French national rose museum, Roseraie de l'Hay, listed in its catalogue more than 3,000 named varieties.

Nor is there any question which nation was primarily responsible for the increase. The man who reviewed Samuel Parsons's book for *The American Gardener's Magazine and Register* in 1848 adopted a patriotic stance on the achievements of American hybridizers—there were a few—and took Parsons to task for his use of foreign terminology. The French word *remontant* might do very well for those conversant with that language, but what was wrong with "the good old word *perpetual*"? Even this love-it-or-leave-it horticulturist, however, had to give credit where credit was due. "To the French almost exclusively belongs the credit of bringing the rose to the perfection it has now attained," he admitted. "More than nine tenths of the immense number of varieties which the last twenty years have produced have been the growth of French cultivators."

Driven by his ambition for a suitably imperial marriage, Napoleon divorced the base-born Josephine at the end of 1809, but left her the house at Malmaison and continued to pay her debts. She died in 1814, little more than a month after her ex-husband's abdication. The police bulletin noted that "The death of Mme de Beauharnais is the source of much regret. . . . Excessively unhappy during her husband's reign, she had taken refuge, against his brutality and his disdain, in the study of botany. . . ." The artist she had commissioned to record her botanical rarities, Pierre-Joseph Redouté, produced a large folio of rose portraits, *Les Roses,* that is generally acknowledged to be a masterpiece and that has done much to keep Josephine's reputation bright among gardeners. But in actual fact, most of the 169 watercolors were not painted from Josephine's collection. Redouté didn't finish the series until three years after his patron's death, and by then the empress's rose garden had perished.

Caroline Ferriday worries that her garden might go the same way. "Getting things taken care of is not such an easy matter these days," she confided as we sat on a bench overlooking the garden. "You call up young men of fourteen and fifteen, and they are all tied up with other things." She can do little besides weeding any more, but the big names of the gardening world have begun to take an interest. Nurserymen who sense a new market in old roses have visited, and the garden won a respectful mention in a recent guide to old roses. In addition, Miss Ferriday has established a land trust, the Bellamy Preserve, that will protect the Yankee minister's homestead against future development.

Meanwhile, she keeps a special bed of antiques to give to visitors. If I saw anything I wanted, she told me, she expected she could find me a clipping or a root. I made my selection, and, her delicate face made beautiful by a smile, she sent me on my way with a single perfect bloom of 'Superb Tuscany.'

5

Twice-Blooming
Roses
of Paestum

Noisette rose

MIRIAM WAGNER had shown me her collection of rose-deco-
rated china, odds and ends of Victorian services that she'd
found in thrift and antique stores. She had been able to identify every blossom on every bowl and chipped tureen. But
now, as we strolled through her garden along the Old Albany
Road in Garrison, New York, I found that I couldn't identify
the rose she was showing me. The bush was low, around three
feet tall, and the flowers were modest, no more than two and
one-half inches across, semi-double, pale pink rounds of crepe
petals. The stems of the blossoms were so short that the buds
jostled one another for room, and the central flower hadn't
space to expand fully. I forgave the flowers every defect,

though, as soon as I picked one and held it to my nose. The
fragrance was essence of rose, a rose perfume stronger, clearer,
sweeter and somehow purer than any I'd experienced before.

That should have tipped me off to the rose's identity, but I
stooped to read the label: *Rosa damascena bifera*. This I knew
was the benchmark against which all other rose perfumes are
measured. At least, that is what Léonie Bell wrote in *The
Fragrant Year*, my favorite study of plant fragrances. Old roses
are one of this talented woman's many enthusiasms, and she
sampled more than two hundred different species and cultivars
for the book she illustrated and co-authored with Helen Van
Pelt Wilson. As I read this work, I'd been impressed with the
depth of research. Yet when I got to know Léonie through a
series of long telephone calls, I learned that what had appeared
in print was merely an extract, a fine distillate from years of
rising early to sample perfumes while the roses were fresh.
It was essential, she insisted, that all the flowers should be
"smelled through one nose."

Léonie admitted that *R. damascena bifera* didn't offer a
showy blossom. But that didn't compromise its impact, since
the perfume was "so amazing that it blinds us to the muddled
flowers." She termed the fragrance "elemental rose" and suggested that any modern hybrid that still "smells like a rose"
probably does so because it counts Damascena among its ancestors.

"Autumn Damask" is the rose's common name; according
to legend, it came originally from the Syrian city of Damascus.
This is the rare case, however, when a Latin name is not only
more exact but also more apt, since this is an ancient Roman
rose. I'd read all about it in my Latin agricultural manuals. I'd
even visited Paestum, the Italian town that won fame as its
home two thousand years ago. I spent a day and a night there
in 1974, though I didn't see any roses then.

I hadn't gone to Paestum looking for roses. I'd ridden south
in a bus from Rome, 280 kilometers, past Naples, Sorrento
and Amalfi with my fellow students from the "Centro" (more

properly, the Intercollegiate Center for Classical Studies in
Rome) to visit the ruins of the ancient city. Paestum had been
a Greek colony back in the days when Sicily and southern
Italy were the land of opportunity for immigrants, the America to which poor Greeks went to make their fortune. The
city's remains include two temples and a basilica lined up in
a stark white row along a ridge, among the best-preserved examples of ancient Greek architecture anywhere in the world.
Well-intentioned and sensible guides had forbidden us to wander through the ruins at night, but after supper, I made my
escape. Equipped with a blanket and a book of Shakespeare's
sonnets, I climbed back to the temple of Hera. The weathered
columns seemed to whisper and moan. As my eyes adjusted to
the darkness, I saw that all around me were Italian couples
who obviously understood romance far better than I.

Eventually my neighbors went home to bed and I fell asleep
on the marble pavement. Soon after dawn, I awoke to the
sound of hoofbeats and opened my eyes to see a man on horseback driving a herd of sheep past the temple. Immediately I
knew the experience had been worth the embarrassment and
the stiff back. In the soft early-morning light I was seeing
Paestum as it had looked two thousand years ago. Or so I
thought. It wasn't until I returned to the United States that I
discovered the landscape should have been covered with roses.

I learned this from the poet Virgil (Publius Vergilius Maro,
to give him his Latin name), whose verse forms an inescapable
part of every classics curriculum. I had dipped into the *Aeneid*,
his interminable epic of Rome's mythological origins, and found
it not to my taste. To graduate without some knowledge of
Virgil's work would, however, be unthinkable. On the occasions when I went back to visit my high school Latin teacher,
Dr. MacKellar would inevitably ask me if I had learned my
Virgil yet. I would admit that I hadn't, and a look of disap-
proval would cross his eighty-year-old face. I hated to disap-
point him. Ours had been one of his last classes before retirement. (My day school had been his refuge after New York

University forced him out at sixty-five.) He had introduced me to the pleasures of scholarship, and I not only respected him, I was fond of him. His diminutive height, hardly more than four feet, his hair neatly parted in the middle, and his bow tie gave a special flavor to his stories of life in our county at the turn of the century. My fellow students and I had spent weeks perfecting our imitations of the sniffle and sigh with which he began every speech, his formal, slightly archaic diction, and the way he pounded the table when our ignorance drove him to fury. So finally, I compromised.

I persuaded my professors at Brown to give me credit for an analysis of a book that all but the most dedicated classicists shun, Virgil's *Georgics*. This is the poet's knowledgeable and affectionate study of agriculture. It is a work full of gossip about crops and weather, advice on viticulture, stock raising and beekeeping, even a word now and then about roses. Among the poet's references to this flower is a line of praise for the twice-blooming roses of Paestum: *"canerem biferique rosaria Paesti."* Had he time and space, the poet says in John Dryden's wonderful translation, he would sing "The Paestan roses and their double spring." Virgil's reference to a double spring was an allusion to the fact that with this one exception, the roses of his day were spring flowers, once-bloomers. But the bushes of Paestum bloomed not only then but also, after a summer's rest, in the fall. This was a source of not only pride but also wealth to the town, since it enabled ancient Paestum to do a brisk business in cut flowers.

I didn't actually encounter "Autumn Damask" until I travelled to Garrison eleven years later. I've since seen the rose in the garden of many other collectors; it's not especially rare. But that day opened my eyes and, more important, my nose to Rome's legacy of roses. And it also introduced a Roman rose, or at least one of classical descent, into my garden. Miriam gave me a plant to take home, a sucker of a Gallica. This race of roses is held to be quintessentially French since it dominated the gardens of that country until Josephine's revolutionary endeavors, but actually it is far older. It arrived in Gaul (all three parts) with the Roman legions.

Miriam calls her bush "Route 301" because she and her husband found it on the shoulder of that highway one night as they returned home from a dinner party. Spotting it in the dark was no feat, for the rose had spread into a sprawling thicket of stout canes, each one tipped by neat, vibrant pink flowers. Miriam cannot even guess its age. In the weeds around it she found day lilies and overgrown lilacs, two indestructible plants that used to be the basis of rural landscaping and whose presence usually marks the sight of an abandoned farmstead. There wasn't any cellar hole, and long-time residents told her that there had been no house on the site for a century and a half at least.

Miriam didn't recognize the exact identity of her found rose, but she was sure that it must be a variety of *Rosa gallica:* each leaf was divided into five leaflets; the prickles (a proper botanical name for the thorns) were needle-like, gray and widely spaced; and the flowers were flattened, tightly packed, neat and round. The fragrance of the blossoms was also characteristically Gallica, fainter than the Damask but possessing the peculiar virtue of persisting after death; unlike other roses, which fade in fragrance soon after they are cut, the Gallica keeps much of its perfume as the petals wither. This trait made *Rosa gallica* an important commodity in Roman times since, dried and powdered, it found a place in ancient salves, oils, bath waters and all sorts of culinary confections.

A heady perfume is typical of nearly all old roses—indeed, many collectors rate it as a definitive trait. In her book of plant fragrances, Léonie Bell quotes an earlier authority, Alice Morse Earle, a prominent garden writer of the turn of the century who wrote:

> The fragrance of the sweetest Roses—the Damask, the Cabbage, the York and Lancaster—is beyond any other flower scent. It is irresistible, enthralling; you cannot leave it. You can push aside a Syringa, a Honeysuckle,

even a Mignonette, but there is a magic something which binds you irrevocably to the Rose. I have never doubted that the Rose has some compelling quality not shared by other flowers. I know not whether it comes from centuries of establishment as a race-symbol, or from some inherent witchery of the plant, but it certainly exists.

In fact, roses owe the special allure of their fragrance not to sorcery or atavism, but to the Romans. The gardeners of that ancient empire made odor the primary criterion of a blossom's excellence, setting a style that lasted two millennia. Only with the introduction of the modern everblooming rose did the primacy of perfume lapse—since then an emphasis on regularity of bloom and form of blossom has pushed fragrance into the background. As Léonie Bell observed, if you find a modern rose that still smells like a rose, it owes that perfume to a Roman ancestor, the Autumn Damask.

The Romans did not introduce the rose into the gardens of Europe; even my rambling exploration of rose history has taught me that. As long as twenty centuries ago, the Romans found a tradition upon which to build. Sir William Flinders Petrie discovered the oldest surviving specimen of a garden rose in Egypt; but it was closer to Rome, just across the Adriatic, that the Romans found their inspiration as rosarians. Through my reading in the Brown library I learned it was the Greeks who were the prodigies in that field, as in so many others. (At times when I studied classics I resented the Greeks—they were like the older brother who always does better in school—but I had to admire them. With little resources other than their fertile imaginations, the inhabitants of the rocky Balkan Peninsula called up new sciences, arts and crafts, imposing themselves over half of Asia and Europe through sheer nerve and force of intellect. They hadn't conquered their enemies, it seemed to me, so much as they had simply overawed them. One imagines the despair with which the Indians watched the thirty-year-old Alexander of Macedon stride down from the Khyber Pass at the head of his weather-beaten band. How could you stop those men who had marched unsupported from three thousand miles beyond the horizon?) Archetypical intellectuals, the Greeks created gardens more impressive in concept than in fact, but their ideas provided the basis for what came after. And it was the Greeks who elevated the rose to its special place in our gardens.

Exactly when they began to cultivate this flower is lost in prehistory, but it seems certain they had made it the object of a cult long before they first transplanted a wild briar into their dooryards and courts. The Greeks' earliest poets, Homer and Hesiod, shadowy figures who didn't rely on writing but chanted their verses from memory, were frank admirers of the rose. "Rhododactyla Aurora," Rosy-Fingered Dawn, they called the goddess who reached out to open the gates of morning. Unlike the collectors of my acquaintance, these early Greeks were more apt to call the place after the rose than vice versa. Rhodon was their word for rose, and Rhodos (Rhodes) they named the flowery island that became famous as the home of the Colossus. The Rhodians, in turn, stamped a rose blossom on their coins and named their Spanish colony Rhoda. Rhodios was a river that ran to the sea near Troy, and the Rhodope mountains bounded the southern border of Alexander's home-land, Macedonia. With the cities of Rhodopolis, Rhodountia and Rhodoussae, the maps of the Greek cartographers (another science they virtually invented) were full of rose names.

Always restless, always curious, Greek traders, pirates and mercenaries sailed and marched to every corner of their world, bringing back, among other marvels, tales of strange roses. Herodotus, a native of a Greek community in Asia Minor and an inveterate traveller, won the title "Father of History" with the researches he made in the course of his trips around the Mediterranean and to the Black Sea. In the *Histories* he published around 446 B.C., he found space among accounts of wars, intrigues and exotic customs to describe the roses that flourished in a region of Macedonia known as the Gardens of Midas (named, suggestively, for the king with the golden touch). "Wonderful blooms," he reported, "with sixty petals apiece, and sweeter smelling than any others in the world." Presumably, Herodotus didn't stop to take a slip, but somehow the roses found their way south into the Greek heartland within the century to become a garden favorite.

Greek custom made the rose the flower of the graveyard, but this was in part because life, even the afterlife, was unthinkable without this flower. In her poems, Sappho bestowed on one lover the pet name "Rosebud" and likened the tint of another's bosom to that of a rose. By calling the rose "Queen of the flowers," she made it clear that by the seventh century B.C. roses were already the flower of love. According to Greek myth, the first rosebush sprang out of the ground as Aphrodite, the goddess of love, rose from the waves, and it was a drop of her blood, drawn from her foot by a rose thorn as she ran to join her lover, that dyed the rose's blossoms red. A wreath of olive leaves is due the athletic champion, wrote Philostratos the Athenian; a diadem is the perquisite of kings; the helmet belongs to the soldier; but a crown of roses is reserved for the beautiful young boy.

The ancient Greeks' taste for boys arose at least in part because they sequestered their women as rigorously as a Turkish pasha. Except in Sparta, women were barred from almost every activity except homemaking and child rearing, so it was only with male lovers that a man could carry on an affair and bestow his bouquets. Banquets, too, were reserved for the male sex, and chaplets perfumed with roses, wreaths to wear on the head, were an integral pleasure of such evenings. The only way a young woman might enjoy rose garlands was through the money they brought her; so great was the demand for this kind of headgear, noted Aristophanes, the great Athenian satirist, that many girls earned a living through their manufacture. But if women wove the chaplets, it was young men who wore them, even before noon as they went to study with their philosophers. Perhaps it was the spectacle of roses draped over his students that caused Theophrastus, the head of the Athenian Lyceum and the "Father of Botany," to classify the rose as a "coronary" flower—a flower fit for a crown.*

Theophrastus' book *Inquiry into Plants* was the first attempt to fit the flora man found around him into any rational system of classification, and it is from this work that our most detailed knowledge of ancient Greek roses comes. Actually, many scholars claim that Theophrastus owed his method and probably his research to his teacher, Aristotle, who had already made a similar investigation of the animal world. This, of course, is the kind of insoluble dispute in which classicists delight and which has kept them employed since the fall of the Roman Empire. It was a question that the two philosophers never considered, since apparently they saw themselves not as competitors but as co-contributors to a single body of work. Theophrastus probably organized this particular work into its finished form, but undoubtedly, Aristotle had a hand in its production. Evidence of this can be found in the descriptions of roses.

Since both philosophers lacked any standard terminology (as pioneers, they were obliged to invent their sciences as they went along), they could not describe the roses of their day accurately enough for modern botanists to do more than speculate about the identities. What the material reveals clearly, however, is a special familiarity with the flowers of Macedonia. Herodotus's sixty-petalled rose, the one he had found in the Gardens of Midas, was promoted to "hundred-petalled" in the *Inquiry*, where it enjoyed a much more detailed treatment. This work reveals that the rose grew wild on the slopes of Mount Pangaeus, from which place local people used to transplant it to their gardens. This sounds like an eye-witness ac-

* It is possible that the students' fondness for roses was typical only of a later, decadent period. The description of academic headgear comes from the Natural History of Pliny the Elder, which was written in the first century A.D.; Theophrastus lived some three and a half centuries earlier and the students of his age may well have exhibited more sober sartorial tastes.

count; as such, it was most likely Aristotle's contribution, for he was a native of that country.

Even if the roses in the *Inquiry* cannot be identified, their number proves that the gardeners of Greece had their choice of several different strains. The book mentions only three by name but alludes to many others, distinguishing the different types not by their sexual parts (as a modern botanist would) but by those characteristics that interest the gardener: the number of petals, the "roughness" of the bush (what a modern gardener would call "habit"), the beauty of the flower and the sweetness of the perfume. For the sweetest of all, the *Inquiry* looked farther afield to Cyrene, a Spartan colony in North Africa. The notorious militarism of the Spartans may make them seem unlikely rose growers, but as any gardener can testify, growing good roses demands both method and discipline, qualities in which these soldiers had been thoroughly schooled. Not all the roses that the *Inquiry* cites are exotic types, however. The text begins its discussion of the genus with a description of the "Dog's Bramble," a wild rose (*R. canina*) that furnishes one of the most dramatic examples of the gardener's innate conservatism. This small five-petalled pale pink blossom still goes by the name of "Dog Rose" in rural England.

Wild roses were the main source of supply for the rose garden until the end of antiquity. Although the *Inquiry into Plants* bears witness that the Greeks had some understanding of plants' sexual nature, ancient gardeners never adapted to plants the breeding practices they used to improve their cattle, sheep and horses. All they could do was watch for and collect superior roses whenever such plants appeared in the wild or as "volunteers" in some neglected corner of the garden. They did propagate clones through cuttings, and the *Inquiry* recommends that technique as well as Douglas Seidel's preferred method of digging up and removing a rooted sucker. All the roses of the day must have been of the hardy own-root variety, a lucky circumstance in view of the style of pruning the book proposes.

Some of the other technical advice passed along in the *Inquiry* shows remarkable insight, for example, the recognition that the quality and fragrance of a given type of rose varies in different climates and soils. This is indeed a fact, but it was not generally accepted among modern rose growers until recently. Even in 1967, Léonie Bell was breaking new ground when she insisted on growing every rose whose fragrance she described on the same plot, and on sampling all the blossoms at the same time of day (in the morning, before the sun vaporized the volatile oils of the perfumes; on the same basis she excluded from the ranks of true rosarians all smokers). In other matters, the *Inquiry* is barbaric. Five years was the average lifespan the Greek botanist allowed a rose—after that length of time, the bush would lose vigor, and the quality of the bloom would decline. To renew an aging rosebush was simple enough, however. Just cut the bush back, the treatise advised, then set it afire.

A less drastic alternative was also recommended, and that was to practice a form of therapy Carl Cato still espouses. When a friend came to Carl for help in saving a venerable but declining rosebush, a specimen he knew that Carl coveted, Carl insisted that it must be transplanted. The man refused, perhaps because he suspected Carl's motives, but finally yielded when a third party echoed the prescription. The rose recovered, Carl told me proudly, and its offspring grows in the National Arboretum (not Carl's yard). Unconsciously echoing the advice of the ancient Greek botanists, Carl explained to me that a change of soil almost never fails to pump new life into a failing rose.

If the Greeks never developed extraordinary skills as cultivators, they excelled as propagandists. Always pleased to tell their neighbors how they should live and think, the Greeks exported their attitudes and customs wherever they went. It was they, apparently, who taught the Egyptians to grow roses

(the roses that Flinders Petrie exhumed all dated from after
the Greeks' arrival in the land of the Pharaohs). The manufacturing of perfumes had been an important industry in
Egypt since the dawn of their civilization; Egyptian perfumers
exported their wares all around the Mediterranean until the
flasks in which they packed them were nearly as ubiquitous
in their world as the Coke bottle is in ours. To supply the factories, Egyptian peasants nursed crops of lilies, lotus and nar-
cissus from the Nile's rich silt, and in the papyri that have
survived from the Pharaonic Age, there are recipes for cosmetics compounded from all kinds of flowers except roses. An
appreciation of this particular blossom seems to have arrived
only in 332 B.C. with Aristotle's pupil Alexander the Great.

Alexander didn't stay long in Egypt after completing its
conquest, but his lieutenant Ptolemy Soter settled there,
founding a dynasty of Graeco-Egyptian Kings. To appease his
subjects, Ptolemy adopted many of the trappings of a pharaoh,
but he seems to have insisted on at least one foreign innovation, the introduction of roses. Ptolemais, the port the king
built twelve miles from the future site of Cairo, must have
been planted with this flower, for Jewish scripture (*Third
Maccabees*) reports that the town was "called rose-bearing
. . . because of a characteristic of the place." Rose-bearing
tombs also appear with the arrival of the Ptolemies, and it was
during their rule that Egyptian growers developed the first
international floral trade. Roman poets and correspondents of
that period mentioned with wonder the roses that arrived in
their winter markets from Egypt. They offer no information
about how the Egyptians kept the blossoms fresh as they sailed
and rowed across the Mediterranean, though some historians
have theorized that the ancient florists grew the bushes in tubs
and transported them entire. Undoubtedly, the demand justified almost any measures. For under the Greeks' tutelage, the
Romans developed an insatiable appetite for roses.

Of course, the Romans had known roses long before they
fell under the Greeks' cultural spell. Though they built the

ancient world's greatest city, they sprang from the simplest country stock—shepherds, herdsmen and farmers. Virgil's attitudes were typical of the sincere affection they kept for rural life even as they strove to rival the Greeks in urbanity (a term, incidentally, that the Romans coined). The founding fathers whom the Romans loved to invoke had surely known the roses of the field. Their descendants, however, discovered the sophisticated pleasures of the garden only when they stepped in to settle the arguments of their quarrelsome Greek neighbors and stayed, despite some misgivings, to rule. In the generation that followed, Greek became the second language of the educated Roman as the conquerors learned an appreciation of the arts from their subjects. This newfound aesthetic appreciation combined in horticulture with something else the Romans learned from the Greeks: a dangerous taste for luxury.

The popular portrait of the Roman is, of course, one of complete debauchery. I have never believed it. It is true that this is an old, deeply rooted stereotype. It originated actually in what I was taught to call "the primary sources," the Latin authors. The chroniclers and letter writers of ancient Rome relished tales of orgies as thoroughly as any Hollywood producer, but that seems to have been a literary convention as much as anything else. It was the custom among learned Romans to scold their fellow citizens for their moral laxity and to close every oration with a reference to the fine traditional values of the old days. The lurid accounts of degeneracy in high places played well to the crowds; they also suited the prejudices of medieval monks, the semiliterate critics who later chose what of Latin literature would be preserved. But it doesn't make sense. How could a race interested only in blood, gluttony and perverse sex conquer half the world, and shape it into an empire that lasted more than half a millennium?

The Romans were materialists, as their taste in roses proves. They were often crass. Their attempts at spirituality were halfhearted, their gods embarrassingly childish and often borrowed from abroad. All of which seems to me typical of an unsophisticated, provincial people who suddenly rise to great power or great wealth. They had worked hard for generations, those Roman farmers, enjoying few luxuries. Now that they were rich, by God, they were going to have the best of everything and as much as they wanted.

Yet they never seemed entirely at home in their new life. As I read about them in college, I recalled the prospector I met the summer I was fifteen. He was my landlord in Yellowknife, the capital of Canada's Northwest Territory, where I had gone to work for *The News of the North*, a newspaper with a circulation of only a few thousand but a beat of a million square miles. Living with the man who had found the town's first gold mine seemed wildly exciting to a teenage boy*—but for most of the summer he was off working a claim. I heard plenty about him from his wife; according to her, he'd struck it rich not once, but twice. Both times he'd sold his claim, and they'd moved to Edmonton, the nearest city. This marked the beginning of a nightly round of restaurants, night clubs and shows, but the big expense, according to the wife, was the taxicab he always kept with its meter running outside the door. Both times, a few months of cab fare exhausted their funds, and they had to move back to the bush.

I looked forward to meeting a rowdy hell-raiser when the prospector finally came in to resupply. He turned out to be a

---

* *I've heard the town has changed, but landing in Yellowknife then was like stepping off an airplane and into the pages of a western. The town itself was a drab huddle of low wooden buildings, but its sidewalks were bright with the embroidered parkas of Dogrib Indians. To replace the clothes the airline had lost with my luggage, I went to the Hudson's Bay Company, and I took my lunches at the Gold Rush Cafe, a restaurant operated by an enterprising Chinese short-order cook. One of my co-workers, the photo-editor, offended an old trapper and had to hide for several days while the old-timer stalked him with loaded gun. That was taken as a great joke, except by the photographer, of course. He survived to take me "prospecting" one Saturday. While he scowled at bits of rock, I wandered into a thicket of Rosa acicularis. I hadn't much interest in plants then, yet I recognized the five-petalled pink blossoms as roses. I remember how odd the familiar, domestic flower looked in the midst of that wilderness.*

quiet, neat old man with a fondness for boiled potatoes. Taxi-
cabs, I eventually realized, had been his escape in more ways
than one—their meters had furnished a convenient means of
shedding a fortune for which he really had no use.

Unfortunately for the Romans, they lacked the prospector's
good sense, and their round of Greek-inspired pleasures never
ended. In general, the conquerors showed remarkably little
talent for inventing new diversions, merely expanding on the
ones they had learned with the theory that more must always
be better. In gardening, though, the students far outdid the
masters. In that art, the Romans' love of the countryside and
their hardheaded talent for organization combined to yield
remarkable results.

Along with the rules of prosody, the Romans picked up the
poetical cult of roses from the Greeks, and even before the
conquest, rose garlands began to appear at the better dinner
parties. Yet when the Romans saw L. Fulvius the banker appear on his veranda at midday, his brow wreathed in roses
even though the city was locked in a desperate war with Hannibal, they hauled him off to prison. There he stayed, too,
until the war was won. Later, gossip had it that Julius Caesar
had popularized the wearing of rose chaplets in public mainly
as a means of hiding his premature baldness. Roman historians
recorded it as one of the disgraces of the emperor Nero's reign
that he once spent 6,000,000 sesterces on roses for a single
party, a sum sufficient to pay the salaries of one of his legions
for a full year. And when 150 years later Heliogabalus adopted
what must have been a pleasant custom, that of releasing
showers of rose petals through the ceiling to drift down over
guests as they dined, a disapproving biographer claimed the
decadent emperor dumped such a deluge that several diners
smothered.

Most vitriolic, though, was the orator Cicero's denunciation
of Verres, an ex-governor whom the Sicilians were prosecuting
for corruption. Was this man's military prowess really essential to the empire, as he claimed? Cicero demanded. Any com-

mander must be able to cover ground in a hurry, and how did
Verres tour his province?

> When spring began, whose coming was marked for him
> by no zephyrs or constellation, for it was when he saw the
> first rose that he recognized spring's arrival, then he be-
> took himself to the toilsome work of travelling, wherein
> he showed himself so hardy and active that no one ever
> saw him on horseback. No; following the custom of the
> old kings of Bithynia, he rode on a litter carried by eight
> bearers, which contained a cushion of transparent, em-
> broidered cloth stuffed with rose petals, he himself wear-
> ing one garland on his head and another round his neck,
> and putting to his nostrils a fine-meshed bag of delicate
> linen gauze stuffed with rose petals.

Verres abandoned his defense and fled into voluntary exile.

But even as they indulged in these extravagances of con-
sumption and recrimination, the Romans never lost sight of
reality. In his official capacity of censor, Marcus Porcius Cato
(the author of the agricultural manual I discovered in Rome)
might struggle to curb the luxurious habits of his newly rich
countrymen. Without doubt he disapproved of their expen-
ditures on roses. Yet he strongly recommended growing them,
since the demand for garlands made roses, violets and other
"coronary" flowers among the most profitable crops for a suburban property. Two centuries later, when another agricul-
turist, Lucius Junius Moderatus Columella, composed a poem
about market gardening (an interesting but awkward bit of
verse that he intended as a sequel to the *Georgics*), he sang
of horny-handed rustics piling wicker panniers high with roses
and returning from market "well-soaked with wine, with staggering gait, and with pockets full of cash."

Typically, these soldiers-turned-gardeners put production on
a systematic basis. Large tracts of land were given over to rose
growing, until Horace, a Roman poet of the last century before
Christ, complained that the fields of Italy were being transformed into one vast nursery. Paestum's dry, sunny climate

and fertile volcanic soils proved especially suited to roses, and it became the center for this luxurious branch of agriculture. At the same time, Italian growers developed a number of methods for extending the rose's season of bloom. This was essential if the emperor was to have roses for parties whenever he wished.

The *Inquiry into Plants* had described the rose as one of the last spring flowers to bloom, and the one with the shortest season. The common wild roses of Italy fit this description only too well. Since they never discovered the principles of hybridization (and for once the Greeks offered no instruction), the Romans couldn't breed roses with longer periods of bloom. What they could do, however, was to ransack their empire for its every existing strain, and capitalize on the natural variations in the flowers' schedules.

Paestum's twice-blooming roses were the Roman collectors' greatest find, but they remained an anomaly, the empire's only remontant rose. An inventory of the other species and varieties revealed the odd rose that bloomed earlier than the average, and others that bloomed later. Individually, these eccentrics offered only the usual short season, but by planting them together, the gardener might patch together a longer harvest. Eventually, certain strains became famous and much sought after. The best account of these comes from Pliny the Elder, the Roman who criticized Athenian youth for its excessive love of rose garlands—apparently, he had a weakness for the flower himself. In his masterwork, the *Natural History,* Pliny described thirteen distinct cultivars, a remarkable number when one considers that the French horticulturist Claude Mollet cited only six in his *Théâtre des Jardinages* of 1663.

This Pliny was the uncle of the villa builder I had encountered during my college days. The older man epitomized Roman drive and discipline, though he devoted himself primarily to the pursuit of knowledge rather than empire. His literary output would be the envy of any freelance writer; this was the result, the younger Pliny explained in a letter to a friend, of his uncle's remarkable life style. He regularly rose from his bed many hours before dawn, no later than 2:00 A.M., and often as early as midnight, to clear away any business related to the public offices he filled. "To live is to be awake," the uncle wrote in the preface of his *Natural History*. He addressed this to another early riser, the emperor, with whom he conferred every morning before daybreak. Upon his return home from the palace, Pliny sat down to his studies.*

Pliny produced works on a bewildering number of subjects, from the art of throwing the javelin from horseback to the finer points of Latin grammar, but only the *Natural History* survives. In its introduction, the author advertises it as "a work of a lighter nature," one whose subject was merely "the world of nature, or in other words, life." Pliny admitted that his manuscript was mainly a compendium of older works, for in that pragmatic age, there was no blame attached to plagiarism. He claimed to have consulted 100 authors and 2,000 volumes to amass his "20,000 notable facts." He was too modest. The real tally is 347 authors, and 34,707 facts.

Without question, the *Natural History*'s thirty-seven books betray all the faults of secondhand learning, mixing fable and error with genuine fact, but no one could read the table of contents without feeling at least a twinge of curiosity: "Showers of stones—their reason (Book II, chapters xlii, xliii) . . . The first clock (II, lxxviii) . . . Signs of impending earthquakes (II, lxxxi–lxxxvi) . . . Cases of the dead coming to life again (VII, lii–lvi) . . . Beavers, otters, the sea-calf, geckoes (VIII, xlvii–xlvix) . . . The fish that shines by night (IX, xliii) . . . The earliest painting competition (XXXV, xxxiv–xli)." Significantly, Pliny devoted ten chapters to gar-

---

* *Pliny's devotion to his books was absolute. Whenever the need for food or a bath forced him to lay them down, he summoned a servant to read aloud, and he criticized his nephew for travelling afoot when he might cover the same ground in a sedan chair and study en route.*

lands and roses. Among these pages he was careful to include data that detailed which strains of roses were early bloomers, and which were late.

The "Campania" for instance, the flower the author described as Italy's most famous rose (Campania was the region of southern Italy that included Paestum; all of Pliny's roses are identified by their place of origin) was an early-spring bloomer. The "Milesian," a "fiery red" that bore the name of a Greek settlement on the eastern shore of the Aegean, withheld its blossom until late spring. The "Praeneste" (named for another southern Italian city) was the last to fade. By planting these together, the gardener could keep the rose bed in bloom over several months, and to extend the rose season even further, he could plant the "little chaplet," a fragrant, autumn-blooming sort (a Musk rose perhaps), or the "Carthage," a rose that, like Hannibal, had come to Rome via Spain. This last bloomed all winter, according to Pliny, though he doesn't make clear whether it needed artificial stimulation to do so. If it did, the growers had perfected a couple of tricks.

Pliny described in another part of the encyclopedia the cold frames Roman gardeners used. These were rude, unheated greenhouses made from panes of talc, a translucent stone. Pliny writes of these structures in connection with techniques of forcing cucumbers out of season, but obviously any gardener who could ripen cucumbers in January could bring a rose into bloom then, too. There was, in addition, a simpler technique: "Those who try to get their roses early," Pliny noted, "dig a trench a foot deep about the root, pouring in warm water as the flower buds begin to swell."

However they managed it, Roman gardeners harvested roses year-round. Where once they had depended on Egyptian imports for out-of-season flowers, by 98 A.D. (a generation after Pliny's death) the Roman poet Martial was satirizing the Egyptian city of Memphis for sending a gift of winter roses to the emperor. "The sailor from Memphis scoffed at the gardens of Egypt," the poet wrote to the emperor, "when he first stepped over the threshold of your city." In Rome, Martial claimed, the Egyptian found every path twined with roses. The poet offered the Egyptians a deal: send Rome your harvests (Egypt was the breadbasket of the empire), and we'll send you our winter roses.

As with Theophrastus's roses, identifying Pliny's flowers—the "Campanian," the "Milesian," the "Praeneste," the "Trachinian," the "Cyrene," the "Mucetum," the "Alabandian," the "Hundred-Petalled," the "Prickly Rose," the "Bramble," the "little chaplet," the "little Greek" and the "Carthage"—has proved problematical. Some historians profess to see in Pliny's "Campanian" the Cinnamon Rose (R. cinnamomea), a reddish purple blossom that is native throughout Europe and has escaped from American gardens to colonize the northern United States. All agree that most of Pliny's roses were varieties of that other European native, Rosa gallica.

There's widespread support for the identification of Paestum's twice-blooming roses with the Middle Eastern remontant rose, R. damascena. Yet some scholars disagree. They point out that R. damascena doesn't grow wild in southern Italy, and that writers of the Renaissance described this rose as a novelty, a rose newly arrived from the East. How could it have dropped from sight for a thousand years? Of course, the same argument could be used to cast doubt on the authenticity of the many works of classical literature that returned to the West during the Renaissance from the Arab countries, or on the authenticity of the countless Roman buildings that, like the Pantheon, were made of hydraulic cement. The formula for that material was also lost with the fall of the Roman Empire, and was not rediscovered and reintroduced, by an English engineer until 1756.

None of this really matters. If the botanical identity of the Roman roses was lost, their type was not. The roses may have disappeared from Paestum, but archaeological excavations have exhumed some very pertinent evidence at Pompeii. The two cities had much in common; like Paestum, Pompeii began as a Greek colony and finished as a part of the Roman province of Campania, and it shared the rich, light volcanic soil that made Paestum a rose capital. But while Paestum's ancient gardens disappeared without a trace, there is little trouble reconstructing those of Pompeii. Almost every house of any pretensions in that unfortunate city was built around a garden, and to lend their courtyards an illusion of space, householders used to paint the walls with garden scenes. Vesuvius's rain of glowing ash incinerated the living blossoms, but it preserved their portraits.

In the building archaeologists have named the "House of Venus Marina," for instance, one wall of the inner court offers a vista of flowers and birds clustered round a fountain. From behind the fountain, a rose struggles, reaching up with its blossoms for the light. The flowers are small, as ruddy as any Gallica I've seen, and their form is the same: compact, regular rosettes. In the building that archaeologists call the "House of the Fruit Orchard," a fountain also serves as the focus of the painted garden, though in this case it's framed with a stylish fence of latticework. In marked contrast to this formal setting are the painting's roses: pale pink, semi-double blossoms, modest wheels of fluttering petals. To a modern eye, these don't look like garden roses at all; they look like flowers you would find in an overgrown field or on the shoulder of Route 301.

In this case, however, "Via dell'Abbondanza" would be a more appropriate name, because a very similar rose has been recovered from a ruined building on that Pompeian avenue. In a ruined house there, excavators found a ceiling panel decorated with roses. Perhaps the painter intended dinner guests to pause in the midst of their meal, gaze upward and imagine themselves at a decadent capital at the banquet where it rained petals. At any rate, the roses and rosebuds on this ceiling are all pink, all the same tight whorls of petals with a tuft of stamens and pistils at the center.

If the form of these Roman roses seemed uninspired, their

fragrance was unmatched. In those days, a poet's reference to
the rose's sweet perfume was more than a cliché. Léonie Bell
pointed out in *The Fragrant Year* that of the 765 roses introduced in the United States from 1960 through 1964, 264 were
described by their creators as of "slight" scent, while only 20
were of "very strong," "rich," or "heavy" fragrance. Pliny admitted that three of the breeds he knew were without fragrance, but he indicated that, in his opinion, this deficiency
made them unworthy of the name of rose. "In so many ways,"
he complained, "is spuriousness possible!" This insistence on
perfume continued to shape rose fashions through the whole
history of old roses. What a Roman would say about our
scentless Hybrid Teas is easy to guess.

No classicist, not even a former would-be one, can resist
the opportunity for an apposite quote. I remember struggling
through one of Horace's odes in the fall of 1973. "I have
created a monument more lasting than brass," the poet boasted
of his verse. "Nothing can corrode it, no rain, no wind, nor
the endless years flying past." By contrast, the perfume of his
neighbor's roses must have seemed the most ephemeral of
pleasures, something to be washed away by the first breeze or
ray of sunlight. Yet I don't need a dictionary and a grammar
to decipher the scent of old roses. When I pick an Autumn
Damask to smell its "elemental rose," I think of the lost rose
fields of Paestum. In June, when my garden reaches its peak
of bloom, the bushes collapsing under the weight of thousands
of sesterces' worth of blooms, and the mingled perfumes spill-
ing out a hundred feet downwind, I remember the older
Pliny's words. I waken, and I live.

6

The
Flowery Kingdom

Indica fragrans

THE WHITE-COATED CURATOR set the roll of silk carefully on the long table. He set a weight, a polished marble block, on the scroll's free end, and began to unroll it Chinese fashion, right to left. Suddenly, there on the fabric were flowers, handfuls of them, casually scattered across the pale background, paintings only, but so fresh and vivid that I sniffed unconsciously for the perfumes. First to appear, in the place of honor, was a rose.

I had come to the Metropolitan Museum, New York's temple of the fine arts, in search of the ancestors of our old roses. China, I knew, had made a crucial contribution to Western rose gardens. Four roses in particular, which came to Europe

at the end of the eighteenth century, are credited with causing a revolution among our garden roses. "The four stud
Chinas," English experts have dubbed them, since like great
stallions they have each sired a long line of champions. Indeed,
virtually every new hybrid rose to appear today counts these
four studs among its ancestors. Yet so far my search for authentic Chinese roses had been in vain. Histories of the rose
offered little information about those flowers other than the
part they played in Western breeding programs, and no gardener I knew had tried to collect them. So I'd fallen back on
the art museums. If I couldn't view the roses in the flesh, at
least I'd find their portraits.

The scroll spread out before me, "The Hundred Flowers,"
was the work of a seventeenth-century artist named Yun Shou-
p'ing, the greatest master of what the Chinese call "bird and
flower painting." This is not a prestigious genre—landscape
painters are taken far more seriously by Chinese critics—but
bird and flower painting is very popular with the general public. The difference in opinion arises from bird and flower
paintings' precise, detailed realism; this appeals to the un-
studied eye of the average person but has always aroused the
disdain of literati. Chinese art texts inevitably quote Su Shih,
a twelfth-century poet: "To judge a painting by its verisimili-
tude, betrays the intellectual level of a child." Maybe so, but
I didn't care. I hoped "The Hundred Flowers" would deliver
traditional Chinese roses in something like their original form,
and help fill a gap in my collection. In addition, I found the
artist intriguing. Yun Shou-p'ing epitomized in many ways the
classical scholar/artist, the men who shaped China's culture
and, of course, her gardens. Profoundly different from their
counterparts in the West, these individuals had urged the rose
down a very different path.

The story of Roman roses is one of prodigality, of a constant
drive for more: more blossoms, through more months, to yield
more petals and perfume. The Chinese gardeners looked for
harmony and balance; they found their pleasure in the perfec-

tion of a single blossom rather than the creation of a floral extravaganza. While the Romans sought sensual gratification in the garden, the Chinese viewed it as a philosopher's retreat, a center for spiritual refreshment. The two cultures also displayed a fundamental difference in attitudes toward the rose. The Romans put it on a pedestal, in poetry and art as well as the flower bed. The Chinese regarded it with suspicion. The garden was the center of household life in China. To introduce a thorny shrub into this nest, the gardeners feared, was to invite dissension in the family.

Yet even if they distrusted this flower, Chinese gardeners could hardly ignore it, for their empire was the world's richest natural repository of garden-worthy roses. North America is home to approximately thirty species of roses (the count varies with the botanist you consult), yet of these only one, *Rosa setigera*, the 'Prairie Rose,' has contributed significantly to the creation of garden hybrids. *Rosa virginana, R. carolina,* and *R. palustris,* the 'Swamp Rose' of our eastern seaboard, have been taken up occasionally by adventurous landscapers, but only for use in their native state. They often figure in "wild gardens," those idealized versions of the natural environment that are so fiendishly tricky to maintain. China, by contrast, with an estimated fifty species of roses, has contributed to virtually every one of the modern rose garden's blossoms.

Besides the four studs, China has supplied the smallest rose in my collection, a dwarf that doesn't exceed a height of eighteen inches in the Texas garden I now share with my geologist-wife.* Much smaller specimens have been recorded; the tiniest was the bush that a Colonel Roulet found in a Swiss window box in 1917. Only six inches tall, it was nevertheless

---

* *Marriage has made gardening much more interesting. Unwilling to give up New York, I commute now from there to Central Texas, where my wife is employed, maintaining gardens in both places. So I may get up one day to plant the first spring lettuce in New York, fly down to Texas and harvest a mature head the following morning. The contrast in climates also allows me to grow a much broader selection of roses.*

perfectly formed in every particular, even to its generous crop of nickel-sized fragrant pink blossoms. The Swiss villagers testified that they had been cultivating the strain for a century, but botanists insisted that the rose must still be Chinese in origin, a midget form of R. *chinensis minima*. How this came to a remote mountain village the scientists can't say, but the literature of imperial China's last dynasty, the Ch'ing, reveals that such dwarves were popular in early nineteenth-century China.

They're increasingly prominent in twentieth-century America. Harmon Saville, a Massachusetts nurseryman who is this nation's leading grower of miniature roses, has described them as "the hula hoop of the flower industry." At a time when rose production as a whole is experiencing little growth, Saville cannot keep up with the demand for his "Minis." Most of Saville's stock is the product of his own breeding program; almost all of his creations trace their descent, at least in part, from Colonel Roulet's rose, which circulated through the nursery industry as 'Rosa Rouletii.' With their compact size—six to twelve inches—miniature roses seem specifically designed for our modern world, where space has become so precious that many gardeners' plots are limited to rooftops and balconies. But populous China faced the same problem centuries ago.

At the opposite end of the scale is another Chinese rose, a monster that I covet but cannot accommodate, R. *odorata* 'Gigantea.' Though first sighted in the Shan hills of Burma, this variety of Tea rose is also native to south central China. Reportedly, it sends its canes climbing fifty feet to bear creamy white blossoms six inches across. A planting of 'Gigantea' would astonish the neighbors, I'm sure, but it's too much like kudzu for me to allow it into my yard.

The Chinese roses that seized the fancies of Western growers were everblooming types, but the Flowery Kingdom (as the Chinese used to call their land) has also yielded a number of very fine once-bloomers. The "Memorial Rose" (R. *wichuraiana*), a summer bloomer whose two-inch white blossoms

blanketed the graves of many Northern cemeteries a couple of
generations ago, is native to eastern China, though it came to
the West via Japan. This, along with R. *multiflora,* another
Chinese/Japanese once-bloomer, between them spawned the
bulk of our modern climbers. *Rosa multiflora,* incidentally, is
also the preferred rootstock of many European rose nurseries
because it matches an exceptional disease-resistance with a
tenacious root system that adapts well to a variety of soils.
Western growers sow seeds of this Chinese rose by the millions every year to provide hardy hosts on which to graft their
more delicate hybrids.

With this wealth of material growing just outside the garden fence, one might reasonably have expected Chinese gardeners to become the most prolific rose breeders who would
flood the market with wonder-hybrids. But that was not their
way. Gardening, to the educated Chinese at least, was a gentle
exploration of nature, not a campaign to force it to man's will.
Confucius's teachings ruled in horticulture as in every other
branch of classical Chinese culture, and it was said of the
master that he even refused to eat fruit out of season because
he would not violate the natural order. Nor would his disciple
Chou Tun-i cut the grass outside his window. When asked
why, he replied that he preferred to see it grow without harm.

There was a select group of flowers that the Chinese did
breed intensively, sculpting and coloring them almost beyond
recognition. These were blossoms that, like the chrysanthemum
or tree peony, had a special symbolic significance—the frost-
resistant chrysanthemum, for example, represented fortitude
in the face of adversity. The flowers were cultivated in pots
usually, often to be displayed as set pieces at seasonal festivals.
Because of its inauspicious nature, the rose was spared that
treatment. It never served as anything more than a landscaping shrub, and as such the Chinese appreciated it in its natural
state. A lively aesthetic sensibility did prompt them to select
and promote choice clones, roses of purer line or color. Yet
they never seem to have joined their Western colleagues in

seeing how far they could push this flower. Instead, the Chinese improvement of the rose seems to have been entirely adventitious, a gradual, unhurried process of refinement.

Yun Shou-p'ing, the artist whose work I had come to explore at the Metropolitan Museum of Art, served as my introduction to the special sensibility of the Chinese gardener. His whole career was a demonstration of his devotion to the classical tradition. Yun was born shortly before Manchu tribesmen rode in to conquer China in 1644, and though he was the descendant of an aristocratic line, he was penniless from boyhood, because his father chose the life of a fugitive rather than coming to terms with the invaders. Even though the Manchu leader, after declaring himself founder of the Ch'ing, or "Pure" dynasty in 1680, chose to rule through a Chinese-staffed bureaucracy, Yun wouldn't accept service under the new regime. All his life he styled himself an *i min,* a "leftover person" from the preceding, native-Chinese dynasty. Rather than compromise his principles, he chose to earn a precarious living by his brush.

Turning to bird and flower painting was another subtle form of rebellion, a means of avoiding a responsible position in a society of which the artist did not approve. It was a decision that could have been based on greed, since bird and flower painting also offered a huge and potentially lucrative market. But Yun refused to work for anyone he considered spiritually unworthy or unable to appreciate his art. It is said that one determined, if unworthy, client was reduced to kidnapping the artist and forcing him to trade a painting for his freedom. The result of this behavior was predictable: though generally accepted as a master, Yun died so poor that a friend had to pay for the funeral.

A comparison of the roses in Yun's painting with those in contemporary European paintings is tempting, but would be of a purely academic interest since in Yun's lifetime (1633–1690) there was no contact between the two horticultural traditions. After a brief flirtation with the Jesuits under the preceding dynasty (the Ming), China had turned inward intellectually, choosing to ignore the barbarians beyond its borders, as far as possible. This prejudice nourished a stubborn resistance to the Manchus throughout their reign, yet it was a prejudice that the conquerors themselves chose to adopt; the emperors of the new dynasty closed China's borders to all foreigners, allowing trade and communication at only a couple of carefully controlled ports. Science and technology were stunted by this policy, since it isolated the Chinese from the great strides being made elsewhere. But in the field of floriculture, the Chinese succeeded admirably on their own.

Certainly the artwork of the period reveals a remarkable range of roses. "The Hundred Flowers," for example, though it includes just three types, makes clear that the Chinese gardener could choose from the luxurious or the chastely simple—in either case roses of a most sophisticated grace.

The first of the scroll's flowers, for instance, the rose in the place of honor, was plump and pink, a demure ball of ruffled petals; the second, juxtaposed with a frilly pink flowering plum, was a sprig from a very different bush. Borne in clusters of a half dozen or more, the small single flowers sported only five petals apiece, pure white with a knot of gold-and-black threads at their centers. Last of the scroll's three roses was a flower that I immediately wanted for my garden: a large, airy bloom set on a languorously curved stem. Two blossoms of this were shown, one from the front and the other from the rear. In both, the petals were delicately scalloped along the edge; the facing flower was a soft pink deepening to darker rose at the petals' bases with, half-hidden in the flowers' center, another knot of golden stamens. Turning from heads to tails to look at the other, reversed flower, I found a rose of a similar form but markedly different color: palest rose along the perimeter, shading to gold where the flower's green base gripped the petals.

To learn anything more about these particular roses I knew

that some sort of botanical identification was essential, but that is a skill I have never mastered. The trick of research, however, is not having all the answers yourself, but knowing where to turn and whom to ask. In a situation of this sort, I knew I could do no better than turn the problem over to Charles Walker, Jr., of Raleigh, North Carolina.

Charles, who is pursuing a doctorate in horticulture at North Carolina State University, is a rare combination of (self-confessed) bookworm and man of action. He is an intellectual browser with, unlike myself, a tidy mind, someone who collects information ceaselessly for the satisfaction that comes when he can fit two seemingly unrelated facts together into a seamless, orderly whole. This proclivity, plus a longstanding interest in genealogy, made him a natural target for the old-rose passion.

He discovered these flowers while reading through a gardening encyclopedia in 1971. The roses he'd known previously, Hybrid Teas, he'd thought pretty, but too delicate; the staying power of the old roses seized on his imagination. "You plant one of these things a hundred years ago, it's still there," he explains in the soft, deliberate accents of the American South.

Reproduction through cloning he recognized as "both a blessing and a curse. What other antiques do you have that you can multiply at will? But let 'em go until they're gone, and you can't bring that rose back. You've got to have at least one little plant to get it going again."

The sense of urgency Charles felt about preserving the old roses he found around him was heightened by the years he spent working at the U.S. Department of Agriculture Plant Introduction Station located in, appropriately, Experiment, Georgia. One of the station's functions was to serve as a "seed bank," to preserve germ plasm of food crops such as field peas and peppers. To protect the genetic diversity of these plants, the government stores seed of valuable varieties; many of the older regional vegetable varieties retain characteristics such as disease- and pest-resistance that may be needed by plant breeders of the future.

"To me, it made a lot of sense," Charles explained. "So I got to thinking, 'Well, what about roses? What's being done to preserve them?' " He visited a number of botanical gardens that maintain collections of old roses but always came away disappointed. Inevitably, the roses were treated as a footnote to horticulture; they never received the care Charles believed they deserve. He became convinced that a special institution was needed, one that would be exclusively devoted to the preservation of old roses. For years, he carried in the back of his mind an idea of a living repository of old roses. Finally, someone asked him what he really wanted to do with his life. Charles replied that he would very much like to be the curator of an old-rose garden, and soon afterward he began to organize the Heritage Rose Foundation.

This organization, as Charles envisions it, would support not only a garden, a germ plasm bank for the rose breeders of tomorrow, but would also work to reintroduce old roses back into the nursery trade. An essential preliminary to repopularizing old roses, Charles believes, is sorting out their nomenclature. Though collectors may love bickering over the identity of a rose, the average gardener does not. He or she does not want to order 'American Beauty,' the classic florist's rose, from one nursery (as I did), only to find it identical to the 'Ulrich Brünner' purchased from another. To date, the garden of the Heritage Rose Foundation remains a dream—Charles only recently completed the seventy-six-page application necessary to win the foundation tax-exempt status, and the search for a suitable site has just begun—but Charles intends it eventually to serve as a living index to old roses, an accurately labelled collection against which nurserymen can check the identity of their wares.

Charles had completed a master's degree in mathematics before he discovered his vocation in rose research; he returned

to school to get the formal training he needed in horticulture
and genetics. But his hardest labors were in a task he set himself—acquainting himself with all the literature pertaining to
old roses. When he found an author whose opinion he valued—
and Charles's respect isn't easily given—he made a point of
collecting everything he or she had written. In the case of Mrs.
Keays, for example, Charles searched far beyond the obvious
sources such as the *American Rose Annual* (the limits of my
exploration). In the *Gardener's Chronicle of America,* a
monthly journal that once issued from Jersey City, he found
nine overlooked articles; in *Country Gentleman,* a Philadelphia magazine that was an impossible anachronism even by
1955, the year it closed, he found another. Eventually, he
assembled twenty-three pieces of this classic author's work,
articles that had been lost almost as long as the roses they
described.

While borrowing books from university libraries, Charles
also ransacked secondhand bookstores to amass his own research collection. He recalls with amusement the consterna-
tion of one bookseller when he bought at one blow nearly all
her painstakingly assembled collection of rose books. If Charles
finds a book he likes at an attractive price, he'll buy two, three
copies; the Foundation will have a use for any overflow, and
rose books make fine presents. Charles used the skills he'd
developed as a genealogist to develop biographical files on the
major breeders, and he now has a file cabinet full of census
records, wills, birth, marriage and death certificates. With
these materials, he has exposed many discrepancies in accounts
of rose introductions. Journalists of a century past were just
as liable to confuse two men with a similar name, or two generations of the same family. But age has lent authority to their
accounts, and now their mistakes are accepted as gospel.

In a pair of articles for *The Rose Annual,* a publication of
the Royal National Rose Society of Great Britain, for example,
Charles addressed the problem of the "Ramanas Rose." This,
the Swedish botanist Carl Thunberg claimed, was the name

the Japanese gave to the big-hipped species (also of Chinese origin) that he described for Western botany as *Rosa rugosa* in 1784. The name has long puzzled rosarians, since contemporary Japanese call the Rugosa *Hama Nashi*—the "beach pear," referring to the fat red fruits of a salt-tolerant rose that often colonizes in the sandy soils of beaches (highway crews in the northeastern United States have found the Rugosa to be an excellent planting for our salt-poisoned roadsides). Consultation with a Japanese native revealed that the final *i* is hardly voiced; since Charles knew that Thunberg had visited Japan as a guest of the Dutch East India Company, he next contacted a Dutch native. This person added another vital bit of information: the guttural rasp with which a Dutchman pronounces an *R* makes it sound like an *H*. If he had been relying on Dutch interpreters, or if his ear had become accustomed to Dutch pronunciation, this certainly could account for Thunberg's confusion of one letter for the other, and the final step in the transformation of *Hama Nash(i)* to *Ramanas*.

The method of rose identification Charles has adopted depends on the same evidence used by other authorities: descriptions from old catalogues, articles and books, and a painstaking, point-by-point comparison of living roses with those in antique portraits. His interpretation of this material, however, is radically different and more time-consuming. It doesn't satisfy Charles to find a description or portrait that matches the rose at hand, he only allows the rose that name when he has eliminated every other possibility. "We're shortchanging people when we don't tell them the whole story," he insists, and he calls any approach less thorough not true identification, but only a comparison.

"To me truly identifying it means proving that this unidentified rose is one and *only* one rose from the past. There's the rub. Usually the old descriptions are so brief and so indeterminate that you can indeed find one that fits your rose, but if you looked harder, you could find yet another one, maybe three or four, maybe twelve. I think if you really want to identify a rose, you must eliminate those other possibilities; you must eliminate all the possibilities but one.

"You see, you've got a unique situation here; you've got a rose that at one time had a name. What you're trying to do is match it up. You're not trying to get close, you're trying to make a perfect match. You're trying to reestablish something that was lost."

Perfection, Charles has found, is hard to achieve. His style of identification often takes years of intermittent work. And after seventeen years of study he has become convinced that he never will sort out all the confusion—the sources of information are too incomplete. So Charles is agitating for a clean sweep—after assembling all the "mystery" roses and sorting them by physical characteristics, he wants to assign to each a properly documented new name. The search for original names could continue, he hastens to add, but in the meantime his program would rescue old-rose collecting from the nomenclatural swamp into which it has fallen.

My own impression is that this very sensible reform has little chance of being accepted. Old-rose collectors enjoy their learned bickering too much; those to whom I've mentioned Charles's suggestion looked uncomfortable and immediately changed the subject. It is ironic, then, that because of his reputation for scrupulousness, Charles remains the court of last appeal in matters of rose identification. I turned to him for this reason and another: unlike the other authorities, he apparently lacks the urge to pontificate. From Charles I would get a simple but complete answer, if one existed, and not the customary condescending lecture that I might deserve but had never been able to enjoy.

I borrowed photographs of the Chinese scroll from the Metropolitan Museum's library and sent them to Raleigh. I told Charles I was anxious for an answer. He responded in less than a week, with a two-page single-spaced typed letter. Over the telephone, Charles had cautioned me against too great hopes, and in his report he stressed that the portraits were "artistic rather than botanically accurate." A single detail was enough to prove that point: one of the roses on the scroll sported red stipules. Stipules are tiny winglike appendages that are found on either side of the petiole (the leaf stem), right at the point where it joins the cane. Stipules vary greatly in size and shape, depending on the type of rose—they are one of the details Charles looks to in his identifications, and he has never found them to be red. Yun Shou-p'ing had obviously allowed himself some artistic license. But, Charles ventured, "The artist apparently recorded some useful features."

The analysis that followed offered a fine illustration of Charles's method of detection. Where I would have contented myself with a glance at the color of the blooms, their forms and (in the case of real roses) a whiff of their perfumes, Charles picked out the flowers' anatomical details. These were his clues. There were the receptacles, the enlarged end-part of the stem that forms a base for the flowers—the "distinctively shaped receptacle of the upper bloom in portrait number one (the first rose on the scroll)" suggested to Charles a China rose. A China rose would be any variety of *Rosa chinensis*, a species that included two of the four stud Chinas. The globular shape of the flower, he told me, probably ruled out my immediate guess, 'Old Blush.' Stipules? Though unnaturally reddish, narrow, "and rather laciniate (cut like a fringe or beard), a combination which is not present in any rose I can think of." The prickles (the proper name for a rose's thorns) were red, which, regrettably, "is typical of several varieties."

We had better luck with the second portrait, the single white. "I perceive this," Charles wrote, "as a recognizable portrait of *Rosa multiflora* Thunberg," the ancestor of our rootstocks and a species that was another of Carl Thunberg's discoveries. Not only the form and color of the flowers but the shade of green used to depict the foliage suggested this identification to Charles. He noted that Yun had been "perhaps a bit generous in his depiction of internodal prickles [the thorns found between the joints from which leaves or branches spring], but the emphasis on the prominently laciniated stipules suggests that his subject was probably this cluster-flowered, single white species."

All this botanical terminology was a bit hard to digest. However, I grasped immediately the significance of another detail that Charles now brought to my attention. I had noticed that the threads at these flowers' centers (Charles identified them as stamens, male sexual organs) varied in color, appearing either gold or black. I had assumed the difference was more or less random. Not so. Golden stamens adorned only fresh flowers, while the black ones marked the older blossoms, those that were beginning to drop their petals. Charles—and Yun Shou-p'ing too, apparently—recognized this as a habit of *Rosa multiflora*. In an aside, Charles endowed the scroll with an entirely new significance. If his identification was correct, he said, then "The Hundred Flowers" was the oldest portrait of this species that he knew, since it predated by a century the description in the *Flora japonica* that Thunberg published in 1784.

Unfortunately, Charles could help me less with the rose that interested me most, the large and elegant parti-colored blossoms that came toward the scroll's end. The receptacles' shape indicated another China, or else a Tea rose (*Rosa odorata*—the species that supplied the other two studs), though definitely of a variety distinct from portrait number one. The difference in color between the two blossoms pictured troubled Charles. He attributed it tentatively to a difference in age. Many roses fade as they age, he pointed out, and the darker hue of the lower blossom could be an indication that it was fresher when the artist took it for a model. This would suggest a Tea rose rather than a China (members of that race tend to darken in color as they age—most visibly *Rosa chinensis mutabilis,* whose blossoms open a sulphur yellow and deepen to crimson). Charles also proposed a simpler solution: that the two blossoms were of similar but different varieties.

I was sorry that he hadn't been able to supply me with

more exact identifications, but I wasn't surprised. Matching
the flower with a name is especially complicated in the case of
Chinese roses, because their nomenclature reflects the clash
of two traditions. Western collectors and botanists usually took
no notice of these flowers' original Chinese names. Instead,
they rechristened each according to Western tastes, naming
it usually for its European "discoverer." This was a logical ex-
pedient in a less cosmopolitan age. The average European or
American gardener of the eighteenth century might never
travel more than a hundred miles from his native village, and
he would have found a Chinese name unacceptably foreign. I
understand the Western nurserymen's rationale, but still it ir-
ritates me to find some Chinese horticulturist's masterpiece re-
labelled with the name of a Western acquisitor.

There's 'Slater's Crimson China,' for example. This red ever-
bloomer was the first of the four "studs" to reach England, arriving sometime around 1792. A captain of the British East
India Company found the bush in Calcutta, the capital of
Bengal; how the rose got there no one knows, but historians
suspect it had arrived in India some centuries previously with
one of the Arab merchants who pioneered the sea route to
China. The captain presented it to a director of the company,
Gilbert Slater, and he grew the rose in his garden at Knot's
Green, Leytonstone. In all fairness, Slater seems to have been
a modest man, and when he shared cuttings with his friends
he called them "Bengal Roses," but his name was the one that
stuck. Hazel Le Rougetel, an English garden designer and a
most accomplished rose historian, showed me in her garden a
rose that she secured from a Chinese correspondent, one that is
very like portraits of Slater's prize. She had hoped this might
prove to be the missing antique, until she showed it to Graham
Thomas. "Graham was very firm about not calling it the true
one," she told me when she took me into her garden to see
the rose. "He said this flower is too rounded, too globular."
Though he can say with some certainty what is not 'Slater's
Crimson,' however, Mr. Thomas cannot say what is, other

than that the original bush was some variant of *R. chinensis* 'Semperflorens,' a variety of the rose that the Chinese call Yueh Yueh Hung, the "Monthly Red."

'Parsons' Pink China,' the second stud, appeared in England in 1793, just a year or so after 'Slater's Crimson.' This rose took its name from a Mr. Parsons of Rickmansworth, who was the first person in England to bring the shrub into bloom.* The proud gardener made no mention of the source of his bush, but a geneticist from the Cambridge Botanic Garden (Graham Thomas's alma mater) may have found a clue in the Banksian Herbarium. This collection of 23,400 pressed and mounted botanical specimens was the greatest instrument for taxonomic research in the world when it was presented to the British Museum in 1827. It was assembled by Kew Garden's famous superintendent, Sir Joseph Banks; it was his wife, the reader may recall, for whom the 'Lady Banks Rose' was named (see chap. 2, p. 57). Among Banks's specimens, Dr. Hurst has identified a number of pink China roses; one is closely similar to Mr. Parsons's pink, and is marked "China prope Canton, Lord Macartney." George Macartney was an Irish peer who led a diplomatic mission to the court at Peking in 1792, and he passed through Canton on his way both into and out of China. Since he didn't report back to England until 1794, he could not have been Parsons's supplier, but it seems likely that Canton was the source. This city was the regular port of call for merchants as well as diplomats and was home of a famous nursery named Fa Tee (Flowery Land).

Fa Tee is known to have been the source of the last two studs. 'Hume's Blush Tea-Scented China' was named for Sir Abraham Hume of Wormleybury, Hertfordshire, but the rose was his only by purchase. It was bought for him in 1810 by an

---

* *This achievement loses some of its luster when one considers that, under the name Yueh Chi, this type, if not this exact clone, was widely grown in China at least a century earlier, while its portrait has been found on a sixteenth-century fan. Yueh Chi means "Monthly Rose," a reference to the fact that this bush blooms and reblooms monthly through the growing season.*

agent of the East India Company who was posted to Canton.
Fa Tee was also where John Damper Parks discovered a straw-
yellow Tea rose in 1824, when he went to China on a shopping expedition for the Horticultural Society of London. His
patrons distributed it as 'Parks' Yellow Tea-Scented China,' of
course.*

Finding fault with the practice of renaming roses would be
petty if it hadn't been accompanied by more serious wrongs.
Western gardeners, not only Englishmen but also Americans
and Europeans of all nations, regarded China as fair game for
any sort of plunder. The Westerners who came to visit Yun
Shou-p'ing's gardens in the centuries following his death were
not the type that compete for ribbons at the county flower
show. On the contrary, they were as hard-bitten a bunch of
imperialists as ever dictated terms to the natives at gunpoint.
Their business might have been with flowers rather than tea,
or opium, but the tactics they employed were substantially the
same.

Imperialism and rose collecting had gone hand-in-hand in
China from the very first. This odd partnership resulted from
not only the British love of flowers, but also the restrictions

---

* *"Tea-scented," incidentally, seems likely to be the sole remnant of
the Chinese names to pass into Western usage, for the roses descended
from these studs are still called Teas and Hybrid Teas. This name
could also be the legacy of the tea merchants who imported the bushes,
of course. In either case, its etymology is the subject of ongoing controversy among the authorities; some claim that the blossoms smelled
of fresh tea leaves, while others maintained the fragance was what you
would discover upon opening an old-fashioned wooden tea chest. Recently the trend has been to dismiss the name as rooted in fancy
rather than fact, a skeptical view I shared until a rustle took me to
the Texan town of Weimar. By the foundation of a cottage, we found
that day a low, rather anemic bush that bore one overblown double
blossom of flesh pink. A typical Tea rose blossom, it was too heavy for
its stem and hung nodding groundward. I pinched the blossom from
its bush, lifted it, and started. I had inhaled the fragrance of a strong
cup of Oolong. A rooted cutting of "Weimar Tea" grows in my wife's
Texan nursery bed now as proof that the old-rose growers spoke the
simple truth.*

the Chinese placed on the merchants of the British East India Company. Confined by Chinese law to the environs of Canton and Macao and rigorously restricted in their contact with Chinese nationals, the English tea merchants found boredom their most formidable enemy. Many took up botanizing as a hobby; a few became truly outstanding plantsmen. James Cunningham, a Company surgeon who sailed to China in 1698 and again in 1701, sent home pressed and dried specimens of 600 Chinese plants that later formed an important element of Joseph Banks's herbarium. Lord Macartney's mission to Peking in 1792 has already been mentioned; its purpose was to protest the Manchu's restriction of trade, but Macartney also interested himself in the flora of the country. He took two gardeners along as part of his suite, and though the embassy failed to open China's doors, it did bring home a number of roses. Besides the herbarium specimens, these included at least one live bush, a vigorous Rambler whose single white blossoms, according to contemporary accounts, breathed a cloying scent of overripe apricots.

I haven't found the 'Macartney Rose' to have any scent. Like most of its compatriots, it didn't take kindly to England's climate, but it thrived when Thomas Jefferson planted it at Monticello in 1799. Our third President may have been a visionary, but he didn't foresee the effect of this introduction. The 'Macartney Rose' spread south and west, to become such an aggressive weed in pasturelands that planting it is now prohibited in Texas. Not that the law has had any perceptible effect on the rose. Its thorny canes and suckering roots have defeated all attempts at eradication; mounds of its glossy foliage swell up along Texas roadsides to bloom white through the summer like drifts of unseasonable snow.

Nearly as vigorous, but legal, is the 'Macartney Rose's' offspring, 'Mermaid.' The result of a cross with an unspecified yellow Tea rose, this hybrid was introduced by an English nurseryman in 1918 as a "pillar rose," a type suitable for training up a pillar or post. In Texas 'Mermaid' grows so rapidly that it is the rose of choice for covering an unsightly shed or wall. Belle Steadman, a rose collector from Dallas, had warned me that when she planted 'Mermaid' at the back of her yard it immediately vaulted the boards and set off at a run down the alley. In fact, the bush my wife planted in July clothed half the carport with polished jade leaflets and four-inch disks of yellow by the following May.

But if the first Chinese roses to filter into the West arrived with tea chests, the great bulk came as the result of a more sinister trade, opium smuggling. Western merchants discovered toward the end of the eighteenth century that the Chinese had a ravenous appetite for Indian opium, and this eventually surpassed caffeinated stimulants as the most profitable article of trade. When the Chinese emperor tried to say no and confiscated the smugglers' stock, the British parliament responded with an expeditionary force. By August of 1842, the Tars and Tommies had extorted indemnities totalling $26,500,000, the right to trade in four more ports, and the title to Hong Kong. China had been split open like an oyster, and foreign merchants rushed in to the feast. The Horticultural Society appointed a China Committee, and by the 28th of December, despite the cautions of the British government, the committeemen had already selected a plant collector and were meeting to choose his gear. They had found their man in the Society's own garden at Chiswick. He was the superintendent of the hothouse department, a young Scots gardener named Robert Fortune.

To encourage Fortune's cooperation, the Society promised to keep his post open for him while he was away and to pay him £100 a year for the duration of his expedition, over and above expenses. In return, he was to search for "seeds and plants of an ornamental or useful kind, not already cultivated in Great Britain." Besides this broad mandate, the Society supplied a list of twenty-two plants it particularly desired; number four was "the Double Yellow Rose of which two sorts are said to occur in Chinese gardens exclusive of the Banksian."

The Banksian was, of course, the yellow form of the *Mu Hsiang,* the "Woody Fragrance Rose," that furnished the Arizonan giant, the pride of Tombstone. For any funds Fortune might need while in China, the Society referred him to Messrs Dent & Co., one of Hong Kong's most notorious opium dealers.

Fortune was a man it is hard to like but almost impossible not to admire. He came up the hard way: born in Berwickshire, a county along Scotland's southern border in 1812, he had apprenticed at an estate in his home town of Kelloe. There he earned a sufficient reputation that at age twenty-seven he was offered a position at the Royal Botanic Garden in Edinburgh, then one of the foremost horticultural institutions in the world. Two and a half years later, his supervisor recommended him for the position at Chiswick. By age thirty Fortune had risen to the pinnacle of his profession and could expect no further success in Britain. Only in the more fluid society of the colonies could he hope to make the leap from gardener to gentleman.

The only photograph of Fortune I have been able to find was taken some years later in early middle age. It shows a lean man with side whiskers, a beaky nose, a cool stare, and a tight, humorless mouth. After his death, a female descendant destroyed all his papers in a fit of spring cleaning, so that little information of a personal nature remains; there are only the asides that Fortune chose to include in the books he wrote about his Eastern travels. These bear witness to a typical Scottish Borderer, a representative of a race that had survived for centuries through raiding, rustling and playing one side off against the other. Though brave, Fortune was also canny and wholly disinterested in lost causes or heroic gestures. He was relentless in pursuit of his goals, a man of a remarkable physical toughness blessed with a self-confidence that only the conviction of complete moral superiority can bestow.

A hint to the path Fortune took in China can be found in his only serious argument with his employers. When he re-

quested that a small arsenal be included in his equipment, the
China Committee demurred, quite possibly from motives of
economy. In a letter of January 1, 1843, Fortune replied:

> I am much disappointed at the resolution of the Commit-
> tee with regard to firearms. . . . I think that Mr. Reeves
> is perfectly right in the majority of cases—that a stick is
> the best defence—but we must not forget that China has
> been the seat of war for some time past, and that many of
> its inhabitants will bear the English no good will. Be-
> sides, I may have an opportunity, some time, to get a
> little into the country, and a stick will scarcely frighten
> an armed Chinaman. You may rest assured that I should
> be extremely cautious in their use, and if I found that
> they were not required they should be allowed to remain
> at home.

Fortune's arguments carried the day and he brought with
him to China both a double-barrelled fowling piece and a pair
of pistols (the China Committee suggested he might be able
to sell these articles at a profit before returning to England).
Fortune did indeed find plenty of use for this extra baggage.
When five boatloads of pirates attacked a junk on which he
was travelling and the crew were disposed to surrender, Fortune, though prostrate with fever at the time, dragged himself on deck. He forced the helmsmen back to their post by
pointing out that if they did their duty they *might* survive the
pirates' attack, whereas he would certainly kill them if they at-
tempted to desert. Disdaining the pirates' marksmanship, Fortune held his fire until they were almost within boarding range
and then raked their decks with repeated blasts of ball and
shot from his double-barrelled gun. After a couple of doses of
this treatment, the pirates chose to depart. In another, less
creditable, incident Fortune used his shotgun to fetch himself
and his servant across a canal. When a boatload of Chinese
refused to ferry him and made as if to escape, Fortune changed
their minds with a shot across their bow.

In *Three Years' Wanderings in the Northern Provinces of*

China, Fortune's published account of this trip, he recalled that his first view of China hadn't inspired much enthusiasm. When his ship, the *Emu,* sailed into Hong Kong's harbor on the sixth of July, 1843, after a four months' voyage, Fortune found himself confronted with a "scorched" coast of barren, almost treeless hills, all granite and red clay. "Was this," he wondered, "the land of camellias, azaleas and roses of which I had heard so much in England?"

Visits to more fertile locales reconciled Fortune to China's flora, but to the people and culture he took an immediate and permanent dislike. The inhabitants of Canton, the first mainland city he visited, he characterized as "a strange people full of peculiarities and conceits." Later he broadened this view to include all the southern Chinese. The whole region was "abounding in characters of the very worst description, who are nothing less than thieves and pirates." The northern Chinese he liked somewhat better; they were "quiet, civil and obliging," but also "sleepy," "dreaming," and "stupid." Typically, his description of any encounter with the natives relied heavily on such words as "laziness," "cunning," "deceit," and "blackguards."

In contrast, he had nothing but praise for the British he encountered in China. Perhaps this was because a disproportionate number were Scots like himself. Jardine and Matheson, for example, Hong Kong's largest trading house as well as the colony's busiest narcotics trafficker, was entirely directed by Scots (the company still recruits from Scotland, though it has long since given up its interest in opium). Surely it was Jardine and Matheson Fortune had in mind when he addressed the topic of opium smuggling in his book. He had come to China, he asserted, expecting to find these men "little else than armed buccaneers." He found them instead "men of the highest respectability, possessed of an immense capital, and who are known and esteemed as merchants of the first class in every part of the civilized world. The trade in opium, although contraband, is so unlike what is generally called

smuggling, that people at a distance are deceived by the term."
Fortune also included a lurid description of opium addicts in
his book—he wasn't entirely blind to the evils of the situation—
but he had to forgive the smugglers. Their trade was too much
like his own.

Fortune found the exploration of China's gardens full of
hardship. Fever proved his worst enemy, felling him repeatedly and leaving him near death on one occasion, but he also
suffered a host of lesser misfortunes. In the course of his collecting he was set upon by mobs, beaten and robbed. Once he
tumbled into a water-filled pit that had been dug as a trap for
wild boars, and had he not grabbed a twig at the trap's mouth
he would surely have drowned. He nearly drowned again
when a sudden squall almost swamped the boat that was taking him through the Chusan archipelago, and he weathered
two typhoons, one ashore, the other at sea. None of this damp-
ened his optimism, however, or distracted him from his quest.

A more serious annoyance was the Chinese's reluctance to
supply him with plants. Fortune soon found his way to the Fa
Tee Nursery. Lying two to three miles upriver from Canton,
this establishment actually included a dozen or more separate
nurseries, one next to the other, and each offering rows of
azaleas, tree peonies, camellias, oranges, and, of course, roses,
all potted in tubs. Fortune's description of strolling down Fa
Tee's paths when the azaleas were ablaze with color and magnolias filling the air with their melon-scented perfume makes
it clear why this was a favorite springtime recreation of the
foreign colony. He found the place thoroughly picked over,
and pushed on.*

* The best history of Fa Tee is found in Hazel Le Rougetel's recent
book, A Heritage of Roses. Apparently, by the date of Fortune's arrival, the Chinese government had restricted Europeans' access to even
this meager pleasure. Foreigners could visit the nurseries no more than
two or three days a month, and then only after paying an entrance fee
of eight dollars each time. The most remarkable aspect of Mrs. Le
Rougetel's account, however, is an incident from the horticultural tour
she made through China in 1981. Having stopped to visit a horticul-

When he arrived in Shanghai, Fortune tried questioning a florist, who insisted that all his sources were too distant to visit. It was purely by chance that Fortune stumbled on the man's nursery a few days later while out shooting birds in the countryside. The florist slammed the gate in Fortune's face and remained deaf to all entreaties for several days. It was only when an officer from the English consulate came out to intercede in Chinese that Fortune was finally let inside.

In his book, Fortune railed against the ignorance of a people who always ascribed a suspicious motive to his scientific interest in plants. The reality was that Fortune was all the while engaged in an attempt to break the Chinese monopoly of tea production. On this first trip he collected only information, but he returned five years later to spirit off 2,000 young tea plants, 17,000 seedlings and six Chinese tea processors. His backer in that venture was the British East India Company, which was developing tea plantations in India.

Whether or not they guessed at Fortune's intentions, the commercial plantsmen of China stubbornly resisted his advances. It was the hospitality of private gardeners that proved his salvation. In their plots he found a wealth of new plants, materials that would make him one of the most successful collectors of all time. On an island off Amoy, he visited the gardens of some Chinese merchants and *discovered* (his term; undoubtedly the merchants would have described the incident differently) "some very pretty Roses, producing small, double flowers of great neatness and beauty, although destitute of perfume." He sent them back to Chiswick. At a Buddhist temple on the island of Poo-to he found the priests cultivating small private plots of favorite flowers. He took more unspecified

tural commune outside Canton, she was told of a neighboring nursery that was reputed to be two centuries old. She hastened to the site and found a scene, rows of bonsai lined up in pots, that agreed very closely with Fortune's description of Fa Tee. And in fact, the inscription over the nursery gate was Hwa Di; when translated from Mandarin to the Cantonese dialect, this reads Fa Tee.

roses from here. In a Shanghai garden he came upon *Rosa anemoneflora,* a spring-flowering double white that resembles the Musk rose so nearly that some authorities have suspected a relationship. He also found roses on a gravesite outside Ningpo, a coastal city that he made a base of operations from the fall of 1843. It was inside the city walls, however, that he really struck gold.

By the time that the spring of 1844 arrived, Fortune had mastered enough Chinese to begin paying social calls. He used these occasions to make an inventory of Ningpo's gardens, finding several valuable plants in this way. His greatest coup came, as he reported in a letter to the Horticultural Society, "on a fine morning in May."

He had entered the home of a local official, what Western visitors called a mandarin, though that is properly the name only of the north Chinese dialect such bureaucrats spoke. Fortune parroted his few polite phrases and was ushered into the garden. There he was dazzled by the mass of yellow blossoms that completely covered a section of garden wall. "The color," he recalled for the benefit of the Society's newsletter, "was not a common yellow, but had something buff in it, which gave the flowers a striking and uncommon appearance. I immediately ran up to the place, and to my surprise and delight found that it was a most beautiful *new double yellow climbing rose.*" Fortune didn't reveal the means by which he collected this specimen, whether he helped himself to a cutting or whether the mandarin saw fit to present him with the plant. However it happened, Fortune secured the rose, the very one that the Society had requested him to find.

He did not stop with this success. From another garden in Ningpo he recovered a China rose (*R. chinensis*) that the Chinese gardener called "five-colored" because of the streaks of pigment that mark its ivory blossoms. He did not say where he picked up the white-flowered evergreen rambler that John Lindley, the Horticultural Society's secretary, dubbed *Rosa fortuniana.* Fortune also found room in the cases of plants he sent back to England for a dark red climber and "a purple garden kind"—this last seems to have been a specimen of the Rugosa rose. But it was on the double yellow climber that he pinned his greatest hopes.

The Society announced the arrival of 'Fortune's Double Yellow' with great fanfare in its *Journal* of 1846, and planted the shrub at Chiswick. Like so many other Chinese roses, it proved a disappointment in England. In a report of 1851, the *Journal* dismissed the rose as "a straggling plant."

"In its present state," the review continued, "this plant has little claim to English notice." It couldn't survive a Chiswick winter unless nestled in the shelter of a south-facing wall, and even then the flowers didn't color properly; in the damp English gloom, they never achieved the lustrous red-gold Fortune had promised. (This is a problem English growers commonly experience with the older yellow roses. English growers have complained to me also of 'Lady Hillingdon,' the magnificent buff-yellow Tea rose of 1910. She doesn't do much out in the middle of the garden, they snicker, but she's great when you get her up against a wall.)

The Horticultural Society forgave Fortune this failure. After all, the collections he sent back included a number of treasures: tree peonies of new and finer reds, purples and lilacs; a winter-flowering jasmine; and an upright variety of the forsythia that has become spring's cliché. A few wealthy gardeners continued to grow the yellow rose. It behaved better in a greenhouse and picked up a couple of additional names: 'Gold of Ophir' and 'Beauty of Glazenwood.' It was hoped that it might father a new race of yellow climbers. Why this failed to occur isn't clear, but one old rose genealogist I consulted noted that the hybridizers of Fortune's day still relied on bees to do their cross pollinating—perhaps its isolation under glass kept Fortune's rose chaste.

The borders that Fortune helped to pry open in 1843 snapped shut again a little more than a century later, in 1949. Limited exchanges with Western botanists have resumed in the last few years, this time on a more equal basis. Graham Thomas has begun a study of the Chinese ancestors of our garden hybrids with seed and plants from China. One of the tragedies of the Cultural Revolution was the deliberate destruction of many of China's finest old gardens. The current regime has undertaken a program of restoration, but one wonders how many of the classic roses still survive. A nation with so many pressing concerns can have few resources to devote to such luxuries. Yet it is hard to imagine a Flowery Kingdom without roses.

The determination shown by Robert Fortune, and other horticulturists who followed him, has however, ensured that some of China's old roses will survive. They linger in odd corners. I'm waiting for some expert like Charles Walker to put a name to my "Weimar Tea"; *Rosa fortuniana,* I understand, remains popular in Florida as an understock for Hybrid Tea roses; and when my wife and I went to Mike Shoup at the Antique Rose Emporium for a climber, something more mannerly than 'Mermaid' to train over the kitchen door, he recommended 'Fortune's Double Yellow' (the "Wang-jang-ve Rose," Fortune's mandarin called it).

This expatriate, Mike assured me, had made itself perfectly at home in Central Texas. Sure enough, soon after transplanting, our specimen began pushing out new growth, and within a month it bore two blossoms. Something about the flowers stirred a memory. With great extravagance, I cut one from the bush and took it indoors. In my study, I laid the rose on a photograph of Yun Shou-p'ing's scroll. The match with rose number three, the large-flowered climber I had wanted for my garden, seemed nearly perfect. I wondered if the darker of the two blossoms wasn't simply the result of an unusually cold or wet season—one like the English springs that discolored Fortune's find.

Charles Walker shook his head when I mentioned this identification. I hadn't the evidence, and I hadn't even begun to eliminate the other possibilities. Moreover, he added, it would be at least two more years before my new bush would have matured sufficiently to produce typical blossoms—the roses of a young bush may differ markedly from those of a genetically identical adult specimen. So I won't claim that my rose is the same as that in the old Chinese scroll. But it is surely Chinese—and like the artist, it is *i min*, a leftover rose that will always remind me of that leftover man.

7

A Journey
to the
Mother Lode

Rosa rubiginosa

CALIFORNIA PRODUCES the finest roses in the United States. That is not opinion but a simple statement of fact. For proof, you have only to consult the professional growers, the men and women who produce roses for the floral trade. The most recent report published by the United States Department of Agriculture listed 239 American growers of florist's roses. Of these, eighty, more than a third, were located in California. New York, in second place, listed only fifteen, down by two from the previous year.

The reason for California's primacy is its climate, of course. This varies dramatically; one of the state's fascinations for a horticulturist is that a few hours' drive from the Mediterranean landscape of Santa Barbara takes you to the lush meadows and forests of Sequoia National Park, and a few more to Death Valley. Along the coast, though, and through the valleys, the winters are mild so that even the tenderest roses may be cultivated without protection, while the monotonously reliable sunshine of southern and central California (3,600 hours annually in Fresno, an average of ten hours every day) fuels remarkable growth. Rainfall is strictly seasonal, but the Californians have compensated by organizing one of the world's most remarkable irrigation systems; the state claims to have more than one sixth of all land under irrigation in this country. Indeed, the long, dry summers play an essential role in producing perfect blooms. The low humidity (outside of the fog preserves along the coast) thwarts the spread of fungal diseases like mildew and blackspot, two of the rose's principal enemies. With more than 15.6 million square feet devoted to Hybrid Tea roses, the California growers harvested 232,493,000 blooms in 1985, for an approximate wholesale value of sixty-five million dollars.

The economic value of California's old roses is negligible by comparison, a few millions annually maybe, but the state dominates that smaller market just as thoroughly. More important than the numbers of old roses that come from California, however, is the leadership the California collectors have provided. There are outstanding experts in every region of the country, and other states may surpass California in the cultivation of a particular class of rose. The Old South, for instance, yields to no one in the matter of Noisettes. Everyone agrees, however, that as a group the Californians' enthusiasm is unequalled. Nowhere else are there so many gardens, such a wealth of old roses so well grown. And the greatest credit for this is owed to a slight, shy Englishman named Francis Lester, who worked almost as hard at preserving his own anonymity as he did at preserving California's rose heritage.

Forty-three years after his death, Francis Lester's name insinuates itself into almost every discussion about old roses you may have with a Californian fancier. They refer to him casually, as a matter of course, and rightly so, since his work was in-

strumental in restoring their roses to popularity. Lester founded
a nursery he called Lester Rose Gardens and established a tradition of attractive, chatty catalogues calculated to infect their
readers with Lester's love of the subject. These informative,
readable booklets have been the old roses' most effective prop-
agandist—under Lester's successor, Will Tillotson, this catalogue drew Lily Shohan to collecting and inspired most of the
other founders of the Heritage Roses Group as well. I receive
the catalogue in its current incarnation, *Roses of Yesterday
and Today,* and find that its affectionate descriptions make me
want to order every rose it lists.

Yet if everyone is familiar with Francis Lester's work, no
one seems to know anything much about the man. I tracked
him for more than a year and can report only meager results.
My most determined digging unearthed just a few scraps of
biography; even his obituaries made reference only to his love
of roses. Nor could his heirs help me. When I wrote Patricia
Wiley, the current owner of *Roses of Yesterday and Today,*
she replied kindly, if cryptically, that the three people who
might have been able to help me are dead, and she was afraid
she couldn't tell me much since she hadn't known Lester until
he was terminally ill with leukemia.

So Francis Lester eluded me, but in the process he taught me
a great deal about old roses. For it was the pursuit of him that
introduced me to his old hunting grounds, the area of the Sierra
Nevada foothills that the Forty-Niners called the Mother Lode.
Old-rose collectors call it that still, and with good reason.

"Mother lode" is a term that requires some explanation.
Few of the miners who came to California in 1849 understood
anything of geology, but most believed (rightly) that the placer
gold they panned from sandbars in the valleys had washed
down from a richer source, a "mother lode" hidden somewhere
in the mountains. It was the quest for this that drew fortune
hunters up into the Sierras by the tens of thousands through
the 1850s. Few stayed longer than it took to exhaust the de-
posits of gold they found; they covered hillsides with cabins,

stores, hotels, banks and theaters, then walked away a few
years later. Eighty years later, when Francis Lester followed
the same tracks up into the hills, he found that isolation had
kept many of these ghost towns virtually intact—Lester, who
was looking not for gold but roses, had struck it rich.

He was born in England's Lake District in 1868, and so
made the acquaintance of the old roses while many of them
were new, or at least still young. In the last half of the nineteenth century, England was the place to see roses—the nation
was in the midst of a love affair with this flower—and Lester
profited by his opportunity. He came to gardening early. In
My Friend, the Rose, the book he wrote about his favorite
flower, he alluded to the experience he gained in the four-by-
four-foot plot his parents set aside for him as soon as he could
walk. His main field of endeavor, however, was not England
but the American West. He emigrated to Mesilla Park, New
Mexico, sometime around the turn of the century and grew
roses in a two-acre garden there for a quarter of a century, an
experience he distilled into an article for the *American Rose
Annual* of 1924. This makes clear that he found New Mexico
missionary country for a rose enthusiast—or at least that he
found nothing there that was old.

Lester didn't arrive in California until he had reached his
mid-fifties, and there he really found his calling. California's
more benevolent climate had nursed many rosebushes along
to an extreme old age. There were Damask roses growing wild
around the old mission, for example, that were reputed to
have come into the state with the Franciscan fathers from
Spain. Lester rejoiced to meet old friends again. He appreciated the best of the new introductions, but he wrote several
times to the American Rose Society to protest the fraud per-
petrated by nurserymen who ballyhooed new, "improved"
varieties every year in the hope of seducing gardeners away
from what long experience had proved to be good. Like a
Hebrew prophet, he berated those of his fellow gardeners who
"worshiped the false god of rose novelties." He himself felt

like "raising my hat, here in Monterey, every time I pass one of the many Mme. Lambard Tea roses that luxuriate in some of our oldest gardens, although they are utterly neglected."

By 1932, Lester had found his way inland to the gold fields. He went camping in the Sierras that year and stumbled upon one of the rose-filled ghost towns. Fascinated to find the roses of his childhood in such a different setting, he returned again and again and reported his finds in a series of articles for the *American Rose Annual*—the last of these appeared in 1944, the year before his death. I came upon his reports while browsing through old periodicals in the library and found that one whetted my appetite for the next. Though not an accomplished writer, Lester understood the value of brevity; he furnished just enough information to excite the reader's interest but never enough to sate it. Passing references to rose gardens then seventy years old, to a Tea rose with a trunk a foot thick that climbed to the top of a two-story house, of huge thickets of 'Harison's Yellow,' a hardy descendant of the Scotch briar that left its New York City birthplace in westbound wagon trains, persuaded me that I must see the gold rush roses for myself. The following May, I booked a flight to San Francisco.

I confess that I also had a personal motive. My grandfather Gloyd was a native Californian, a mining engineer descended from one of the many Welsh families who used the skills they had mastered in their native coal mines to make a new start in the gold fields. He filled my childhood with stories of mining camps and miners, of dusty towns in the midst of pristine streams, peaks and forests. He died two years ago, but among the things he left me, the shotguns, fly rods and wool shirts, was a pocketknife. Sweat has stained the walnut handle almost black, but the gray carbon-steel blade keeps a keen edge; Grandfather told me it was a grape-cutting knife from the San Joaquin Valley, that the blade was hooked so that it would sever a stem without slipping. I use it for pruning, and I carried it with me to California on a trip that was as much an investigation of my own past as that of the roses.

My plan was to drive Route 49, the "Mother-Lode High-way" that follows the great artery of gold the whole of its 160-mile length. From Columbia, the "gem of the southern mines," I'd travel north, stopping wherever a blossom caught my eye. Friends in the Heritage Roses Group had put me in touch with several of Francis Lester's successors, modern-day collectors, and I had arranged to meet them at intervals along the way. Having established an itinerary, I settled down with my guide books: the journals, letters and newspaper accounts of the original Forty-Niners.

They came to California from all over the world, I learned, not only from Wales, but from England, Ireland, France and Germany, from Chinese villages and Australian penal colonies, from Mexico, of course, and also from Chile and Peru, even Hawaii. They found a nearly virgin wilderness—in January of 1848, when gold was first discovered at Sutter's Mill, California's non-Indian population had been less than 15,000. Despite the climate, which most of the Forty-Niners praised as freely as my grandfather, life in the camps was brutal. Scurvy was a common affliction among men who subsisted on bacon and biscuits, and the prevalence of cholera suggests the caliber of town planning. California was a harsh environment for human transplants—10,000 died during the first year of the gold rush.

Not surprisingly, homesickness was the common thread running through all the diaries and letters. Mementoes of a former life assumed talismanic importance; in 1885 a correspondent of a California literary magazine, *The Overland Monthly*, asserted that this had played midwife to horticulture in the state. Many a letter, according to him, left California saying, "Mother, send me a head of ripe dill, a pinch of portulaca seed, a poppy seed case from the fence corner." The author recalled visiting an old lady in Trinity County a decade previously and finding in her yard "geraniums, carnations and roses, the lineal descendants of plants she had watered and cared for during the weary weeks of the journey from Western New

York to Weaverville, California, by way of Jim Beckwourth's Pass and the town of Shasta."

Gold fever also played a role in bringing roses to the Mother Lode. As twenty-dollar gold pieces stamped "Cal" began to issue from the Philadelphia mint, the merchants of the Northeast realized that a new and fabulous market had appeared. Under the heading "Ho for California!" the New York *Herald* began to run a full column every day of advertisements aimed at gold seekers. "California boots—made expressly for the mining region" sold alongside "California" tents, hammocks, camp hampers and cooking sets. There were sheet-iron cottages that could be shipped in pieces for assembly in the gold fields, nine-foot metallic boats that nested one inside the other so that miners could more easily sail up the gold-bearing rivers and streams; there were rifles, revolvers, carbines, Bowie knives, life insurance policies for miners, even daguerreotypes to send home to the loved ones. Buy now, the *Herald* advised; the pair of boots that cost three dollars in lower Manhattan might easily set the purchaser back two hundred dollars in the gold fields.

Mark-ups like that had every Yankee with capital loading freight onto westbound ships. Californians complained that more often than not, the goods were useless, like the 4,000 ladies' hats that arrived in 1849 when California's Caucasian female population was limited to a few barmaids (a euphemism, surely, for practitioners of a far older profession). A Mrs. Farnham, a former matron at Sing Sing, tried to remedy that situation; she developed a scheme to export young women. She chartered a boat and advertised for volunteers. Though her "California Association of American Women" sailed with only three members, it illustrates the lengths to which entrepreneurs would go to serve those who found gold. The curious result was that while staples continued in short supply, at least at the mines, any conceivable luxury—canned lobster, French champagne or the latest French rose—was available at the docks of San Francisco and Sacramento.

It was disillusioned gold seekers, men who realized there

was a better living to be made from California's climate than
her mines, who pioneered the trade in old roses. A. P. Smith
had been a dry-goods clerk in Troy, New York. Horticulture
was his hobby. He was growing mulberry trees and silkworms,
hoping to found an American silk industry, in 1848 when he
heard about the gold strike in California. He joined with thirty
others in buying the bark *William Ivy* and sailing it around
Cape Horn to Sacramento. The men passed the voyage gam-
bling and swapping shares of the ship, and by the time it tied
up in California, only six men held any claim to the title. One
of these was Smith, and he used his winnings to buy fifty acres
of land along the American River. He began by growing fruit
trees, but by 1856, when he published his first "Annual De-
scriptive Catalogue," he was offering ornamental trees, shrubs
and vines as well, together with an "unusually fine" stock of
"choice roses."*

I have seen the catalogue, and Smith's selection *was* remarkable. It included 81 different varieties of Hybrid Perpetuals,
Bourbon roses, Chinas, Noisettes, Teas, Moss roses and Climbers. Some of these were only a few years old—'Madame Tru-
deaux,' for example, had first appeared in France in 1850—so
Smith could claim with justice that he was offering his customers the latest Paris fashions. No price was listed for any of
these items, but it must have been steep. To bring roses out
to California, Smith had to order them from Eastern nurserymen and then transport them in pots by horse-drawn wagon
across the continent, or by ship around the Horn. He must
have suffered huge losses, yet by 1857 he claimed a stock of
15,000 plants.

Smith wasn't California's only source of fine roses. James
Lloyd Lafayette Warren, a nurseryman from Brighton, Massa-

---

* *This and other information about California's pioneer nurseries was
very generously shared with me by Thomas Brown, a landscape architect practicing in Berkeley. His monograph,* A List of California Nurseries and Their Catalogues, 1850–1900, *must be the basis of any serious study of this subject.*

chusetts, also came to seek his fortune in the gold fields in 1849 and settled for a seed store on J Street in Sacramento. Warren returned to New England in 1853, but only to move his old nursery west. The catalogue he brought back with him, though printed in Boston, was California's first, and it listed 31 varieties of roses. William Connell Walker, a lawyer from Philadelphia and likewise a Forty-Niner, founded the Golden Gate Nursery in 1850 on three acres near San Francisco's South Park. By 1854 his establishment boasted a conservatory and rose house; by 1859 he had added several more greenhouses to bring a total of 10,000 square feet under glass. Walker's catalogue of that year (1858–9) offered 156 different types of roses, a figure that few Eastern nurseries could have matched.

These were the flowers that Francis Lester rediscovered in the 1930s and '40s. As I left the plane and drove across the San Joaquin Valley, I wondered how many still lived. I watched cherry and almond orchards change to ranches as I climbed into dry, grassy hills and followed the roads to Tuolumne. I had arranged to meet Fred Boutin there, a botanist who had worked at the Huntington Botanical Gardens in San Marino, whose personal collection had helped to establish that institution's outstanding display of old roses. Like Lester, Fred had come to the gold country originally on a vacation and been fascinated by its roses. After returning again and again, he finally stopped there in 1979, settling permanently in Tuolumne at the heart of his hunting ground.

Like every town in the region, Tuolumne owes its birth to the gold rush, though Summersville, as it was called in those days, figured in only a minor way in the events of 1849. Its period of greatest prosperity came later, with the building of a narrow gauge logging railway and the Westside Lumber Mill. The street names bear witness to that past: I came into town along the Old Tuolumne Road, crossed Chestnut, Fir, Willow and Laurel, turned left up Elm, passed Madrone and rounded the block to pull up in front of a two-story house on

Cedar Street—a suitable address for a botanist. As I climbed out of my rented car, a slight sandy-haired man opened the front door of the house. Fred was dressed in what I later observed to be the uniform of Tuolumne County: work boots, blue jeans, red suspenders and a flannel shirt. Most modern residents of the region could have stepped out of one of the daguerreotypes the New York *Herald* advertised.

So could their roses. I had noticed that every house I passed on my way through town boasted, in addition to a vintage pickup in some stage of disassembly or restoration, an old-rose bush. Fred agreed with my observation, and after helping me in with my suitcase, he took me to see those he had collected.

His backyard bore the unmistakable stamp of the collector— the rosebushes, hundreds of them, growing in five-gallon plastic tubs, were all carefully labelled but arranged more like a mob than a garden. He explained that he had been preparing to move them to his ranch outside of town when a forest fire swept through that property last spring, temporarily delaying the project. Now the roses wait, packed together by family and type like immigrants at Ellis Island, wherever Fred has found a sunny spot among the pines. The resulting thicket of canes and flowers might not satisfy a landscape architect, but it does provide a properly flamboyant setting for Boutin's Old English game cocks, who strut in and out of the roses in pursuit of the family's hapless tomcat.

Despite the unconventional treatment, the plants flourish. As he took me round, Fred handled the plants with the unconscious, automatic care a farmer gives his stock. He'd reach over to shake the water from a drop-laden cane without missing a beat in the conversation; he'd tease a bud open with a fingertip as he talked, or bend down as he listened to blow into a blossom and help it finish unfolding. He knew the name of each shrub without stooping to read the label—or at least he could tell me what the shrub was not.

He showed me the double red blossom that another old-rose fancier had sent to him as 'Slater's Crimson.' Fred can't agree.

"It has proliferating carpels," he explained to my complete confusion; "there's no mention of that in the original descriptions." He gestured at a Tea rose with an apricot blossom. The Huntington Botanical Gardens lists it as 'Madame Jules Gravereaux," but Fred doubts that too. The bush of that name he has found illustrated in old catalogues is a "lustier" rose with larger flowers. His bush bears modest flowers, midway in size between a China and a Tea rose, whereas the roses in the portraits are nearly as big as a prize-winning Hybrid Tea. Furthermore, the original catalogues advertised the rose as a semi-climber, and his shows the disposition of a shrub. Fred wishes he could put a name to his rose. He was its discoverer—it was, he recalled for my benefit, the first rose he found in Sonora, the Tuolumne County seat. But Fred won't move until he is sure, and that time may never come.

"Mystery" was the word he used most often as we moved round the collection. There was the "mystery rose" he found on the way to Angel's Camp, a double-flowered Damask-type climber. The bloom he pulled over for my inspection was quartered with a button-eye center, and colored a luscious, fruity pink. "Looks like raspberries and cream," he observed. The name? He responded with his easy laugh and a shrug.

"Then we come to the mysteries of the early Noisettes," he informed me as we arrived in an area of long, arching canes and clustered blooms. "We're finding batches of them up here." A sigh. "Some of them are beautiful. But what are they?" We stopped at bush after bush as Fred displayed his special prizes, a wild Banksia collected in China, and a rose he has raised from seed, a silvery pink blossom he held up to survey critically.

"That could be one of the old portraits . . . oh, batches more unknowns back here—mystery after mystery."

There were plenty of roses to which Fred could give a name. There was 'Champion of the World,' an offspring of 'Hermosa,' a pale pink China rose I knew from Francis Lester's articles. Lester had found 'Hermosa' all over the Mother

Lode. Near to the champion was 'Madame Lambard,' the me-
dium-pink Tea rose that Lester had admired in Monterey's
older gardens, and that Fred hailed as an "extremely important parent." I recognized 'Marie Pavié,' the Polyantha I grow
along a path in Texas. Fred pointed to the foliage, different
from other Polyanthas, evidence, Fred suspects, of intermar-
riage with *Rosa arvensis*, the Ayrshire rose of England. Fred
has more rose names at his fingertips than anyone else, quite
literally. With his file of "accessions," the three-by-five-inch
cards he makes up for every rose he acquires, he also includes
cards of related roses he has read about but never seen. Some
of these roses survive only in a single description in an archaic
text—he never expects to find those. Even if he did, in many
cases the physical descriptions are so vague as to be useless.
Yet these phantoms serve a purpose. They are all part of Fred's
program to reconstruct family trees.

"I used to be *very* name-oriented," he explained. "That's
just something that appealed to the cataloguer/collector instinct, I guess." When he began collecting the old roses, he
felt the need for some sort of "handle." But having worked on
several groups of woody plants, he was aware of how completely artificial systems of nomenclature are. And old-rose
names are more artificial than most. Fred's readings in botanical and horticultural literature have been omnivorous; he'll
quote old herbals as well as catalogues in support of a point,
manuals of rose culture from 1920 or 1820, botanists' field
notes and correspondence, exotic floras and accounts of fif-
teenth-century Chinese expeditions to Africa. This research
has made him aware of the inconsistencies to be found in even
the most authoritative sources.

'Hermosa,' for example, is dated 1840 in all modern texts,
and credited to the French nurseryman Marchesseau. Yet Fred
has found a description of this rose in a catalogue of 1839,
circulated by Philadelphian Robert Buist. In fact, Fred has
found references to 'Hermosa' dating back to 1834. He believes
that Marchesseau got the credit for this rose simply because

his firm was well known, that the rose historians of the last
century never bothered to look farther than Marchesseau's
catalogue. How many other roses are misattributed in this
manner? Many, according to Fred. When I mentioned the
bickerings over rose identifications I had witnessed, he laughed.
He believes that the need to tag everything with the "right"
name is part of the way our minds function.

Fred's interest in parentage is part of a different approach
to rose identification. He studies roses now by groups and
families; he was deeply involved with the Bourbon roses when
I visited. Though he knows only a few dozen of these roses at
first hand, he had uncovered references to hundreds, and was
assembling all the information into a sort of botanical collage.
By scrutinizing all the roses in a group, tracing all the permu-
tations of the gene pool, he learns to recognize family traits.
Often, as in the case of 'Marie Pavié,' he can spot the inter-
mingling of different strains. By placing the roses in a com-
parative chronology, he charts trends, watching how a family
developed and changed with time. Erecting this "pyramid of
knowledge," as he calls it, serves him well in trips around the
Mother Lode. It allows him to put most discoveries in context
immediately, even before he has identified a rose by name. He
doesn't wait for an exact identification to continue his research.
Like Charles Walker, he knows it may never come.

In the letter I wrote Fred before going to California, I had
expressed my interest in collecting, and after our walk he suggested we set out without further delay. With an ice chest in
the back of his station wagon, just in case, we set out on a tour
of Fred's discoveries. After directing my attention to two regal
'Louis Philippe d'Angers' (medium red, China rose, intro-
ducer: Guerin—1834) in the garden across the street, and
'Madame Joseph Schwartz' (white, Tea rose, Schwartz 1880)
Fred turned toward Sonora, the home of the putative 'Madame
Jules Gravereaux.'

We passed a bank of egg-yolk-yellow blossoms brighter than
any old rose my Yankee eyes had seen before, and Fred iden-

tified it as 'Persian Yellow' (R. *foetida Persiana*), a centuries-old garden rose from Iran that was the source of the yellow shades in the twentieth-century Hybrid Teas. With its luminous hue, 'Persian Yellow' is also supposed to have passed along a particular susceptibility to the fungal disease blackspot. If so, it is the instigator of the chemical warfare that has become the central experience of modern rose gardening. When I cared for a garden of Hybrid Teas a decade ago, I found it necessary to spray once a week and within twenty-four hours of every rainstorm throughout the growing season to keep those prima donnas healthy. Spraying absorbed more of my labor than any other single operation. So I looked away from 'Persian Yellow' and asked Fred about Francis Lester.

Fred asked me if I knew that Lester had been a cactus nurseryman, too. That was what he was doing all those years in New Mexico. Indeed, it was a measure of Lester's devotion to roses that he continued to grow them in a locale best suited to succulents, a desert climate at an elevation of 3,800 feet. He became an authority on which roses performed well under those trying conditions, testing ninety varieties and publishing a list of those he found "satisfactory." "Satisfactory," is, of course, the highest praise an English gardener can accord any plant; "unsatisfactory" is utterly damning and consigns the delinquent to the compost heap. Lester found that old standbys more often than not proved the most stalwart—'Frau Karl Druschki,' the white Hybrid Perpetual, and 'Madame Caroline Testout,' a pink Hybrid Tea of 1890, headed the honor roll of satisfactories. Naturally, this reinforced his prejudice for the old-timers.

Not only had Lester grown up with the old roses, Fred pointed out, he had arrived in the Mother Lode just in time to meet a generation who remembered the roses' arrival. The task of identifying a rose was simpler then; Lester could consult with aged residents who had known individual rosebushes since their planting. Fred meets with gardeners two generations removed. All they can tell him, usually, is that they call the bush "Grandma's rose." Did Lester assemble any collection of gold rush roses himself? Fred has never been able to learn; Lester eludes him, too.

Sonora offered a city plan far more typical of the Mother Lode than Tuolumne's; Tuolumne was laid out in a grid by timber barons, while Sonora is the typical gold-rush town where streets grew up from miners' winding footpaths. We paused on a height at the town's edge to peer across at the county courthouse and its cluster of Washingtonia palms, and the knob of a hill that supports a date palm. After pondering the survival of these subtropical anomalies in a mountain town, we plunged down a labyrinth of twisting streets to visit the garden of Fred's friend Diane. This garden has been in the possession of the same family since the 1860s, and it preserves some remarkable roses. On the way, we paused to inspect a primitive Bourbon climbing over a stone wall. The flat double and quartered red blossoms resemble those of 'Rose Edouard,' the first Bourbon rose and the founder of that class. Our examination of this rose caused Fred to voice doubts he harbors about the 'Rose Edouard's' parentage, indeed of the origin of the whole class.

According to the received story, the first Bourbon rose, 'Rose Edouard,' originated on the Ile de Bourbon, a French colony in the Indian Ocean, sometime before the year 1817. It was standard policy of the European powers in those days to establish a botanical garden in each colony to help in cataloguing its natural assets, and to increase its wealth by introducing new crops. In 1817, a Monsieur Bréon found himself a post as curator of such a garden on the Ile de Bourbon. There, he found 'Rose Edouard'; according to his tale, it sprang up in a hedge from a natural crossing of 'Old Blush China' and an Autumn Damask, the so-called Red Four Seasons (a rose that has been lost but which old-time growers agreed was not red but rose-pink).

Semi-double in form, a vivid rose-red in color and very fragrant, 'Rose Edouard' was a pleasant flower, but not a showstopper. When Bréon sent seed of it to Jacques, the chief gardener of the Duke of Orléans, however, an unsuspected virtue emerged. The new rose (which was distributed incidentally, as 'Bourbon Jacques') combined a degree of the China rose's repeat-blooming habit with an exceptional hardiness. Though definitely not everblooming, the rose was nevertheless a step in that direction, and since it survived northern winters, it met with great acclaim. Nurserymen bred a new class of "Bourbon" roses from seedlings of Bréon's find and Hybrid Bourbons proliferated like rabbits. By 1846, America's foremost plant importer, William Prince of Flushing, New York, offered 144 varieties of Bourbon roses, ranging in price from thirty-seven cents to three dollars apiece. Bréon had achieved immortality, in rose-growing circles, at least.

Fred believes the man to be guilty, at the very least, of jumping to conclusions. Bréon was not a botanist, Fred has ascertained, only a florist who was willing, like Fortune, to gamble the dangers of the long, uncomfortable journey to the East against a chance at professional advancement. Aside from the rose, Bréon apparently did no other collecting during his brief tenure as curator of the botanical garden, nor did he leave notes or any other evidence of an interest in botanical exploration. Instead, he returned to France to reestablish himself in the floral trade, where the tale of his discovery could only boost his business. In his search for 'Rose Edouard's' origin, Fred prefers an account he has found in *Prince's Manual of Roses*, the guide-to-roses-cum-catalogue that William Prince published in 1846.

Prince himself believed Bréon's story but appended another, conflicting account, one that the nurseryman said was current on the Ile de Bourbon. According to this, 'Rose Edouard' belonged to a Madame Edouard, a widow who had asked a friend, a naval officer, to find a new and unusual rose for her husband's grave. He brought her the remarkable remontant rose—probably from India, where it is still used in religious rituals, Fred notes. Pointing to the extreme conservatism of such customs, Fred suggests that the rose is much older than currently believed. Nor does he think it could be the offspring of 'Old Blush' and a Damask. It seems unlikely to him that crossing a pale pink flower with a rose-pink one would produce the intense red of the first Bourbon.

Fred proposes a descent from a red China rose, such as 'Slater's Crimson,' with an admixture of some sort of Gallica blood—the leaves of 'Rose Edouard' and many other Bourbons, leathery and rounded, suggest a Gallica influence, as does the Bourbon's exceptional hardiness. He further speculates that the ancestor of this rose was brought to India by medieval Arabic merchants on their way home from China. Constrained by a Chinese law prohibiting the export of gold or silver, foreigners could exchange their wares only for goods such as silks. A small balance they would make up with odds and ends of porcelain or lacquerware or, Fred suggests, a rose. Support for this theory comes from sixteenth- and seventeenth-century accounts of reblooming red roses in western India and Arabia, other staging points on the Arabs' route. Fred suspects that a search of old gardens along the Malabar Coast might turn up more clues and specimens. But that will be someone else's task. Fred has work to do in the Mother Lode.

Looking at my notes from that afternoon, I find them almost unreadable, for Fred kept my pencil running flat out. As we looped up, down and around the sunlit hills with their buxom profiles, I wanted to absorb all I could not only of roses but also wildflowers, trees and shrubs. I hadn't outgrown the need for names, and when goaded by questions, Fred responded with a flow like a Gilbert & Sullivan patter song. Blue oak, black oak, valley oak; lupines, penstemons, Escholtzia; native buckeyes in white bloom at the edge of ponderosa pines, and Digger pines that dropped enormous cones like bombs. We pulled over to inspect a climbing Bourbon rose. Fred put his nose to a globular pink bud and inhaled: "Hmmm, not bad." Then he directed my attention to the 'Jersey Beauty' beside it, a rambling rose with simple but fragrant butter-colored blossoms that New Jerseyan W. A. Manda introduced in 1899. We saw a climbing specimen of 'Hermosa,' a 'Little Gem' (Moss rose, red blend, William Paul, 1880) and a 'Champneys' Pink Cluster' that was three thousand miles from its South Carolina birthplace. We entered a forest of bizarrely sculpted gray limestone pillars, and Fred announced that we were nearing the site of the Columbia Diggings. The hillside, he explained, had been washed bare of soil with high-pressure hoses more than a century ago to sluice out the gold.

At its height Columbia boasted thirty saloons and 143 faro games, but as the mine played out in the 1870s, the town's 15,000 citizens began to drift away. Columbia never was entirely deserted, though the hydraulic strip mining had torn right through the town center to leave it looking like nothing so much as some monstrous oriental rock garden. Even more surprising was the persistence of the roses that had been planted in the community's heyday. They flourished amid the desolation and even outlasted Columbia's conversion into a state historic park in 1945. Only a few of the human residents stayed on to watch as the old brick and frame buildings were restored to furnish a home to strolling banjo-pickers, pan-your-own-gold concessions, historic stagecoach rides and shops that sell authentic penny candy at a quarter a piece. When Fred and his friend Karen Gustafson began a couple of years ago to collect and preserve the roses on the 273-acre tract, they found sixty distinct varieties. With cuttings of these they established a display garden next to Columbia's Old Fallon House Theatre.

Trouble with the automatic irrigation system had set the garden roses back that spring, so Fred took me around the park to show me their parents, original gold rush roses that continue to flourish in neglect. A hybrid of the Chinese Multiflora rose that Vibert introduced four years before the gold rush, 'De la Grifferaie,' had sent its thorny canes and lilac-pink flowers over the veranda of one old cabin. Around the corner we found 'Félicité et Perpétue,' a hybrid of the European species *Rosa sempervirens*. Monsieur Jacques, the same man who had raised 'Bourbon Jacques,' named this sweet-scented white pompon-flowered Rambler in honor of his two daughters in 1827. A "Climbing American Beauty," a relation of the famous florist's rose only in name, rambled over the door of another cottage. Fred dashed my enthusiasm for the huge single deep-pink blossoms with the warning that they age to a color he described as "day-old liver." At the edge of town we came upon the prize exhibit: the largest 'Fortune's Double Yellow' I had ever seen. The canes climbed thirty-five feet up an oak tree to hang halfway to the ground in golden-flowered festoons. Fred and I would be the last to enjoy this spectacle, though, for the garlands of flowers were wilting and dying. The rose's owners, proprietors of a bed-and-breakfast, had cut its canes at ground-level to keep it from climbing into *their* tree.

Far less showy, but with a story to tell, was a rose that wasn't even in bloom when we found it. Fred picked a leaf, crushed it, and held it to my nose. I smelled apples, and realized that the bush must be *Rosa rubiginosa,* the only species whose fragrance lies not in the flower but in the foliage. Glands around Rubiginosa's leaf margins release a scented oil when bruised or moistened by rain; this wild "brier rose" laces the hedgerows of England and has worked its way through the verse of that country from Shakespeare to John Keats. You'll find this rose not only in poetry, however; you'll also find it, according to Fred, in any California town where Welsh or Cornish miners settled. I thought about my grandfather as we drove to Angel's Camp.

Gloyd had never worked at mining gold, but his profession had taken him, his wife and daughter (my mother) to a succession of Western towns stamped from the same mold as this one. My mother recalls planting her first garden in Park City, Utah, by a house so close to the mine that one night a blast sent a boulder hurtling down the mountainside to punch a dent in the wood-shake roof. The spring she was eleven, she ordered a packet of perennials from a mail-order nursery and planted them in a space she grubbed out along the climb to

the front door. The next fall she went away to school in Salt
Lake City, but she returned to visit the garden in summertime
just as an Oriental Poppy was blooming; the picture is still
fresh in her mind, of how exotic the flower looked, and how
huge that splash of color seemed in the endless expanse of
uncultivated green.

Angel's Camp had its splashes of color, too. There were
roses on every corner—this was new territory for Fred; he'd
never collected here before and he found himself too distracted by the quarry to figure out the system of one-way
streets. After a couple of frustrating circles we parked and set
out on foot. Almost at once we came upon a 'Champneys' Pink
Cluster,' the primordial Noisette, then a copper-colored Tea:
"Probably 'Mademoiselle Franziska Krüger' (Nabonnand—
1880) in one of her many disguises," Fred observed. "She's
constantly causing problems." Past a couple of Hybrid Perpetuals and a 'Hermosa' in excellent bloom, then we found
what Fred identified as a Rambler of the Wichuraiana clan.
'Excelsa' (Walsh, 1909)? Probably.

We arrived at a hill and a sign that said "Hardscrabble." It
pointed up a road like a goat path, so steep that cleats had
been nailed across the wooden sidewalks for traction. There
was a rose on the corner, huge and pink, a primitive Hybrid
Tea: "One of those 'La France' things that probably isn't,"
Fred explained to me, as he invited me to share the perfume.
I opened my notebook to record the fragrance ("sweet, sweet,
& fruity"), when I was interrupted by an unfamiliar voice,
one full of suspicion.

"What are you writing in there?"

The interrogator was a tall, thin man with a long black
beard, clad, inevitably, in boots, jeans, suspenders and flannel
shirt. As soon as I began explaining my errand, I realized how
unlikely it sounded, so I changed the subject by asking him
what he was doing with the rosebush in his arms. Still eyeing
me, he explained that it was a climbing 'Peace' rose he was
going to plant in front of his house. He and Fred were soon

exchanging views about rose fragrances, and presently we were all looking down at a Hybrid Perpetual on the bearded fellow's scrap of vertical real estate, a remarkable pink rose with a blossom for all the world like a peony.

Down the street, we took our first cutting of the day, from a single dark-red rose that was struggling through a hedge. Fred pronounced the rose (perhaps, for he is too experienced to commit himself prematurely) 'Vesuvius,' an Irish Hybrid Tea of 1923 vintage. Why this parvenu, I had to know. Because he likes it, Fred explained as he borrowed my grandfather's knife.*

It came to the point that I couldn't stand the sight of another rose, though Fred had shown me only a small fraction of the 200 varieties he has found around Tuolumne County. "What you soon realize," Fred told me, "is that there is an unending supply." He laughed. "I sometimes think they multiply overnight, just to keep me fascinated." Fred is helping that process along by breeding new roses himself. He began crossing China and Tea roses several years ago, repeating crosses he knows were crucial to the development of the garden rose. His intention was to further his knowledge of family traits by observing what kind of offspring the roses produced. What he learned, he admits, is what every old-time nurseryman knew.

"Crossing two roses is like putting your quarter in a slot machine." He has hardened his heart toward the seedlings. Mildew is the most serious pest of roses around Tuolumne; some roses are naturally resistant, and Fred insists on this quality in his creations. As soon as a single leaf betrays mildew's gray, powdery presence, he roots that seedling out.

"I don't wait to see the flower; I don't *want* to see the

---

* *An odd consequence of the old-rose revival is that a gardener can now purchase ancient roses as well as new ones—yet middle-aged cultivars such as 'Vesuvius' remain unobtainable from commercial sources. If Fred wanted that single red Hybrid Tea, he had little option but to take a cutting.*

flower," he says in the desperate tones of a parent whose child has brought a stray dog home.

How are the purists going to regard a Boutin–1988 old rose? I asked. "Keeping the old roses pure," Fred mused. "What does that mean?" He laughed once again.

As I drove north the next morning, I thought about a story Fred had told me the night before. I had mentioned the quest for the Musk rose, and he responded with a tale of his search for a counterfeit Musk. In the garden of a friend, in Fort Bragg, California, a collector whose accomplishments awe even Fred, he saw an unusual hybrid of R. brunonii, the rose that was formerly passed off as the Musk. His friend told him it came from the Mother Lode, and gave him directions to an old house back in the woods. He'd find the rose there, she assured him, climbing to the very top of the trees. Fred followed the directions but never found the house. After a couple of attempts, he went back to his friend. She was no longer sure of the way either, and the man who had originally tipped her off had decided to keep the rose to himself. If he hadn't seen the rooted cutting, Fred told me, he'd wonder if he'd imagined the whole affair. "There are these rumors of gardens . . ."

The radio returned me to a more modern world as I left Tuolumne County behind. I cruised around switchbacks in time to the Beachboys—from time to time the disk jockey interrupted the songs of sun, surf and blondes to test the audience's knowledge of television trivia. He played an old theme song (when had I last heard that?) and asked his listeners to call in the program's name. Everyone called from the highway on their cellular phones:

"Hi, I'm Dave from Carmichael."

"Carmichael? Say, you *must* be driving a BMW!"

"No, a Saab Turbo 9000."

"I knew it had to be something like that—and I'll bet you're wearing a *real* Rolex."

"Sure, style's important. Let me guess . . . that was *Meet the Munsters*, right?"

The descent from wooded hills into the city of Auburn completed my re-acculturation. The uniform changed to fitted
jeans and tooled cowboy boots, and the gold-rush town seemed
to have been swallowed up by a more recent boom. From the
guide book I'd picked up that morning, I learned that the
town's name was the legacy of a party of homesick fortune
hunters from Auburn, New York, who arrived in 1849 when
a miner could expect the gravels to yield $1,000 to $1,500 a
day in dust and nuggets. I wondered if I should stop, too, but
decided I couldn't. I had an appointment to keep with Angie
Slicker up at the Empire Mine in Grass Valley.

Angie had assured me—I would swear without tongue in
cheek—that her area was "just a gold mine for roses." This may
be due to the town's peculiar settlement; as late as 1890, 85
percent of Grass Valley's residents were Cornish by birth, and
I suspect that its public library is the only one in California
with a Cornish/English dictionary in its collection (I was the
first to pull it off the shelf in some time, though—the librarian
was as surprised to see it as I was). Cornwall is famous for its
gardens. A tongue of land that sticks out into the Gulf Stream,
this ancient kingdom includes patches of subtropical climate
where palms grow out-of-doors, and English rosarians of the
last century had written with envy of the tender roses, the
'Maréchal Niels,' the climbing 'Charles Lefebvres,' that
bloomed to perfection in Truro. A gardener of my acquaintance served her apprenticeship as a potter in Cornwall, and
she has told me often of the perfumed once-blooming rose
that climbed the door of the house in which she lived. Once
when he was seeing off a visitor, the master potter gathered
an armful of blooms and presented them to the woman.
"There," he said, "that's smelling salts for the soul." Cornwall
was full of such medicine, according to my friend.

Gold brought the Cornishmen to Grass Valley. It sparkled
in the sheets of quartz that surfaced at Ophir Hill, the rise
that the prospectors named for King Solomon's legendary
mines. None of the Americans knew how to extract the pre-

cious metal from the hard rock, so they imported the skilled labor they needed from Cornwall's declining tin and copper mines. The "Cousin Jacks," as the Americans called them, dug 367 miles of tunnels under Grass Valley, burrowing to a depth of 11,000 feet and recovering six million ounces of bullion. Franklin Delano Roosevelt closed the works, along with all the other gold mines, as a "nonessential industry" during World War II (my grandfather never forgave him), and labor troubles after the war shut down the Empire Mine permanently.

A real estate speculator was sniffing round the 784-acre property when, in 1975, the state of California stepped in and, at a cost of $1,250,000, turned the site into a historic park (a bargain price when one considers that there is still more gold in the mine than ever was removed). The result was more to my taste than the Columbia park; the centerpiece of the Empire Mine Park is the English-style manor house built by one of the mine's former owners in 1897 and a scrupulously maintained formal garden of 950 old roses.

Angie had joined the park as a docent in 1980, the year before work on the garden was begun. Recently retired from a career as a pediatric nurse, she recalls that she wasn't much of a gardener at that time. Like most people, too, she had a rose mixed up in her childhood memories. It was a pink Multiflora, a 'Seven Sisters' rose, that climbed the porch railing in front of the family home (this name has been applied to any number of Ramblers, though strictly it belongs only to R. multiflora platyphylla; its origin lies in the seven shades from pink to white that are to be found in each cluster of the Rambler's sweet, feminine blossoms). Yet when Angie volunteered to help the park's gardeners, Ernie and Richard, with the new roses she found the work familiar. Roses, she explained briskly, are like "little babies; in both cases you're taking care of them, nurturing them and making them grow, right? So basically it's the same."

Angie admires the old roses' will to live. As Ernie and

Richard cleared the neglected landscape of brush, canes began to reemerge, survivors from the original plantings. One of these they identified as 'Fortune's Double Yellow,' though I suspect that the original gardeners cultivated the rose under its alternate name, 'Gold of Ophir'; that would explain its presence on Ophir Hill. Cuttings from this supplied the bushes that now clothe the rose garden's central arbor. Angie showed me also a bank of 'Félicité et Perpétue,' but she confessed that she hasn't done much collecting. The park had purchased almost all of its stock from the *Roses of Yesterday and Today* catalogue. But Angie took me into town to see a rose that a former resident had written to say was an original Rose of Castile, the Damask that came to California with the Spanish.

It may have been that once, but the rose growing next to the Mount St. Mary Convent wasn't a Rose of Castile anymore. Undoubtedly, the convent's rose had been a grafted specimen, and a too-enthusiastic pruning had removed all the scionwood. At any rate, the rose Angie and I found, a two-inch disk of white touched with pink at the center and here and there along the edge, was a fine specimen of Odorata understock.

"So-called Odorata" was how Fred Boutin had identified this rose when he had pointed out another specimen to me at the Columbia State Park. According to the history books, this understock rose's Chinese name was 'Fun Jwan Lo.' Frank Meyer, a collector in the employ of our Department of Agriculture, saw it in a garden in Chihli province and, admiring the rose's vigor, sent it back to the United States for use as a rootstock in 1924. Meyer had identified the rose as a hybrid of the Tea rose *R. odorata*, but Fred sees more resemblance to the European species *R. sempervirens*.

Actually, Fred thinks he may have found a match for this understock in the 'Sempervirens of Italy' described in *The Rose Fancier's Manual* of 1838. This was the work of Catherine Frances Gore, a popular novelist who took time out from

her potboilers (she produced as many as four a year) to trans-
late and adapt a French rose grower's treatise. Several other
books of that period mention the same rose; Fred suspects it
was a hybrid of the native European species *Rosa sempervirens*, a chance cross of the native species with an early Bourbon or 'Old Blush.' So if the rose was European by birth, how
did it come to be in China? There's no reason roses couldn't
travel east as well as west, Fred maintains. Italian Jesuits had
made the trip as early as 1583, and in the mid-eighteenth century one of their successors, the French priest Father Benoît,
laid out a European-style garden for the Chinese emperor. A
couple of generations later, the British East India Company
maintained a garden at Canton—the company ships could well
have carried roses on the eastward legs as well as the westward
legs of their voyages. Robert Fortune mentioned in his memoirs that he had taken a whole shipment of plants out to China
with him, to test the glass cases in which he hoped to bring
his collections back. Fortune never related what had happened
to those transplants. Had he traded them for Chinese plants
or distributed them as gifts? As I sketched the rose struggling
up next to the Grass Valley bell tower, I reflected that this
bush might be even more exotic than Angie had hoped.

Angie took me back to the mine, and I spent the rest of the
afternoon among the park's impeccably grown roses. Since
these had been arranged in chronological order, I could watch
the garden rose evolve, the blossoms grow and color, the petals
multiply and the perfume wax and then wane, just by strolling
down the paths. Angie took me to inspect the mine too. We
peered into the cold stillness of the main shaft, down which
wooden "skips" filled with hymn-singing Cornishmen used to
slide at a rate of 600 feet a minute. We visited the blacksmith
shop, which had been recreated by the park's "over-the-hill
gang," a group of retired men who had built the building and
then hunted through the community tracking down the original tools that had been dispersed when the mine equipment
was sold at auction in 1959. Angie agreed with Fred that my

next stop ought to be Downieville, one of the northernmost gold camps and, because of its remote situation, a special preserve of old roses.

The hills rose higher, steeper, rockier on both sides of the highway, into Sierra County, and the bridges that jumped the rocky streams narrowed to little more than a lane. As an Easterner raised amid scrubby second growth, I was most impressed by the size of the trees. Two or three of the enormous pine sticks made a full load for the logging trucks that roared past me on their way out to the mill. For the last forty-eight miles before reaching Downieville, I didn't pass another town, hardly even a cabin.

Downieville *was* full of old roses, though the town itself was little more than a crooked street along either side of the Downie River. Sunset ended my first quick reconnoiter, but I was out again at dawn, shivering and hoping to catch the early light for photographs. So deeply was Downieville sunk into its ravine, though, that the sun didn't penetrate to street level until after eight o'clock.

In the meantime I continued my prospecting. I found a neat little rose like a violet-colored zinnia (though I didn't recognize it at the time, I later learned that this was 'Hippolyte,' a French Gallica that the handbooks will categorize only as "very old"). Nearby, the "so-called Odorata" had hooked its canes over the lower branches of a tree, while a more compact shrub offered fat pink buds that opened into big cupped blooms—I never learned any more of this than that it was undoubtedly a Hybrid Perpetual. Toward the edge of town, I came across an incongruously robust specimen of the "Sweetheart Rose," a treelike 'Cécile Brünner' espaliered along a fence. As I stared at this rose with its four-inch trunk, the owner came out to pick up her morning paper. I ventured a hello and remarked on the delicacy of the color, the soft, artless pink of the fresh buds. I said it was nice to find an old rose so well cared for, and the lady of the house replied that people around there really appreciated beauty, that was why they had come to Downieville. Not that there was much beauty in the town, she remarked; they were digging up the streets now and it seemed that they were always mining or something, but nature was beautiful—the sky so blue, the hills forested and green. Then she announced that she smelled the coffee. She reentered her house and I walked back to town to get myself a cup.

A bakery perched above the riverbank lured me in with the smell of fresh doughnuts. I bought a mug of coffee and a buttermilk bar and found a seat at one of the crowded tables. With a floor of rough boards, the darkness and the bursts of laughter, the small warm room had the comfortable air of the local men's club. The talk was of chainsaws—which brands were best for logging—poaching deer, mining, and women, in that order of interest. As he rolled a cigarette, one grizzled individual opined that with the work of skinning and hanging the meat, a bowl of buck stew just wasn't worth it. Another told a tale of helping to break up a ring that was supplying venison illegally to a tony sportsmen's club in San Francisco; the meat was really wild burro. A young man stepped in through the front door and a senior member of the party asked innocently what had gotten him out of bed so early this morning. The hoots and jeers that accompanied this sally were interrupted by another veteran humorist, who turned to me and inquired sardonically if I had ever seen so many bitter old men. I grinned and replied, "Never." But I had, every time I went hunting with my grandfather.

Outside again, I crossed the river by an old iron bridge, near where the miners lynched a Mexican dance hall girl in 1851—she had stabbed one of them to death in what she claimed was self-defense. Downieville was man's country, then as now. As I walked to the end of Pearl Street, I contrasted the carefree laughter of the bakery with the weary tone that had been in my landlady's voice as she told of the shock she'd experienced when her husband had brought her here from Ohio. Cut off from every amenity, the female pioneers must have valued a rose's spiritual smelling salts more than I could imagine.

Four or five blocks later, at the edge of town, I introduced myself to an old couple who had retired to Downieville six years ago. In clearing out the brush on the hill behind their house, they had discovered the site of an old cabin and two roses. One they had transplanted to the front yard; when they showed me this one, I recognized the fat, round buds and cupped pink blossoms as those of a Hybrid Perpetual—it proved to be 'Duchess of Sutherland,' one of the first of its class, a French introduction of 1839. The rose we found up on the hillside was not in bloom, but by its fragrant foliage I knew it for R. *rubiginosa,* a trace of Welsh settlement.

Downieville's roses kept me busy the rest of the day. I met David Wilson, a Hollywood writer who had withdrawn to the mountains to concentrate on his rubber-stamp art (he gave me a copy of *Rubber Times,* the catalogue of his ready-made, reproducible images). David cheerfully offered me all the blossoms I liked of his 'Hermosa.' I stopped to watch a man work at the forge he had set up in his front yard, then passed on to talk with a couple from The Valley (which valley I'm not sure, but they didn't seem to think it needed any identification). They were the proprietors of the 'Hippolyte,' and they also offered to share it with me. I accepted their generosity as I had David's, for I was headed to a "Celebration of Old Roses" the next day and I didn't want to arrive empty-handed.

I was up early again, to cut the flowers before the sun evaporated their fragrance and took the starch out of the petals. The trip back to San Francisco Bay and the town of El Cerrito, one that had taken miners and roses weeks, took me about three hours. The site of the celebration, the El Cerrito community center, was easy to recognize: cars were backed up around the block, and in the parking lot vans and trucks were disgorging a river of rosebushes and cut blossoms. I was half-frozen—I had kept the air conditioning turned on

full the whole way from Downieville to keep the roses fresh—
and I was glad to disembark into the warm, perfumed air.

I had brought the bucketful of blossoms with me in the
hopes that I could get some help with their identification.
Within minutes of plunging into the busy crowd, I had the
information I wanted as celebrants came up to make me welcome, and welcomed the roses, too, by name. I asked for the
affair's organizer, Miriam Wilkins, and got a warm but hurried hello. Miriam passed me along to a friend, Linda Street,
who put aside her own business to escort me around the festival.

We went inside to be met right away with an artificial rosebush from whose branches hung rose-shaped cookies. The
baker, a woman in a straw hat adorned with a band of roses,
explained to me that each cookie had been modelled on a
specific rose, cut and colored accordingly, and flavored with
rose preserves. I selected a pink-frosted 'Baronne Prévost,' took
a bite and made my way to a thirty-foot table covered with
vases.

One of the requirements of the celebration was that every
participant should bring a rose from his or her garden properly
labelled. This was the event's serious side, and I spent a good
deal of time here making the acquaintance of roses which I
had read about but never seen. But as the public-address system came on with a medley of rose music ("Second-Hand
Rose," "My Wild Irish Rose," "The Yellow Rose of Texas"—
any song you can imagine that has a rose in its title), I found
myself drawn irresistibly to the booths of rose crafts.

The owner of a country inn had come with a selection of
rose foods she had made from her own eleven-acre garden.
There were rose-petal jellies, rose-flavored vinegars, rose-shaped
chocolates and rose-print wrapping papers. The Mount Diablo
Porcelain Art Association had come with a table's worth of
rose-painted dishes, pitchers, pendants and vases; the rose
portraits in oils nearby were the work of Pam Bloxom, an
artist from Castro Valley who named to me the garden from
which she had drawn each scene. I crossed the room to inspect

a rose-patterned quilt, and fell into conversation with Marlea Graham, who was stuffing a teddy bear stitched together from rose-patterned fabric. She divides her time between firefighting and horticultural consulting, and has applied her skill with computers to creating a program that generates a list of suitable rose varieties for any application and conditions. Bell's Bookstore of Palo Alto brought selections from its stock of old-rose books and cards—the manager, Barbara Worl, had also contributed a number of elaborate arrangements of roses from her own garden.

Among all these exhibits, the most extreme example of devotion to the rose was Miriam Wilkins's double table of rose artifacts. She had rose-scented soaps on display, little bottles of rosewater, rose-hip teas, rose-patterned pitchers and creamers, silver-plated, rose-ornamented frames and boxes, a Centifolia-rose tea towel, watercolors of roses and a matted cover from an old *Woman's Home Companion,* the "Love Story Number" that featured prominently a lush bunch of overblown roses. This was the purest expression of rose appreciation in the hall. None of the articles was really useful, and none of any monetary value, yet they obviously represented years of shopping.

Had I chosen to stay, I could have attended the series of rose talks delivered in the adjoining lecture hall. I had had my fill; but I returned to El Cerrito the next day to meet Miriam Wilkins. Still recovering from the festivities, she nevertheless took me through her garden, a jungle that very nearly realized my ideal of what a rose garden should be. We walked down paths that tunnelled along under the eight-foot-tall overarching canes, and I climbed into the tree house that her husband had given her as a sixtieth birthday present so that she would have a vantage point from which to view her garden properly. We stopped by the loquat tree, home to the mockingbird that my hostess had taught to sing: "Miriam, Miriam, I need you Miriam." Then she showed me where the badminton court used to be before the roses swallowed it up, and the piece of the neighbor's property that her roses had overrun. The neighbor, with the spirit I was learning to expect in Californians, had ignored her attorney's advice and granted Miriam an easement so that she may grow roses there for the rest of her life.

Miriam took me down to the bottom of her hillside garden to see her 'Francis E. Lester' rose, a Hybrid Musk that was bred by the great old-rose man but released the year after his death by his widow. Once again Lester frustrated my investigation; Miriam could not find a single blossom. The rose had been glorious a few weeks previously, she assured me. (It wasn't until months later that I did catch a specimen in bloom in the garden of the Royal National Rose Society in England.) With just five pink-tipped white petals, 'Francis E. Lester' is a simple but pretty rose, one much esteemed by connoisseurs who wonder why it has never ingratiated itself with the public.

I caught a night flight home from San Francisco. Since then I've returned to the Mother Lode often in my imagination. I think of the sunlit hills and the shabby old towns festooned with perfect flowers. I think of the contradiction the woman pointed out in Downieville, the rough way my friends in the bakery have often treated a place they love for its green, unspoiled beauty. I suspect that contradiction has much to do with the eccentric energy I witnessed in El Cerrito.

In the letter that Pat Wiley of *Roses of Yesterday and Today* wrote to me about Francis Lester, she told me she had only one distinct memory of the man and that it had nothing to do with roses. She'd take him to the hospital for the transfusions that were then the only treatment for leukemia, and he'd talk of fish. Lester had dammed up the creek that ran through the nursery and had trained the trout to eat from his hand— they would even allow him to take them from the water to stroke them. My grandfather had loved trout, too, but at the end of a split bamboo rod or in the pan. I could not imagine a more unlikely partnership than the California miners, men of shovel, drill and dynamite, and the dreamy, gentle rose grower. Yet in California's fertile climate their very different enthusiasms had crossed. Together they had produced a flowering of old roses unrivalled in all the world.

8

"He Who Would Have Beautiful Roses in His Garden..."

Double musk rose

AT AGE NINETY-TWO, Karl Jones spoke with fervor on the subject of roses. He had spent fifty years amassing what was the nation's largest private collection—8,500 bushes—and outside the window of his Barrington, Rhode Island, home I could see rectangular beds stretching, rank on rank, all the way down a five-acre slope. The field, however, was no longer his— he'd sold it the previous August. He was tired of roses, he said.

Or maybe he was just angry. He'd kept the garden open to anyone who cared to visit ever since he cleared the site of bull- briers and rubbish in 1937. The maintenance of the garden had cost him something like fifty thousand dollars annually,

yet it had always been available for the high school's graduation ceremonies, for weddings, or for the pleasure of passers-by.
In 1985 Barrington, though one of the wealthiest communities
in the state, had raised Karl's taxes, and he decided he'd had
enough. He called in a local developer, asked him to name his
price for the property, and shook hands on the deal. When
the townspeople came to remonstrate with him, he wasted no
time in setting them straight. The roses were his private affair; he'd grown them for his own satisfaction and the pleasure
of his late wife, and now he was through. When a *New York
Times* reporter asked him if he had any regrets about his
garden's passing, Karl replied that he certainly did not. "It
was good fun. I didn't do it for the community. I did it for
myself."

Karl was never a particular devotee of old roses. In his garden there had been a wealth of rare antiques, but his appetite
was omnivorous. Any rose of merit that he came across, new
or old, was granted a spot in his beds. His favorite rose, he
said was 'New Dawn,' a sweet-scented blush-pink blossom of
1930 that is generally accepted as one of the finest remontant
Ramblers of all time, but that hardly qualifies as an antique.
Yet as I listened to his reminiscences, I was coming to a better
understanding of the classics. Karl was a rose collector of the
old school, perhaps the last in the line of great private patrons.
They flourished in the last century when labor was cheap and
income tax negligible, conditions that allowed them to grow
roses on a scale unimaginable now. Throughout their reign,
they set the styles in roses; to a large extent, their tastes dictated the direction taken by rose breeders. And they achieved
this not only by their wealth or through the magnificence of
their gardens, but also through the intensity of their com-
mitment.

I knew a good deal about these individuals' accomplishments; I had read descriptions of their gardens, as well as their
own books and memoirs, in the Botanical Garden's library.
But obviously that was not the same as an interview.

Every collector I have met I ask the same question: Why roses? It is a foolish question, like asking Sir Edmund Hillary, Why Everest? and the answers I have got are usually about the same as the mountain climber's famous reply. Karl, however, surprised me with a prompt and cogent response. He told me that he had been frail as a child, and his sickly health had caused his father, a Providence businessman, to buy a house out in the country. It was a very small house without running water, only a cistern in the kitchen. His father was an enthusiastic gardener who liked all kinds of flowers, but he hadn't had any special interest in roses, so he delegated their care to his eleven-year-old son. Since this involved fetching buckets of nutrient "tea" from a tub of manure mixed with water, it was a chore, Karl told me dryly, that he didn't appreciate at the time. He felt amply rewarded, though, when friends came to visit the family while the roses were in full bloom. Who took care of them? the visitors wanted to know. "Karl does," his father replied. "He does a good job, doesn't he?"

"Well, that set me up," Karl recalled eighty years later. "The roses were mine from then on. That was the beginning of my rose career."

It wasn't until he was grown, married and working in his father's company as an engineer, however, that Karl's affection for the flower developed into something more. His father bought the young couple the house in Barrington; though comfortable, it was modest, but it came with extensive property. Whether it was for his own and his wife's pleasure or his father's too that Karl began planting the roses there, he didn't reveal. He did say that when his father died, he took on his gardener, a choleric little "north of Ireland man."

"He didn't want anyone to work with him, he wanted to work alone," Karl told me. Whenever the Irishman was given an assistant, "he'd say, 'I can work circles around him, he makes me sick.'" The tone of fierce approval in Karl's voice made me wonder what kind of driver he himself had been in his younger days.

He hired boys from a local school to clear his back property, working mainly on weekends. His interest in automatic sprinkler systems (for fire protection, not irrigation) caused his company to send him as a salesman all over Canada and the United States, even down into Mexico. He began bringing roses home from these trips. "I'd stop in Philadelphia and, see, there'd be some fine new roses offered very cheap and I'd buy maybe half a dozen, bring them home, sink them in the ground." I tried to establish when this enthusiasm had become an addiction, but like most collectors, Karl didn't see anything extraordinary in his activities. He was just doing what he enjoyed. He did reveal, though, that he presently found it necessary to hire a man who had worked for Walter Brownell, a famous Rhode Island hybridizer. The new gardener was an expert at grafting and could produce new rosebushes wholesale, thus saving lots of money, Karl blandly explained.

By then he had obtained import licenses from the Department of Agriculture and was ordering roses from all over the world. He got his understocks from Holland, "and I'd buy a few roses from Germany, a few from France, a few from England and a few from Ireland, and I'd graft those." A note of impatience crept into his voice. "The only place I had unsatisfactory delivery was in France. I would write 'em, I had fairly good French, and tell 'em just what I wanted and just when I wanted 'em. And they'd send 'em when they got damn good and ready. I'd have to bury 'em for the winter."

For a while, other branches of horticulture threatened to distract the promising collector. He experimented with espaliering, the ancient technique for dwarfing fruit trees by training them in geometric patterns along a wall or fence. Though this reduces the number of fruits a tree will bear, it increases their size, and Karl showed me a blue ribbon he had received from the Massachusetts Horticultural Society for the gigantic Cortland apples he had exhibited at one of their shows. But the new interest didn't last. "I had to stop that because people were driving in and getting out of their cars to take these big, beautiful apples. They had to be worked over all the time, you had to keep 'em pruned, keep the leaves away from 'em so the sun could get at 'em. They'd drive in and pick one of these big apples and take a bite out of 'em. They were so damned hard that they couldn't chew 'em. They had to ripen in a container; see you can't just take those apples off the tree and bite into 'em because they're too hard, they've really got to ripen. That made me so mad, they wouldn't let my apples alone, that I gave all the apple trees away, pulled 'em all up."

He'd tried blueberries too, planting 150 bushes. "We grew beautiful blueberries, some of them were that big." Karl measured an imaginary but most succulent fruit with tips of thumb and forefinger. "We got a new bunch of kids come into town. They wanted some of the blueberries, and I told 'em you've got to wait until the blueberries are ripe. Well, those are ripe, they said. I said, no, they're not ripe. They were big, but they weren't ripe. Well, they decided they were ripe so they decided to have 'em. And they lifted the nets* up and got in there, and they repeated the dose two or three times. I got sick of the whole goddamn thing and I pulled 'em out. Cleaned the whole place out." Roses, with their thorns, could defend themselves, so Karl returned to his first love.

Trouble with his hip had confined my host to bed, and he spoke in a whisper, but memories of bygone battles brought a flush of animation to his face; he related with satisfaction the comeuppance of a woman who stole one of his rosebushes after demanding that he give it to her. As a gardener, I appreciated the annoyance of dealing with the public. You come so close to realizing an inner vision of how the world ought to be, then someone intrudes with ill-considered questions, vol-

---

* A blanket of loosely woven netting does an excellent job of protecting berries against birds; it is not as effective against that other garden pest, small boys.

unteers constructive criticism and steps onto a freshly dug bed to smell a flower.*

To be fair to Karl, he kept, along with the ribbon his apples had won, a photograph of the last high school graduation held in his garden. Unlike many gardeners who open their preserves to the public, he never charged a fee for admission. Indeed, he refused even to host fund-raising events, believing the garden should be free. His contribution to the town's economy was the tourists his roses drew, some from far outside the state. Many returned in rose season year after year.

A constant refrain through all of Karl's reminiscences was the difficulty of finding and keeping help. The invaluable Irishman died of cancer—"poor devil"—and another gardener who began spending winters in Florida was seduced by the Southern climate into a permanent stay after his wife died. The man with the knack for grafting "had a disposition like a full-grown porcupine—the other men didn't like him." More recently Karl drew his help from the community of Portuguese fishermen and sailors who have settled along the Rhode Island coast. He worked out an arrangement with the local school whereby it employed the men in maintenance over the winter, then released them to Karl again in the spring.

Karl's preoccupation with labor problems was one that he shared with anyone trying to maintain a large garden in the United States. Gardening is a skilled craft that requires a long

---

* My wife insists on telling the story of the time she brought an English colleague to see my rose garden at Lamont (I had just begun to court her). I looked up from cultivating a bed to see them standing on a freshly seeded patch of lawn—my howls of protest drove them back out through the gate before I had a chance to add a hello. She has not forgiven me, though I've explained repeatedly that I was not the one at fault. I was abashed, however, the following summer by the small girl who came into the garden, her golden hair wreathed with a garland of marigold blossoms. She asked me if I'd seen the gardener. Why did she want to know? I demanded, preparing a lecture on the awful sin of picking my marigolds. "Because I've heard he's a really mean man," she replied. I was at her mercy until she returned to school in the fall.

apprenticeship or years of study. Yet entry-level jobs in the
private sector pay only marginally better than flipping burgers
at a fast-food restaurant. The income of an experienced gardener, the manager of a really first-class estate, is more reason-
able, but few can endure the lean years it takes to reach that
plateau. Those who do still find themselves dogged by the
low wage scale. Chemicals and power tools have greatly reduced the man-hours required for many basic maintenance
chores, but for some tasks, such as dead-heading a flower bed,
there is no substitute for a careful pair of hands. Apprentices
were the traditional solution to this problem, but with the
beginning wage what it is, any laborer the head gardener can
afford either cannot or will not do the job properly. Expedients
that the fast-food chains are beginning to explore, hiring re-
tirees and the functionally retarded, have long been familiar
to gardeners.

There are rewards for private service. The wages of even a
head gardener or estate manager may not be high by the standards of other industries, but often a free house and car come
with such a position—maybe even homegrown eggs, milk and
vegetables. In the past, these benefits usually went undeclared
and untaxed, a fact that made them especially attractive. My
accountant tells me that the IRS is cracking down on this type
of situation. Payment-in-kind has another disadvantage, as
well. It reduces the gardener from the level of professional to
that of family retainer. When the furnace's pilot light blows
out some winter night, or when the employer needs a ride to
the airport, a call to the gardener's cottage is just too convenient.

Horticultural training programs continue to attract talented
young men and women, but a terribly high percentage burn
out within a few years of graduation. Of the seven who graduated with me from the New York Botanical Garden, only
one still works full-time as a horticulturist (though another
was studying landscape architecture, the last I heard).

Most of my classmates continue to garden as amateurs, I'm
sure; and the most exciting gardens I've seen in recent years

have been those of dedicated amateurs. Amateurs may not be able to match the efficiency of a professional, but they often compensate with a greater enthusiasm. I've seen amateurs do things for love that you couldn't pay me to tackle. Because of the army of do-it-yourselfers, gardening has experienced a boom over the last decade. A Gallup survey in 1987 confirmed that gardening was the number-one outdoor activity in the United States, with sixty-nine million households participating. Throughout this same period, though, the scope of the individual planting has shrunk as professional staffs have disappeared. No single person, however compulsive, can maintain 8,500 rosebushes in his or her spare time. So the era of the great patron has passed.

I thought about this as I thanked Karl and went out for a stroll in his doomed garden. At the entrance to the parade ground of roses stood a covered wooden lectern; inside was a visitors' book. The entries testified to the impression the roses had made. "We came from across the state to look and see if the garden was still here and were very pleased to see that it is still beautiful and we'll be back to visit again," was the breathless promise of someone who perhaps, like me, had been following the garden's vicissitudes in the newspapers. A childish scrawl (but the hand of a high school graduate, I supposed) added:

> I love your roses
> they smell lovely
> You are nice to
> let people have
> ceremonies in your garden

Many of the entries struck a spiritual note. "God bless you for the joy you provided us today in your beautiful garden," the Super Sixties of Calvary Bible Church of Westport, Massachusetts had written. "Thank you and the dear Lord for such beauty," added a visitor from Salem, Arkansas. I wondered about the visitor from Fall River: "I love your rose garden—it's just like Heaven." Who was he, and how did he know?

While impressed by the religious zeal that the collector's garden had inspired, I wasn't surprised. I knew that many great collectors of the past had regarded their work not as a hobby but as a crusade. Indeed, the greatest of them all, the man who set the pattern for Karl Jones and all the other great patrons of the rose, had been a missionary by profession—an Anglican dean who turned his garden into a living sermon.

His name was Samuel Reynolds Hole, and as Dean of Rochester he presided for almost two decades over that busy provincial city's cathedral. He was well situated to grow roses there; Rochester lies in Kent, the county that has long been known as "the garden of England." Its soils are fertile, its winters mild and the rainfall regular but not excessive: twenty-five to thirty inches a year, a third less than Devon or Cornwall. More important for the rose grower is the four and a half hours of sunlight the Kentish countryside receives on average each day, an exceptional ration by English standards. Even without nature's encouragement, though, Dean Hole would certainly have grown roses.

In many respects he was the quintessential English country gentleman. Born in 1819, the same year as Queen Victoria, Hole was the only son of a wealthy Nottinghamshire squire. His boyhood in the rural village of Caunton was devoted to the pursuits of his class: hunting, shooting, archery, bowls, and, of course, cricket. Though he grew up in the midst of gardens, he showed little interest in horticulture as a boy. By his own account, his early visits to the garden were both hasty and surreptitious. Slipping through the garden gate, he stole in to raid the orchard and bait his father's gardener, Mr. Evans. The results of these exploits were not happy—he recalled later that he paid each time with indigestion and a severe scolding from his nanny.*

* This raises certain questions, obviously, about the fate of Karl Jones's old adversaries from the blueberry patch.

Hole seems to have spent the obligatory years at Oxford sharpening his skills as a raconteur and committing to memory an inexhaustible fund of Greek and Latin tags with which he would sprinkle his writings and stories for the rest of his life.* Upon graduation, he became infected with the piety of his age and took holy orders. But it was only after he had returned to his native village as a curate, he confessed in his memoirs, "that a brighter light dawned upon my darkness." Not born again, Hole had merely fallen in love, head over heels in love with a rose.

It happened, he recalled, as he was "sauntering in the garden one summer's evening with cigar and book," his mind lost in idle reverie. Suddenly a flower caught his eye, a perfect blossom of 'Rose d'Aguesseau,' a Gallica imported from France a decade previously in 1833. Bathed "in the splendour of the setting sun," the rose was a captivating sight, "the tints of vivid scarlet gleaming amid the purpler petals as light in jewels or in dark red wine."† Next evening, the young clergyman was back, this time armed with a pencil and Thomas Rivers's guide** to roses.

To the astonishment of his childhood adversary, the gar-

---

* In later life he came into great demand as an after-dinner speaker. The novelist William Makepeace Thackeray sponsored him for membership in the Garrick Club, and Hole was elected an honorary member of the weekly dinners given by the humorous magazine Punch—there, he noted with satisfaction, "the sparks of wit flew with such profusion as to form complete fireworks."
† I found 'Rose d'Aguesseau' in Graham Thomas's collection at Mottisfont Abbey. I arrived at the end of the Gallica roses' season, and all the shrub's blossoms had faded, save one. Crimson, quartered and flattened like a small shallow bowl, it was undeniably an elegant rose, but to me, nothing more.
** Rivers, the leading English rose nurseryman of the day, was cited in chapter 4 for his observations about French rose growers (see pages 98–99). Shortly before his death in 1857, Rivers paid Hole the compliment of sending the clergyman a copy of the last edition of his guide inscribed: "Once your master, now your pupil."

dener Evans, Hole ordered a dozen new bushes, taking personal responsibility for their planting and care. Rose catalogues became his constant companions, and his collection expanded at a dizzying rate, reaching a total of five thousand in a few years. Poor Evans must have looked on with mixed emotions. For though he could not but applaud the young master's conversion, the long-suffering gardener was powerless to prevent the swelling congregation from overrunning his asparagus bed.

From the beginning, Hole's aesthetic appreciation of the rose was reinforced by a belief in its powers of moral uplift. He took as his motto "He who would have beautiful roses in his garden must have beautiful roses in his heart." An interest in roses, he maintained, was a most effective means of combatting the degradation of the working class. "Get a man out of the dram and beer shops into the fresh, pure air," he preached, "interest him in the works of his God, instead of the deformities of vice, give him an occupation which will add to his health and the comfort of his family, instead of destroying both, then . . . hope to see him a Christian."

Nothing was too good for such flowers, Hole felt, an attitude that occasionally drew him into awkward situations. On one occasion, for example, he returned from a "parochial walk" to find that a visiting party's horse had left a pile of manure in his drive. As he rushed to the roses with this treasure, however, his jubilation turned to confusion, for in the garden he met the visitors, three ladies who were properly shocked to see the reverend gentleman loaded down with that unmentionable. In addition, the most difficult point of doctrine he ever faced was a direct result of his rose growing. The dilemma arose from a confession made by a Mrs. Lawrence about her Double Yellow Provence Rose.* Although a great beauty, this

---

* The nomenclature of this rose is more than ordinarily confusing. You find in old gardening books both a Rose of Provence and a Rose of Provins—despite the similarity of the names, these are very different flowers. Rose of Provence was the catch-all title of various Rosa centi-

rose was a shy bloomer—until Mrs. Lawrence's father, the Colonel, forced it by burying a fox at its roots. This plunged Hole into a quandary. While he applauded the result, he could not approve of the means for, as any gentleman knew, foxes were sacrosanct and their execution by anything other than a properly appointed hunt with horse and hounds was heresy. Deeply troubled, he had to content himself with the knowledge that the Colonel was "a great sportsman" and certainly no common "vulpicide."

Hole devoted much of his adult life to promoting the rose, publishing his own guide, *A Book About Roses,* in 1869. This, he assured his readers in the introduction, he had written "sans étude, and therefore sans humbug." It was a success from the first and developed into one of the all-time best-sellers of horticultural literature, running through at least thirty editions in the sixty-four years it remained in print. Hole's proudest achievement, though, was the founding of the Grand National Rose Show in 1858.

This was a project born of indignation. It outraged the dean that other plants, even "the vulgar, hairy Gooseberry," had their own exhibitions while the rose did not. Determined to remedy this injustice, he besought leading florists and nurserymen to finance a "feast of roses," an elevating occasion "at which the whole brotherhood might meet in love and unity." They responded with a gift of £200, and Hole rented St. James hall in London, hired the band of the Coldstream

---

folia *cultivars, flowers for which the southern French region of Provence was famous. Rose of Provins, on the other hand, was a common name of* Rosa gallica officinalis—*great quantities of this were cultivated near the city of Provins (thirty-five miles southeast of Paris) for the perfume industry. In any case, the Double Yellow Provence Rose is not closely related to either. It is a species rose,* Rosa hemisphaerica, *native to the Middle East. An exceptionally vigorous shrub that rapidly reaches a height of eight feet, it has the annoying habit of bearing abundant crops of yellowish green buds that in northern Europe rarely open. In a hot, dry Mediterranean-type climate the buds unfold to that rarity among old roses, a two-inch double blossom of bright, true yellow.*

Guards, and commissioned thirty-six silver cups to serve as prizes.

At five-thirty on the appointed day, trainloads of roses began arriving from all over England, ten thousand blossoms in all, as amateur and professional growers rushed to mount their displays. The occasion was judged a triumph. Dean Hole termed the scene "beautiful, exceedingly," and the reporter from *The Times* noted that the perfume from the flowers completely overwhelmed the stench of the Thames. To the dean's delight, his own entries won two cups and the show was adopted as an annual event.

In one respect, however, Dean Hole couldn't claim victory. Instead of the love fest he had anticipated, the show fostered a fierce and unscrupulous rivalry. In the scramble for prizes all sorts of sharp practices became common: rose-napping, flower counterfeiting and attempts at suborning of judges, to mention just a few. Yet the competition did have its positive aspects. Endless ingenuity was lavished on the problems of raising flawless roses. Eccentric fertilizers were compounded from bat guano, ground bones and malt; zinc caps were suspended over tender buds to ward off the sun; and revolving clockwork guns were manufactured which, when wound and loaded, fired blanks over the garden at regular intervals to frighten off birds and other intruders.

The publicity resulting from the shows also helped to make the rose even more popular among the well-to-do. The possession of prize-winning roses became a mark of real distinction, and a well-appointed rose garden as essential an appurtenance of the gentleman's equipage as a well-appointed cellar. The dean, however, seems to have felt more at home among gardeners of less pretension. He wrote with genuine delight of a rose show he had been invited to judge in a working-class district of Nottingham; and contemporaries testify that his imposing voice and physique (he stood six feet, three inches), his genial manner and readiness with a pun or joke made him a favorite with the common man. But Hole would proselytize wherever he found a listener. His converts ranged from millionaires to laborers, as the rose assumed the title Hole had long believed it deserved, "Queen of Flowers."

Another effect of the shows that Hole could not have fore seen was the process of standardization they initiated. To judge between roses, it was necessary to establish criteria, to reduce the flowers to a formula. By 1889, a German publication had distinguished ten different forms (including, ominously, the "bomb-shaped") to which all double roses could, and therefore must, belong. Nonconformists disappeared from the catalogues as gardeners opted for proven champions.

Dean Hole did become aware of the losses by the end of his long career. In 1901, the last year of Victoria's reign and just three years before his own death, Hole reflected on the fate of the 478 varieties listed in the catalogue from which he had ordered his first dozen roses. Of all of them, only eleven were still on the market. With typically Victorian optimism, Hole believed the change must represent progress. "Will it be so with our [current] Roses when fifty more years have passed?" he asked the rosarians of 1901. "I believe, I hope so."

Dean Hole died in 1904; Karl Jones began feeding buckets of manure tea to his father's (Mr. Jones, Sr.'s) roses the following year. Karl watched Dean Hole's wish come true as one by one the old roses disappeared from the nursery catalogues. Many found a refuge in Karl's garden. Nurserymen of the current old-rose revival have told me that hillside in Barrington was a treasure-trove, and that Karl was always generous with cuttings. One spoke with real anguish of the things that disappeared with Karl's abdication.

I returned to Barrington after an interval of eighteen months, driving up in mid-autumn. This time I just pulled the car over on the shoulder of the road and got out for a look. The beds near the house were as spruce as ever, the bases of the bushes carefully hilled with soil to protect them from the coming frosts. But a blacktopped road, Jones Circle, cut into the hill below from a side street.

A sprinkler played on the lawn of a brand-new Colonial house and a sign advertised "Lots for Sale." Beyond, the trellises along which Karl Jones had trained his roses still stood, but they were choked with weeds and the canes tied to the wires were mostly dead. A red Rambler—it looked to me like 'Blaze'—reached up to lift its fiery blossoms above the overgrowth. It made a fine contrast to the wild white asters that were blooming around it. I wondered if Dean Hole would have had an apposite quotation from the classics; I didn't disturb Mr. Jones.

9

Indica fragrans

Black
Gardeners

Pam had made me promise not to wear my tweed cap or my loafers; they marked me as an outsider, and the older country people didn't care for them. She told me, too, that I shouldn't talk any more than was absolutely necessary—my Yankee accent might frighten Miss Lily Mae.* Besides, she probably wouldn't understand me and I surely wouldn't understand her. Pam said she would do the talking, and I was more than happy to agree. I'd been trying, unsuccessfully, to interview the black gardeners who have supplied so many roses to the old-rose revival. I was running out of leads and Miss Lily Mae looked like my last chance.

* Lily Mae is not this lady's name; but out of respect for her privacy, I have decided to conceal both her name and the location of her home.

We drove a long way down muddy dirt roads to get to her home. The white board-and-batten cottage was set well back from the road behind a neatly tended front yard. The silhouette of a flower was cut into the front gate, and within there was no lawn, just a clean expanse of packed earth interrupted here and there with a crepe myrtle, a crinum lily or a rose. This kind of "swept-yard" was an old cottage-gardener's tradition in Texas, Pam told me, though it was usually located to the rear of the house, where the family kept the chickens. There wasn't any sense in planting grass where the fowl would root it out. Miss Lily Mae doesn't keep chickens, but she keeps her front yard swept because that's the way her mother did it. She's quite proud (according to Pam) that she has kept the yard the same since she inherited the house in 1924.

I admired the row of 'Old Blush' roses arranged around the foundation. Miss Lily Mae had cultivated these as standards, clipping away the lower branches to encourage the formation of a trunk. These stood three or four feet high, a formal ball of foliage and flowers atop a thick weathered stem. Around the side there was a yellow Tea rose, Pam told me as we mounted the steps to the front porch. Pam called out "Miss Lily Mae!" After several minutes of waiting, we heard a noise inside, then nothing. Finally a middle-aged man walked out from behind the house to ask us what we wanted. We explained that we had come to visit Miss Lily Mae, whereupon our interrogator (he turned out to be her nephew) told us that she had looked out but hadn't recognized us, that she wasn't inviting us in. Pam asked him to give Miss Lily Mae her regards, and left a bush of 'Souvenir de la Malmaison' as a gift.

On the way back to the highway, Pam explained that, now in her mid-eighties, Miss Lily Mae was not well; she grows garlic for her high blood pressure, and she suffers from swelling in her limbs. Pam was sorry that I wasn't going to meet her, the last survivor of the elderly black women who had given Pam many of her best roses. Pam mourned that "all the old heads were going under," that Central Texas was seeing

the last of this skillful band of gardeners, that a generation
was passing on and that the younger generation in the black
community didn't seem interested in continuing this horticultural tradition. I had felt a moment of keen frustration on the
porch, but by now I was resigned. It seemed a fitting epitaph
to the chapter I had intended to write about black collectors.

All the collectors I know south of the Mason-Dixon Line, at
least those who have been hunting roses for more than a decade, have secured a large percentage of their roses from the
older women of the local black community. The story of these
women, I suspected, had to be among the most remarkable of
the old-rose revival. They guarded the roses through a time
when almost no one else cared, and very many cultivars survived solely through their efforts. According to friends like
Pam and Carl Cato who had known many members of this
special group, they usually didn't know the names or histories
of the flowers, they just knew they were beautiful. They hadn't
had any other object in view when they rooted a cutting than
the pleasure it might give themselves, their families, friends
and passers-by. Unlike their white counterparts, who won ribbons at flower shows and published their experiences in articles and books, these women had worked in anonymity all
their lives. Should I have been surprised that when a reporter
came to the door, they declined to answer?

Yet there were questions whose answers I wanted to know.
Why had these women shown such an unusual appreciation
of the old roses? I suspected that their perspicacity may have
been partly a by-product of prejudice. They hadn't been welcome at the horticultural society or the garden club, they hadn't
sat through the lectures about the latest trends in gardening,
they hadn't chatted over crustless sandwiches about the rose
they'd seen on their last trip to England. Unjust as this was,
it insulated the black gardeners from the distractions of fashion.* But this is merely supposition; what is fact is that these

* It occurs to me as I write this that the black rose fanciers may have
had meetings, formal or informal, to which the white community was

women consistently showed an instinctive good taste. For several generations they continued to prefer the enduring beauties of the classics to the quick thrill of novelty.

I had other questions. I wanted to know where the black
women had gotten their roses, how they had propagated them,
why they chose the particular cultivars they did. Had they
traded them back and forth among themselves? What did they
see in these flowers that they cherished when the rest of the
country was rooting them out? The collectors I asked for
names all agreed on one thing: I was at least a decade too
late. One and all they told me that the rosarians they knew in
the black community had died.

One of the few stable neighborhoods in my hometown of
Nyack, New York, is the black community that has inhabited
the same two dozen blocks as long as I can remember. Nyack
has experienced a wave of gentrification in the last twenty
years; what was once a sleepy, and admittedly shabby, little
river town has been profiled repeatedly in the real-estate section of the *New York Times*. The old Victorian houses have
been refurbished and painted gay colors, and the brick buildings at the town center have been turned into antique shops.
Property values have risen tremendously, but at the cost of
turning the town into a revolving door. People don't buy a
home now, they invest in a property, planning to sell it in a
few years to cash in on the appreciation. Only the black neigh-
borhood remains much as it was when I first knew it.

I've been through there looking for roses a few times, finding many but nothing really old. I did meet a young man who
is a rose grower, though. I asked him about his experiences
with this flower. He downplayed his skill as a gardener. It's
not a hobby, he told me, just something he learned from his
mother. "She's got a real green thumb." He lived with his
parents, and his mother supervised work in the yard. Later I
telephoned and spoke briefly to her. She told me about rooting

---

*not invited. This again is speculation; all I know for sure is that they
didn't abandon the old roses when nearly everyone else did.*

cuttings under fruit jars and shared her rose-growing skills willingly. But when I asked for an interview, she declined.

Maybe she smelled a taint of condescension in my questions. Maybe she felt I was intruding on her family's privacy. Still, I was disappointed, for I wanted to see her roses. Her son told of roses acquired as parting gifts from older neighbors who were retiring, selling their houses and returning to their families in the South. He recalled with regret a rose he and his mother had let slip through their fingers, one they had been offered in this way but hadn't had room to accommodate. After the neighbor sold her house, it had burned, but the rose survived. The contractors who rebuilt the house had dumped their rubbish on the rose, and still it survived. I wanted to know what kind of rose this was, but the young man couldn't tell me. I felt ashamed to press for a visit that his mother wouldn't welcome.

As an outsider I was reluctant to form any theories about what might be causing the black communities' apparent decline of interest in the old roses. All I had were scattered impressions anyway. So I was particularly interested by an article the *New York Times News Service* ran in September of 1988. This was the story of reporter E. R. Shipp's trip home to Georgia. Shipp (whom I presumed to be black, though the article didn't say) wrote of her visits to black neighborhoods that "retain enough of their former character to be listed as National Historic Districts."

"What the visitor sees," Shipp continued, "is not blocks of restored homes, but living, breathing neighborhoods, blemishes and all. These neighborhoods have remained intact through segregation, the civil rights movement and beyond." The article focussed on vestiges of the rich heritage black Americans maintained through segregation, despite economic injustice. It didn't mention old roses, though it could have. The article admitted that many of the old glories are decayed. Auburn Avenue, the two-mile strip in Atlanta that *Fortune* magazine once described as "the richest Negro Street in the world," has grown "seedy."

"When the civil rights movement opened new sectors to blacks," Shipp explained, "many abandoned the old neighborhoods, leaving behind tawdry mom-and-pop grocery stores, liquor stores, taverns, barber shops." With these, they also left behind some of the world's finest roses, flowers that they had saved from extinction. The buildings survive, but the rosebushes are fast disappearing. Some of the women who grew them are memorialized in study names. "Miss Mary Minor," for example, a superb rose, a three-foot-tall bush that bears large flat quartered blossoms of white with a heart of flesh-pink, has kept that woman's memory fresh for Pam, though she died in 1986. As the roses' "real" names are rediscovered, however, even this paltry tribute fades. In the same year as its donor's death, "Miss Mary Minor" was identified as 'Souvenir de la Malmaison,' a French-bred Bourbon rose of 1843. Subsequently, all mention of Miss Mary disappeared from the Antique Rose Emporium catalogue (though it was her rose Pam brought as a gift to Lily Mae). But then, I doubt Miss Mary would have minded.

10

Bourbon rose

"Thank God
for the
Tax
Deductions"

IT'S NOT EASY to buy roses from Mike Lowe. Mike (though his name is Malcolm, I've never heard him referred to as anything but Mike) does operate a nursery. He circulates a mail-order catalogue, a typewritten brochure entitled, succinctly, "Lowe's Own Root Roses." But by the standards of most competitors even in the old-rose business, his sales are insignificant, less than two thousand bushes a year. And these he grows only to order. If you want one of his roses—and he offers varieties available nowhere else in the United States—you must contact him eighteen months in advance. Then wait and hope. Because if the temperature should dip to twenty below, as it not uncommonly does in Nashua, New Hampshire, then the cold

may damage the roses and you'll be back to square one. Mike
Lowe won't ship anything but first-quality stock.

I'd known of Mike's nursery since 1983, its third year. I'd
discovered it in the course of researching an article about
Rugosa roses, a rugged breed of shrubs that thrive, in the wild,
along seacoasts.* Most nurseries offered only two Rugosas,
wild types: a simple wine-purple blossom and a white-flowering
strain. Mike listed ten, not the largest selection I'd found but
certainly the choicest. There was 'Rose à Parfum de l'Hay,' a
cultivar claimed by some as the most fragrant of roses; 'Mrs.
Anthony Waterer,' a vivid crimson named by an English
breeder for his wife; and an oddity, 'Martin Frobisher,' a rose
old in appearance and lineage but modern by birth, since it
dated only to 1968. Nor was Mike afraid to take issue with
the pundits. 'Blanc Double de Coubert' is probably the most
prestigious of the hybrid Rugosas—no less a personage than
Gertrude Jekyll recommended it to her disciples as "the whit-
est rose known." Mike did not and will not grow it. He doesn't
like the way the rose fades—spent petals hanging on the stems
like rags, a dirty habit.

I had arranged to visit the nursery on a Saturday in late
June, and though I'd called him for directions, I lost my way
in the maze of new streets around Mike's house. When I
pulled over to the curb to check the directions against my
map, another car paused to offer help. I explained my errand,
and the other driver announced: "I'm Mike Lowe, follow me."

I spent the rest of the afternoon doing just that. A middle-
sized, middle-aged man, Mike is possessed by a restless energy
that in the course of our four hours together never let him
pause for more than a moment. Perpetually busy with one task
after another, Mike accompanied himself with a continual

* I had used them to landscape along a parking lot, suspecting that
they would adapt better than most shrubs to the poor sandy soil of the
roadside. In fact they flourished; the salt the groundsmen spread across
the pavement in wintertime to melt the ice killed almost everything
else, but it seemed to evoke only nostalgia in my Rugosa roses.

flow of observations, reminiscences and speculations. He admitted that he loves to talk. But then he has a lot to say.

It was Lily Shohan who urged him into the nursery business; he's a microwave engineer, he told me with a machine-gun delivery. He's been doing that for thirty years, collecting roses for only about twenty-five. Collecting heavily only for the last twenty years—"and we lost everything nine years ago."

Bad winter? I asked. "No, bad builder," he replied.

"It had nothing to do with the winter," Mike told me, simultaneously sorting his mail, eating a sandwich and sipping a beer (I'd met Mike on his way home from a flower show and he was relaxing from the stress of staging an exhibit). "Builder was building us a house. He was supposed to row everything out in a field." (That is, the builder had agreed to plant Mike's bushes in regular nursery rows; Mike wouldn't move without taking his collection along.) "A-n-d he didn't row everything out in a field, a-n-d it ended up in pots sitting in the field, all the plants. Then he went bankrupt. Out of four hundred plants, we had fifty left."

"That must have broken your heart," I commiserated. Mike dismissed my sympathy with a wave of his hand as he took another bite from his sandwich and reached for another letter. "Yeah, but I was already propagating, we were going to start a nursery over in Hudson, Hudson County. That's where we were going to move. I had been propagating and handing out plants for years, so I just called up everybody and said, hey, I want a piece of everything I gave you. It took me about two years to put it all back together, which wasn't too bad.

"It was the rare stuff, actually, the rare stuff was the stuff I didn't lose because those roses were in greenhouses. You know, people had them in greenhouses so it was easier for them to send me things like that. Lily keeps them all indoors; have you been to her house? She had most of the Teas and Chinas, and *she* was the one who was trying to get me to go into the nursery business, so I said, hey, I need my stock back."

How old is the nursery?

"I guess this is the fifth or sixth year." Mike paused to sneeze; he's got an allergy to pollen, he explained with a laugh. "But we've been growing roses forever, or it seems like it. Actually we had a tract out even before we were officially a nursery. Just a little piece of paper that said we had these roses; if anyone wanted them, we'd propagate them. Yeah, we lose money." Mike laughed. "We don't make any money."

How had he reacted, I wanted to know, when Lily encouraged him to start a mail-order nursery?

"How do you react?" Mike mused. "It's a nice idea. Can I afford to do it? Can I make money at it? Even if I can't make money at it, how much is it going to cost me? Is it going to help me in what I'm doing?"

It has helped Mike in his pursuit of old roses. The nursery hadn't yet shown a profit by the date of my visit, but that, I suspected, was because income from sales has been plowed back into expanding the collection. "Thank God for the tax deductions," Mike confided, fishing a bill from an envelope and setting it to one side. "If I didn't have them, I'd really be in trouble." Nursery work has provided an excuse, too, to broaden the scope of his hunting from local to international.

When Mike first developed an interest in old roses, he began his scouting through a network of neighbors. There was the elderly woman who lived in a trailer over in Lebanon. Along with the religious tracts she used to send him, she provided fifteen unidentified roses she'd collected over a period of forty years. Mike had identified eight and was still working on the others. There was also a member of the local rose society, a man whose primary interest was in modern roses but who used to stop by from time to time with a "found" rose that he had rooted. "Here," he'd tell Mike, "try this." It was he who gave Mike his first specimen of 'American Beauty,' the old florist's rose. He also furnished a start of a spiny bush of delicate fernlike foliage that bore sweet-scented large blush-colored roses intermittently throughout the summer and fall. This proved to be 'Stanwell Perpetual,' a rose that like 'Harison's Yellow' seems to have been a spontaneous hybrid of the Scotch Briar, *R. spinosissima;* when introduced in 1838, its "perpetual" bloom earned it widespread notoriety, though it was soon eclipsed by the emergence of the Hybrid Perpetuals.

When roses were a hobby, the farthest afield Mike travelled was Beltsville, Maryland, where he'd gone to explore an old collection established and then abandoned by the Department of Agriculture. But since roses have become his business, he's followed Lambertus Bobbink's example by ordering collections from France, and even farther off in Denmark. ("They were Tea roses," he marvelled of the Danish shrubs. "Who would grow Tea roses that far north?") He has also flown to Britain to confer with his friend Peter Beales, one of that nation's leading old-rose nurserymen.

Many of his discussions with Peter Beales (author of *Classic Roses,* a beautifully illustrated, very substantial volume that furnishes the closest thing there is to an old-rose textbook) have centered on the identity of various roses. That, of course, is the inevitable result when two collectors meet. Often according to Mike, he can type a rose's identity just by turning the blossom over to study the calyx (the cup from which the petals spring). The shape of the calyx can vary widely, and it's common knowledge among rose taxonomists that each species of rose, and often particular varieties, have calyxes of a characteristic form. Mike's skill in recognizing these comes from his nursery work. Each time he makes a cutting, he must turn the length of cane upside down to trim the base with his knife; after surveying tens of thousands of rose bottoms, he has an index in his head. Indeed, he's much in demand for that very reason. When I visited him, he told me that he was recently returned from a trip to the Brooklyn Botanic Garden, where he'd helped the rose curator sort out the labelling of his display. Before that, he'd been to the Hershey Gardens, a notable rose garden in Hershey, Pennsylvania, and to a private garden in Washington, D.C. From each of these trips he returned loaded with cuttings, 120 from Brooklyn alone.

Mike calculated that he had 500 to 600 varieties, and a total of 4,000 bushes (give or take a few) in the double lot around his house, but that's not a big collection by his standards; he began collecting as a protégé of Karl Jones. Mike told me that Karl, who persists in calling him "the kid," provided him with many rarities. Then, handing me a beer and grabbing another for himself, Mike took me out to see.

Tomorrow was to be the nursery's annual open house, and Mike was determined that his roses should look their best. He complained of the blackspot* infesting their leaves, though I could see hardly a trace of the telltale black blemishes. In fact he contented himself with snipping only an occasional leaf as we passed up and down the beds. Striding along on his tour of inspection, Mike demonstrated a bedside manner that would shame Marcus Welby. He addressed each rose by name, commenting on its condition and alternating stern or affectionate remarks as the occasion demanded. One bush he threatened to dig out if it let another summer slip by without a bloom; another, a more forthcoming variety, he spoke to quite differently:

"Isn't that wild? Did you ever see anything so lovely? Oh, look at that hiding in there! Isn't it gaudy? Knocks your socks off. Oh, and there's 'Arthur de Sansal' . . . which is turning out to be a real dog. Don't matter what I do, no matter what I do, no matter how many bushes I get of it, I just can't get any vigor out of it at all. Look at that—guy by the name of O'Neal did that, and he died. So they call it 'O'Neal's Bequest.' No-

---

* Diplocarpon rosae, *while treatable and rarely fatal, is one of the most fiendish diseases to attack cultivated roses. The fungus establishes ring-shaped sooty colonies on both top and bottom of the rose leaves; these release ethylene gas, a substance used commercially in the artificial ripening of tomatoes and other fruits. In roses, the ethylene causes the bush to shed its leaves prematurely. A heavy infection of blackspot can entirely defoliate a rosebush by midsummer, and though the plant will usually return with another, somewhat sparser crop of leaves, it may lack the strength to survive the following winter. There is no cure for blackspot, though it can be suppressed by spraying the bush with an appropriate fungicide at weekly intervals throughout the growing season.*

body wanted to introduce it, so I said, hey, I'll take it. I love anything that's got yellow and red edges. Isn't it pretty? Isn't that a pretty little rose? Hey, it's going to be in my garden. Here's something from Karl's garden. Karl didn't even know what it was—call it our 'Unknown Yellow.' It's getting big enough that I should do something."

Several beds were set apart; these were recent imports which by Federal regulation Mike must keep in quarantine for two years. Dropping to his knees, he searched unsuccessfully for two cuttings of Dean Hole's beloved 'Rose d'Aguesseau.' Both had been trampled by the neighbor's son, who has run a short-cut through Mike's side yard. "What the hell, kids got to live too," he muttered dubiously.

Farther on, we stopped to inspect a bed of "old-fashioned-type" roses that the English nurseryman David Austin has been breeding. Austin, the creator of the 'Graham Thomas' rose (see p. 29),* aims to combine the old-rose form and fragrance with a more everblooming habit, and a wider range

---

* I had the good fortune later to visit David Austin at his nursery in Wolverhampton. I found him out in his rose field, a short, stocky man in the well-worn tweed jacket and rubber boots that are the traditional (and in an English climate, very practical) garb of the English farmer. He told me that he had entered rose growing because the R.A.F. had condemned half the family farm for use as an airfield. The remaining acreage couldn't produce enough grain to support him so he turned to the production of old roses, an interest he had long shared with his friend Graham Thomas. On the day of my visit he was choosing which of his new, and as yet unnamed, roses he would present at that year's Chelsea Flower Show (an event that traditionally opens with a visit from the royal family, this show's prestige is enormous; good reviews at Chelsea can make the reputation of a new introduction). He told me of the creation of this line, of the crosses he had made between modern everblooming roses and old recurrent classics like the Portlands. Austin did not promote his introductions as a substitute for the old roses (he continues to grow one of the world's most extensive selection of those). He calls the new cultivars "English Roses" and bills them as "New Roses in the Old Tradition." I found them a graceful tribute, rather like a new arrangement of an old air. I plan to install several in my garden as soon as Mr. Austin settles on an American distributor.

of colors. Mike admires Austin's roses and showed me several around the garden: 'Wife of Bath,' with its smallish pink blossoms of an authentic cupped pattern; 'The Squire,' cupped blossoms, too, but larger and of darkest crimson; and 'The Reeve,' pink globes with the authentic old-rose fragrance. Named for characters from the *Canterbury Tales* (Austin has since moved on from that conceit), these were undeniably beautiful flowers, but even if they kept their place in Mike's garden, I knew they wouldn't find space in his catalogue. Mike admitted that he, too, raises an occasional seedling, but only for his own amusement. Such roses have no history, and as Mike observed, "What do you do with a Gallica introduced in 1986?"

If Mike didn't wholeheartedly endorse David Austin's experiment, it is not because he resists progress. He is interested in the prospect of a truly blue rose. I mentioned the story of Alexander Dickson's rose (see p. 21), but Mike dismissed it as fable. A gardener in twelfth-century Damascus used to show visitors his blue rose, a blossom "the color of zulite" (celestial blue), but a Spanish Moor, Ibn el Awam, exposed him in his *Book of Agriculture*: the charlatan irrigated his bush with a mixture of indigo and water. More recently, in 1986, Professor Griffith Buck of Iowa State University patented a rose called 'Blue Skies' which observers have described as having "a decidedly blue hue"—on the color chart of the Royal Horticultural Society it registers as heliotrope blue, a brilliant violet shading to deep purplish red. This is not true blue; Buck himself puts the word blue in quotes when he describes his creation. But it is impossible that Buck, who relies on conventional methods of hybridization and selection, should ever arrive at that. As previously noted (see footnote, p. 21), the rose lacks the genetic coding to manufacture delphinidin, the pigment that gives blue flowers their hue.

Mike Lowe pointed out that this should present no insurmountable problems to a genetic engineer, since he or she could remove the genes governing the production of that pig-

ment from another blue flower, a petunia, say, and splice
them into a rose. And later, in California I met a man who
talks of doing just that.

This was Luca Comai, a young Italian plant molecular biol-
ogist who works for Calgene, a genetic-engineering firm that
is headquartered in Davis, down the street from the University of California's agricultural school. "Biotechnology," he
told me, "is really more advanced than people think." So it is,
for what he told me in his precise, low-key manner set my
imagination racing.

I had read in a gardening magazine of Calgene's determination to produce the first blue rose; the reporter had recognized
this as juicy copy, composing his brief article in the style of
pulp science fiction. Dr. Comai obviously found this distaste-
ful, and he strove to put the matter in perspective. Actually,
he told me, the blue rose was just part of a larger project, one
in which he was helping a Calgene affiliate, Calgene Pacific
(based in Victoria, Australia) develop the technology to engineer the color of all sorts of flowers. And this, of course, was
only a minor part of the firm's activities.

The picture of these that emerged from Dr. Comai's descriptions and from the annual report that he gave me were,
quite simply, amazing. With a research staff of 143, including
80 research scientists, and an annual research and development budget of $7.6 million, Calgene was taking steps to
change our world in not-so-subtle ways. In partnership with
Nippon Steel, the company was modifying rapeseed (a plant
of the mustard family whose seed contains as much as 40 percent oil by weight) to produce a variety of lubricants for special industrial applications (the exact nature of these was not
for publication, unfortunately). The firm was also working
with food companies to produce edible rapeseed oils that
would be especially low in saturated fats. Calgene had harvested 1.2 million pounds of oils that year. Yet it cited as the
year's major achievement a successful field trial of BromoTol®.

BromoTol® is a gene so special that Calgene has patented

it. If inserted into the genetic material of a plant, it confers a tolerance to the herbicide bromoxynil. In practice, Calgene has found that it makes tomato and tobacco plants immune to a dosage ten times the recommended application rate. With BromoTol®-equipped plants, a farmer could weed fields chemically even after planting his crops. Another gene, GlyphoTol®, confers a similar tolerance for another popular herbicide, glyphosate. Despite a personal distaste for chemical gardening, I could see how important Calgene's products could be to farmers, to whom weeds spell significant losses in crop size and quality, and often the difference between profit and loss.

Dr. Comai spoke of altering the ripening properties of tomatoes, to make the fruit ripen more slowly so that a truly vine-ripened fruit would survive the trip to the supermarket, spend an interlude on the produce-department shelves and still arrive on the dinner table in a condition more appetizing than the present product. He spoke of transforming cotton, tomatoes, flax and corn to make them more pest-resistant. He told me that color had already been engineered in petunias, on an experimental basis, with the production of a brick-red blossom, a color that does not naturally occur in this flower. Roses, however, were proving recalcitrant.

He stood at a blackboard, outlining the chemical structure of rose pigments, trying to make me understand the difficulties of the situation. Yes, one could transplant the biosynthetic pathway for delphinidin from another plant, but that was not necessary. Actually, only a single enzyme was lacking in the rose's pigment-manufacturing pathway. This enzyme, apparently, is all that is needed to add an extra hydroxyl group to pigments that the rose already manufactures and to convert them to delphinidins. All that, as he observed, is known. He saw no special difficulties in cloning the genetic coding for that enzyme before too long.

The real problem lay in "transforming" the rose, in introducing the new genetic material into a cell and then persuading that one cell to grow into a complete plant. They had mastered this process in other crops—rapeseed, tobacco, etc.—but not yet in roses. While "micropropagation," test-tube propagation of a new plant from a small piece of the parent plant's tissue, is a well-established technique, no one has yet mastered the more difficult task of regenerating a rosebush from a single cell. Though he expected to be producing blue flowers, carnations for example, before too long, Dr. Comai admitted that the blue rose lay farther in the future. How long would it be? Conceivably, he said, it could take ten years. I thought of the centuries that this quest had already exhausted, of the twenty-five years that Dr. Buck of Iowa State specified as the minimum time necessary to start a rose-breeding program, but said nothing.

As he took me around the lab, I noticed that Dr. Comai's running shoes, jeans and tee shirt were effectively the employee uniform (though the technicians all wore white lab coats as well). Yet the atmosphere was hardly casual; we passed through room after room—"A maze, isn't it?"—of fluorescently lit glassware and instruments, gleaming and sterile; racks of petri dishes in which plantlets sprang from plugs of tissue. Dr. Comai commented that within ten years scientists should have a battery of genes that would allow them to "tune" the production of pigments within a flower, generating hundreds of different-hued blossoms from a single plant variety. This would not threaten the role of the traditional plant breeder, he emphasized. It would be merely "an extension" of traditional techniques, a means of providing breeders with new germ plasm.

"Right now breeders might be somewhat uneasy because they don't understand how this extension is going to work." Does anyone? I wondered. "The breeders who have the ability to grasp what this new technology is going to provide," he insisted, "are really enthusiastic."

Mike Lowe hadn't seemed especially excited about genetic engineering on the day of my visit, but he had been very interested in that other aspect of the new technology, micropropagation. As we toured his roses, he talked at length about the potential of this technique. Even in its present crude state, it could prove a very useful tool in the rescue of old varieties.

I had seen at Calgene how an "explant" is taken from the parent plant and placed on a bed of nutrient medium, either liquid or agar jelly, inside a sterile sealed petri dish or flask. Classically, the explant is taken from the meristem (the actively dividing, growing cells) of a bud, but it may come as well from many other parts of the plant: shoot or root tips, stems, seeds, leaves, embryos, pollen grains and even flowers have served as a source of explants. If the explant finds conditions within its laboratory home congenial, the light of the right wavelengths and the right number of foot candles, the temperature not too hot, not too cold, then it may begin to grow. For growth to proceed, however, the nutrient medium must be properly nourishing. The recipe for this may include not only minerals but also vitamins, plant-growth regulators, and organic complexes such as coconut milk or yeast extract— the requirements change not only from species to species but from cultivar to cultivar, and depend also on the type of explant, so that the preparation of media demands a skill equal to that of a Cordon Bleu chef.

Initially, growth is apt to take the form of callus, a rather uninspiring blob of undifferentiated juvenile cells, from which will spring (again, if all goes right) small shoots of new plants. Each of these should be genetically identical to the parent, unless one of the cells that engendered it should have chanced to mutate (in practice, such an event is very rare). When the shoots reach a size sufficient to tolerate disturbance—this too varies from cultivar to cultivar—they may be separated from the explant with a sterile knife and transferred to their own test tubes. As roots develop and the shoots develop into full-fledged plantlets, they are transplanted to containers filled with growing mixtures composed of peat and perlite (a feather-light, water-absorbent but sterile volcanic rock); after a gradual induction to the stress of a normal environment—a process that gardeners call, appropriately enough, "hardening off"—the micropropagated plant is ready for sale.

Obviously, micropropagation is a more involved process than rooting a stem cutting, and it requires a bit more precision on the part of the grower. Sloppiness in preparing cuttings will reduce the percentage of "take"; in micropropagation, it generally results in contamination of the growing medium by bacteria, yeasts, molds, etc., and the death of the explant. But if it is more exacting, micropropagation also offers unique benefits. Propagation by cuttings or by grafting makes heavy demands upon the parent plant. Taking a cutting or a scion significantly reduces the size of the parent and can result only in one offspring. An explant is usually smaller and, properly managed, can produce literally thousands of offspring. With chrysanthemums, for example, it is technically feasible to produce a billion plantlets from a single shoot tip in the space of one year.

Furthermore, micropropagation offers the best means of cleansing bacteria- and virus-infected stock. No one seems to know exactly why, but even in the case of an infected parent, explants taken from apical meristem (the actively dividing cells in the plant's topmost, dominant bud) yield pathogen-free plantlets. Scientists speculate that a high concentration of growth regulators in the meristem deactivates invading bacteria and viruses, or that the bud's dividing cells somehow compete with the pathogens, preventing their replication; whatever the reason, even a thoroughly debilitated plant will produce healthy offspring through this particular type of micropropagation. As a result, micropropagation (or mericloning as it is also known) now accounts for the majority of nursery-grown orchids and is playing an increasing role in the production of strawberry plants, chrysanthemums, garlic, potatoes, dahlias, lilies and carnations—all crops that are normally propagated vegetatively, by cuttings or divisions, and in which viral or bacterial infections were formerly endemic. The ap-

plication to roses is obvious, and in fact experiments with
micropropagating roses began in the 1970s. Researchers have
found that because of the diversity of roses' genetic background, because of the many different species that contributed
to the modern rose, the techniques and formulas that must be
used vary widely from variety to variety, and that whereas
some popular types lend themselves to micropropagation,
many don't. To date, no major grower has made the new
science the basis of his production. I've spoken to only one,
Jack Walter of Grand Saline, Texas, who has even tried.

Jack raised old roses for a while, not from conviction but
because an old-rose nursery contracted with him to do their
propagation. Currently, he works mostly with miniature roses;
his company, Kimbrew-Walter Roses, is one of the biggest
producers of miniatures in Texas, listing more than 100 different cultivars. He was out digging roses the day I called. It
was mid-January; in a few weeks spring would arrive in Texas,
and gardeners would begin dropping by the garden centers to
see what the new season had brought. Jack's wife told me he
worked till 7:00 P.M. this time of year, and that I should call
in the evening. Not this evening, though, because Jack was
going to address a local rose society. We settled on the following night.

Jack proved to be a cheerful man, one whose enthusiasm for
roses had survived the long hours unaffected. He told me that
he had spent nearly $25,000 to equip a micropropagation lab-
oratory six years ago, and that it had been three since he used
it. He was growing full-sized modern garden roses then, and
his hope had been that through micropropagation he could reduce both the labor and the time required to produce a crop.
The savings in labor had been minimal, however, and the
harvest had been roses that, to a Texan, looked dangerously
like runts. Grafting is the method of propagation he favors for
roses: "When we bud them in the field, we get canes after two
years that are as big as your thumb, and not just one to the

plant, but several to the plant, 'cause that's what makes our grade number one."* After the same length of time, his micropropagated bushes had yet to produce a cane as big as his pinkie.

With time, Jack felt sure his micropropagated roses would have caught up, but no one wanted to buy them. As he observed, "People think bigger is better," especially in Texas. That's why he dropped micropropagation. He agreed that the technique's ability to produce disease-free stock was attractive, but only to a grower who wasn't driven by the need for profit.

Operating a nonprofit institution isn't Mike Lowe's goal, either, but nevertheless, he wasn't ready to write off micropropagation. He hoped that it would reinvigorate 'Maréchal Niel' and other virus-infected old clones. As a New Englander he was also intrigued by experiments that have shown that such clean stock is far more tolerant of cold, at least initially. Microbiologists have discovered that common plant-dwelling bacteria, *Pseudomonas,* produce proteins that act as "seeds," or nuclei, for ice crystals. By facilitating crystal formation, the bacteria make the host plants more vulnerable to frost damage. Produce a bacteria-free rose, and you've got a bush that can tolerate significantly lower temperatures, at least until it is reinfected by *Pseudomonas* from the surrounding environment.†

---

* *Nurserymen classify roses by size into three grades: number one (the largest), number one and one half, and number two. Anything smaller than number two roses, Jack Walter told me, has "canes as big as a straw"—he normally discards these as worthless. Most of his micropropagated roses fell into this grade.*

† *These bacteria have served as the focus of one of genetic engineering's bitterest battles. Steven Lindow, the plant pathologist who discovered the microorganism's role in frost damage in 1976, began working to engineer a strain of bacteria that could not produce the crystal-seeding protein. By deleting from Pseudomonas the gene that blueprints the protein, he eventually produced what he called an "ice-minus bacterium." He tested this inside a greenhouse by spraying thousands of different plants with an ice-minus culture; this did indeed help normally susceptible species resist frost damage even when air temperatures dipped well below freezing, as low as 23° F. When*

Mike admitted, however, that pathogen-free stock will not be an unmitigated blessing.

"I mean, you're going to lose some of the striped roses, they're going to lose their stripes, because it's a virus that causes the stripes. Not in all varieties, but in some of them. You are going to lose the spots on some of the roses." He took me to a Moss rose in one corner of the garden. 'Ma Ponctuée' was its name, and sure enough the leaves and pink blossoms were punctuated, pleasantly freckled with dark spots. "If you take the virus out of it," Mike explained as he picked a blossom, "it'll lose the mottled flowers and the mottled foliage, and you'll have just a plain old pink Moss rose."*

"So you lose something to get something," he continued, and made his way across the garden, pinching spent blossoms from the bushes, snipping off the odd yellowed leaf. He pointed to a bed perhaps seventy-five feet long by a hundred feet wide. "This is the nursery field. There are two thousand plants in there, probably less than that, probably sixteen hundred this year. You can see the frost pockets where the frost hit the roses. 'Specially down there, over in that corner. I don't know why. The Hybrid Perpetuals got wiped out this year. I had a lot of orders for Hybrid Perpetuals, and I'm going to have nothing. These are Albas. . . . Albas? Oh, I've got more plants than I usually have. I usually have around a hundred,

---

he tried to test the ice-minus bacterium outdoors, however, he encountered a storm of protests and lawsuits that delayed the experiment for more than three years. His company, Advanced Genetic Research of Oakland, California, spent $600,000 on environmental impact studies and legal fees before securing permission from the Environmental Protection Agency and the community of Brentwood to treat an acre of strawberries. As Lindow predicted, the new bacterium did not migrate outside the treated plot, and it did make the strawberry blossoms more resistant to freezing. The cost of securing permits and the cooperation of local populations, however, threatens to scuttle a product that could save American fruit growers hundreds of millions of dollars annually.
* I have been reassured by other rosarians that, to date, no rose has lost its stripes or spots when purged of viruses.

I got about a hundred and twenty. Bourbons?" He turned to address a young woman who had come from Connecticut to see his roses. "Want Bourbons? I got extras. Boy, have I got Bourbons this year. I'll drink to that." And with a mocking smile, he raised his beer can in salute to the roses.

11

American
Beauty

Moss rose

On November 20, 1986, President Ronald Reagan signed Proclamation 5574, officially recognizing the rose as the national floral emblem of the United States. In doing so, he was simply complying with a resolution the Senate and the House of Representatives had passed two months earlier.* Neverthe-

---

* *The rose was adopted only after much Congressional wrangling. The debate about a national flower began in the late nineteenth century, with various Congressmen proposing the mountain laurel, the columbine, the carnation and many other flowers in addition to the rose. The late Senator Everett Dirksen of Illinois became notorious for his annual sponsoring of a resolution to make the marigold the national flower; my own sympathies lay with John Kyle, a representative from Iowa who fought in the mid-1960s to reserve that honor for the corn*

less, the presidential proclamation is an interesting document. In it, the President cited fossils that reveal the rose to have "existed in America for age upon age." That is true. "We have always cultivated roses in our gardens"—that, too, is fact. "Our first President, George Washington, bred roses, and a variety he named after his mother is still grown today." Here he began to stray from history into folklore. There is a rose known as 'Mary Washington' that has grown at Mount Vernon for many years, a vigorous Noisette, exceptionally hardy for this class, that bears large clusters of very double white blossoms. No one knows its origin, but it can't be traced back past 1891, and it surely cannot be the work of George Washington. The first Noisette, 'Champneys' Pink Cluster,' didn't appear until 1811, twelve years after the first President's death.

As a writer, I understand how easy it is to turn a good and convenient story into fact. Besides, in the case of roses, it is often hard, or even impossible, to separate truth from fiction, to winnow out all the legends, myths, fantasies and outright lies. This is particularly difficult in cases that relate to the garden rose's American heritage. Our horticultural patriots have been so anxious to claim this flower as our own that they have been manufacturing pedigrees for more than two centuries.

This is not to say that there aren't many genuinely American roses. Relatively few, however, fit the category of old roses. A generation after John Champneys, in 1836, two Baltimore

---

tassel. *The rose always led the popularity polls, but even so, its partisans were reduced to a bit of skullduggery to win their campaign. Their resolution was passed hastily through the Senate on Rosh Hashanah, when many opponents were absent. One aide to a pro-rose Congressman had the misfortune to call the New York Botanical Garden Library in search of evidence to support this choice. As it happened, his call was answered by an English librarian who promptly told him off. Did he know that the rose has been the symbol of England for more than five hundred years? she asked. Did he know that the rose was also the symbol of five other countries, the bulk of whom lay behind the Iron Curtain? The rose was a stupid choice, she told him, and then, very efficiently I'm sure, got him the material he needed.*

florists, John and Samuel Feast, began producing hybrids from our wild Prairie Rose (*Rosa setigera*). Their climbers, 'Baltimore Belle' and 'Queen of the Prairies' (both introduced in 1843), still make an occasional appearance in old-rose displays at flower shows. Old nursery catalogues list numbers of other "Prairie" or "Michigan" roses, but these seem to have universally disappeared. Many of the early American breeders would likewise be forgotten if H. B. Ellwanger, a Rochester, New York, nurseryman, hadn't included their names in *The Rose*, the horticultural handbook he published in 1882.

This book marks a milestone, for in it Ellwanger not only describes his own efforts to introduce fine roses into American gardens, he reveals the existence of a young but well-established rose-growing industry. In his chapter "Raisers of the Best Roses," he includes seven Americans; he makes clear, though, that none of them could compete in output with their European colleagues. The leading American contender, the Feast brothers, had produced only three roses Ellwanger thought worthy of mention (in addition to the two roses I have already cited, the author included 'Anna Maria,' a "Prairie Rose" that has disappeared without a trace). By contrast, François Lacharme of Lyon, France, had twenty-one entries. More to the point, when the time came to rank the breeders in order of merit, Ellwanger didn't even include his countrymen. In a monograph on the subject of American roses that he published in *The Gardener's Monthly* of September 1880, Ellwanger felt obliged to close with a long list of American apples, peaches, cherries and plums, to soften the blow to the American reader's self-esteem. He rightly observed that "In the production of roses, instead of having exhausted the field, we have only just entered it; the future possibilities open to the raiser of new roses are only dawning upon us."

Indeed, by the turn of the century, American hybridizers like Dr. Walter Van Fleet and M. H. Walsh were introducing roses that were best-sellers in Europe as well as at home. I came to know 'American Pillar,' Van Fleet's Rambler of 1902, because it blankets an arbor on the old Lamont estate, but I found it clambering just as vigorously up the half-timbered cottage I stayed in at Mottisfont, in England. Jackson & Perkins, the giant rose nursery now headquartered in Oregon, scored one of their early successes in 1901 with the pink-flowered Rambler 'Dorothy Perkins'; look in the literature of the Edwardian era and you'll find English gardeners complaining of the horticultural cliché that rose had become. The United States moved quickly to the forefront of rose breeding in those years, a position it enjoys today, but that story belongs to modern roses and has little to do with this book.

What nineteenth-century Americans couldn't produce domestically, however, they were perfectly content to make their own through naturalization. The first instance of this that I found is revealed in the catalogues of Thomas Hogg, a transplanted Scotsman who in 1822 established what he called the "New York Botanic Garden" on a site at Broadway and Twenty-third Street. I've read through Hogg's catalogue of 1834; the list of roses was limited to thirty-nine cultivars. These included an "Adamsonia," a "Jacksonia," and a "Clintonia"; roses, in short, for enthusiasts of any political party, Federalist, Democrat or Whig. Hogg was a well-respected horticulturist, and he may have bred these roses himself, but for several reasons I doubt that he did. Unlike his competitor in Flushing, William Prince, Hogg was not especially interested in roses—that is evident in the brevity of his list. Nor have I found any other reference, contemporary or modern, to these roses; no one else wrote of them, even though American-bred roses would have been quite a novelty at the time. Finally, I doubt whether Hogg would have seen anything reprehensible in relabelling imported stock. No doubt he would have agreed with Vibert about a beautiful rose's right to many names (see p. 79). Whatever else is true of these roses, however, undoubtedly they sold well in election years.

A far more significant instance of this kind of adoption is provided by the Cherokee Rose, R. laevigata. This was adopted

in 1916 as the state flower of Georgia; that resolution began:
"Whereas, the Cherokee Rose, having its origin among the
aborigines of the northern portion of the state of Georgia, is
indigenous to its soil, and grows with equal luxuriance in
every county of the state . . ." This is not only poor English,
it also runs counter to the opinions of most botanists. This
species of rose is common throughout Georgia, as well as the
rest of the Southeastern states—the whole area, in fact, once
inhabited by the Cherokee Indians. Moreover, the rose has
been established there for a long time. The first scientific description of it appeared in the *Flora Boreali Americana* of
French botanist André Michaux, a work that was published
posthumously in 1803. Michaux, who rambled up and down
our eastern seaboard for twelve years, collecting plants first
for the French monarchy and later for the Republic, wrote of
finding the rose he named *laevigata* in backwoods Georgia.
He could hardly have missed it, since this plant is not only
common, it climbs through the trees to a height as great as
fifty feet. A single specimen may spread over an area of ten
thousand square feet, bearing in May or June a fragrant
shower of golden-centered three-inch white flowers. A spec-
tacular rose, but not a native.

It's Chinese, the botanists agree. This species is also common throughout the warmer regions of that country, where
it is known as Chin Ying Tzu, the "Golden Cherry," a name
that is a tribute to the plant's colorful hips. The first record of
its arrival in Europe dates to 1696—like many of its fellows, it
travelled deck-passage on an East India Company merchant-
man. How and when it arrived in North America is unknown;
how it penetrated to the interior so quickly (if 1696 does mark
its introduction to the West) is inconceivable.

Imaginative rosarians have tried to explain this problem
away by proposing earlier arrivals. They've resurrected legends
of a trans-Pacific voyage by fifth-century Buddhist monks
(surely they wouldn't have left home without their favorite
rose), and proposed an almost equally unlikely chain of trans-

fers by which the rose passed from Chinese gardeners to Arabs, from Arabs to Moors, to the Spanish and with them to Florida in the sixteenth or seventeenth centuries. Roy Shepherd, whose book *History of the Rose* is one of the best general guides to the evolution of garden roses, points out the holes in the latter theory. The Spanish were not very successful in their efforts to introduce European plants into Florida, Shepherd notes, and anyway, *R. laevigata* does not thrive in that state's coast regions, the only area the Spanish settled. But then, seemingly in despair, Shepherd proposes that "an exchange of plants took place in pre-glacial times when there was a land connection between the continents."* How a shrub that is not winter-hardy north of Kentucky could have found its way across Siberia and Alaska I do not care to speculate.

I will leave the problem of the Cherokee Rose's immigration to the Georgians—and I applaud their taste in choosing this most beautiful species as their state flower. The fact is that this rose's bloom is one of the brightest, most lasting memories a visitor takes away from a springtime trip through the Georgia countryside. Besides, if one cares to look for a rose that gained official status under false pretenses, a far more dramatic example can be found in the nation's capital.

The flower in question is one of the most popular roses of all time, the only old rose whose name everyone still recognizes—the 'American Beauty' rose. I don't have a text of the legislation confirming this as the official flower of the District of Columbia. I have only the information that "After considering the suitableness of a number of flowers to become the district flower, the Board of Commissions of the District, on June 6, 1925, adopted the American Beauty rose."† Likewise, I find no record of whether this rose was a popular choice

* *Shepherd's discussion of this subject may be found on pages 91–93 of his book.*

† *George Earlie Shankle,* State Names, Flags, Seals, Songs, Birds, Flowers and Other Symbols. *Transcript of a telephone conversation with the office of Daniel E. Garges, Secretary of the Board of Commissioners of the District of Columbia, February 21, 1931.*

among its constituents, but I'm sure it must have been. What could be more appropriate? This Hybrid Perpetual was claimed as a native Washingtonian, having been introduced onto the American market by the Field Brothers nursery of that city in 1886. By 1925, it had reigned as the premier florist's rose for forty-nine years—for two generations it had been the rose a man bought by the dozen for his wife or sweetheart. And the name, of course, couldn't have been more patriotic. Unfortunately, it, too, is bogus.

Actually, this rose was French. It was the work of a breeder named Lédéchaux, a man of no particular consequence (at least in rose circles) whose roses are otherwise forgotten. This one effort justified a lifetime's work, however. The color of the blossom is hard to describe, but Georgia Drennan, a rosarian whose opinions on the subject of cemetery roses I have already quoted (see p. 59)* characterized it this way: "The unusual shade of carmine-crimson, with a brilliant underglow, has over it a soft violet tinge, as if a film of bluish smoke hovered over the red velvety petals." If this wasn't enough to set the rose apart, then surely its stems were. These were extraordinarily long and stiff—they might stretch to six feet—guaranteeing the luxurious blooms a uniquely dramatic presentation. Naming this tour de force 'Madame Ferdinand Jamin,' Lédéchaux offered it to the public in 1875.

The new rose fared poorly in France and England. It proved finicky, unsuited to cultivation in the open air in all but the mildest climates. Even in the greenhouse it was difficult to raise. It showed a fastidious preference for certain types of greenhouses—the three-quarter span, a saltbox-shaped house, faced toward the south was best—while demanding special soils and temperatures. Bringing the bloom to perfection also required a delicate sense of timing; the grower had to hold the rose back by pinching off all flower buds until the bush had gathered sufficient strength for its single orgasmic display. If

* *The description of 'American Beauty' is quoted from page 46 of the same work,* Everblooming Roses, *by Georgia Torrey Drennan.*

catered to in all these respects, the bush still might be expected to yield no more than six or seven perfect blooms in a season, after which, exhausted, it fell into a fatal decline. The flowers, it is true, were magnificent, but European amateurs shunned this rose, and even florists preferred more accommodating cultivars.

Almost surely, 'Madame Ferdinand Jamin' would have perished in obscurity if she hadn't found her way across the Atlantic. She surfaced in 1882 in the nursery of Mr. Anthony Cook of Baltimore, who claimed her as his own, one of a lot of 900 seedlings he had raised. Sales languished until the rose came to the attention of prominent Washingtonian George Bancroft. A former minister to Great Britain and the author of a widely acclaimed two-volume work, *History of the United States,* he was an ardent rosarian as well, but his daughter seems to have been the one who spotted the rose (stories vary on this point). To Bancroft must go the credit for recognizing the rose's potential for greatness; however, Field Bros., which acquired a cutting from him, made what proved to be the crucial contribution. The nursery gave the rose a new name, one that appealed irresistibly to the exuberant patriotism of its customers. It dubbed the rose 'American Beauty,' and Americans forgave it all its faults.

American amateurs were no more able to grow this flower than their fellows in Europe, but they were willing to pay professionals almost any price to do it for them. Peter Henderson, a Scottish florist who had settled in Jersey City, noted in his 1887 catalogue that a hundred 'American Beauty' roses wholesaled for fifty dollars; in the Christmas market of 1898, a single stem retailed for as much as three dollars and seventy-five cents, the price of a full day's labor from a skilled workingman in those days. Florists who mastered the occult science of bringing 'American Beauty' into bloom made their fortune with it. "A good rose grower, one that can show results and please the public," wrote a florist of the time, "receives as

much pay as a college professor. As a rule, his knowledge has
cost him as much. By a rose grower, I mean a specialist who
can produce heavy-headed 'American Beauties' with yard-long
stems. It is a business by itself. Good rose growers get from
three to five thousand dollars a year and many who cater to
Washington, Chicago and New York, double that sum."[*]

To produce 'American Beauty' roses for the New York
market, one grower in North Wales, Pennsylvania, built a
glass house 150 feet wide and 700 feet long. He planted
100,000 rosebushes in this structure—the "benches" (a greenhouse grower's term for the tables on which he sets his pots)
would have stretched two and three quarters miles if placed
end to end. Though the largest, this was only one of many
similar greenhouses in that town. He and his colleagues covered a total of fifty acres with glass, all for this one flower.
Carloads were shipped as far as New Orleans (it didn't pay
to maintain a greenhouse in that subtropical city, where it
would be used only two months out of the year) and cargoes
of these precious flowers were sent by ship to London. The
best gauge of the rose's popularity, however, lies in the revolution it brought about in the art of floral arrangement. A
tight, formal bouquet of mixed greenery and rosebuds had
been the Victorian pattern; it was well adapted to the weak-
stemmed Tea roses that had been the florists' favorites. This
treatment did not suit the long-stemmed 'American Beauty,'
so an airier, less formal style of floral design became the thing.

Girls' clubs, boys' boats and sleds, silk stockings, flatirons,
fabric dyes and silverware were christened 'American Beauty'
in the hope that the rose's name would enhance their sales.
Many other roses were endowed with a spurious kinship:
'White American Beauty,' 'Pink American Beauty' and 'Red
American Beauty' were not related to the real 'American
Beauty,' though salesmen hoped the public would think they

* *Drennan,* Everblooming Roses, *p.* 47.

were. The exorbitant cost of raising this rose had made growers turn to other cultivars by World War II, yet florists are
still getting requests for "a dozen red 'Beauty' roses."

Georgia Drennan, who knew 'American Beauty' in its heyday, called it "the rose of roses of American origin." Since
then, its real story has become public. The District of Columbia keeps 'American Beauty' as its official flower anyway. Perhaps there is a special wisdom in this. An immigrant rose
spurned in its homeland that came to the New World to find
overwhelming success seems particularly apt as a symbol for
our nation's capital. Perhaps there was an unconscious wisdom, too, in Congress's decision to make the rose our national
flower. Senator Everett Dirksen used to argue that the marigold, an American native, better deserved the honor. Garden
roses, the pro-marigold forces argued, are essentially a European flower, a flower of the privileged class. Surely, though,
the Duchesses and Countesses, the Princes and Kronprinzes-
sinen, through their long sojourn on our soil have earned some
right to that title, too.

"The American people have long held a special place in
their hearts for roses," said the President in his proclamation
of November 20, 1986. "Let us continue to cherish them, to
honor the love and devotion they represent." A small, cynical
voice within me whispers that this is nothing more than a
platitude, a conventional sentiment. But then I am shamed by
the memory of the old-rose collectors I have visited across this
country. Our gardens, at least, must be richer for their simple,
sincere belief.

ACKNOWLEDGMENTS

Of the many people who helped with the writing of this book, I would like to extend special thanks to the following:

To my agent, Joe Spieler, who convinced me that the idea was worth pursuing and wouldn't let me quit

To the staff of the New York Botanical Garden Library, who never failed to find an answer to my most arcane questions

To my editor, Anne Freedgood, for her enthusiasm and her relentless pursuit of quality

To Charles Walker of the Heritage Rose Foundation, whose inexhaustible knowledge of rose nomenclature and history saved me from many an error

To my wife, Suzanne, who always found time for another rustle, another rosebush and another chapter

And finally, to all the old-rose collectors, who shared their experiences and their gardens so generously.

Index of Roses